MW01110382

With warm regards,

5/02/2005

Two Grandmothers From Baghdad

And Other Memoirs
of Monkith Saaid

By Rebecca Joubin

De Weideblik Press

First edition, November 2004

All photographs are from the collection of Monkith Saaid and
Rebecca Joubin.

Book design: Kees Hakvoort
Print: Macula bv, Boskoop/Nijmegen
Binding: Van Mierlo bv

www.weideblik.com

ISBN 90-77767-03-7 (hardback)
ISBN 90-77767-02-9 (paperback)
NUGI 300

For Maya Nora Saaid
and my parents Behnaz and Jahan Joubin

I flee my occupied paradise
Like the river water shuns the filth of the gutter.
The river remains forever constant to its course.

Muzaffar al-Nuwwab

Contents

Author's Note

This is a portrait of an artist in Baghdad during the 1960s and 70s. The story is based on the memories of Monkith Saaid, the tales I gathered during my journey to Baghdad during the Fall of 2003, as well as my own imagination. Although all close family names have remained identical, I have changed the names of neighbors and acquaintances. It was only after Saddam Hussein's rule ended with the fall of Baghdad on April 9, 2003, that the artist revealed the true name of the village he grew up in: Griyat. I have not masked this name.

Acknowledgments

Several friends and colleagues have made the publication of this novel possible. First of all, I would like to thank Ton den Boon at De Weideblik Press for believing in and supporting this project from its very inception. I am grateful to Dominic Coldwell, Laura Kelso, Kira Brunn, and Tyler Golson for reading through parts of the novel at various stages in the writing process and offering invaluable suggestions. I am also indebted to the people of Griyat who welcomed me into their village during the Fall of 2003 and patiently answered my questions. I will never forget the sacrifices made by my parents-in-law, Naji and Nuriya, and my sisters-in-law, Manal, Ibtihal, Iqbal, and Amal, to help me fill the gaps in my stories.

I am grateful to my parents, Behnaz and Jahan, for their unconditional love and generosity. They taught me how to set high goals and go after them with determination and discipline. Even when we differed in perspective, they stood by me. My brother and sister, Cyrus and Kathy, have been there for me unflinchingly during all the ups and downs of my writing career. I thank Maya, my close friend and stepdaughter, for the gift of her brightness and warmth. She listened attentively to my stories about her father and inspired me to carry the project through. And most of all, I thank my husband, partner, and best friend, Monkith Saaid, for introducing me to life. I thank him for his love and for trusting me with his story.

R.J.

My Shahrazad

My insufferable tragedy... I unearth an abysmal pit to bury my memories, so that I may deliver myself of them forever.

"Shall I tell you another story?" he whispered, smiling faintly.

I glimpsed at my watch. It was now three in the morning. We were nestled at the kitchen table, my back against the lit veranda, while he was perched in his familiar position, in his habitual chair. He faced the illuminated porch, as if on the lookout for something, some wrecking recollection that would soon pounce on his heart.

When we had first met, I was used to being in bed by eleven in the evening. Ever since I had been hit by chronic insomnia a few years earlier in Morocco, my sleep was sensitive, any change in schedule unleashed an anxiety that would wrap itself around me like twisted sheets of steel and keep me up, weeping until the break of dawn.

This changed shortly after I met him. After a year of seemingly endless preparation, I had just passed my doctoral orals at Columbia University. I felt a familiar unrest, and had traveled to Damascus to conduct research on exiled Iraqi writers and artists.

"I have a friend, an Iraqi sculptor named Monkith Saaid, who will surely be of help to you," my neighbor's friend, Amina, told me. "He has been living in exile for some twenty-four years now. Following his flight through the desert in 1979, he attended the University in Damascus, and then after several voyages, he settled his oars in the Netherlands and continued his higher studies in sculpture at the Rietveld Academy in Amsterdam. But he always found himself drifting back to Damascus, his first port of safety."

I quickly grew accustomed to carrying a pencil and notebook with me whenever I saw him; his memories and experiences were a bottomless sea and I soon found myself drowning in it. I struggled to remain above the translucent crest of the wave, never foreseeing which direction the mad tide would toss me.

I remember that sultry summer evening when we gathered for drinks in a café in Bab Tuma. This was only our third encounter. His ex-wife was visiting with their daughter, Maya, in the

13

hope of piecing together the shattered window of marital trust, but it took only moments before the fiercely broken fragments they aspired to salvage sliced their hearts. No glass was left to be smashed, and as they wept, his parents were well on their way from Baghdad to see the granddaughter they had not yet met.

But on this day, he crept over the fragmented glass and managed to escape to the shelter of his studio, where he called me and Amina to go out for drinks in the evening. When I saw him, he looked exhausted. His eyes were hazed, his smile drained with sadness. He slumped down on his chair and mumbled ruefully:

"Well, last night she banished my parents from the apartment, and every single neighbor has heard her shrill screams, which fill the malevolent shadows of the night. No one in the building knew me before, and now they pass by me with sinister, sidelong glances. Once the window of trust is shattered, it can never be mended, no matter how much you try. I should have known this, years ago, following her first betrayal. I was living in Syria at the time, and I lost all reason to live. In drunken stupor, I wandered the streets, in search for some anonymous spot to dig my own grave. Iraqi poet, Muzaffar al-Nuwwab, who could no longer watch me commit a slow process of suicide in front of his eyes, gathered my papers and hatched a plan to send me to alcohol-dry Libya. I was devastated. Iraq, my native country had expelled me. Now my adopted refuge, Syria, appeared to be throwing me away, shipping me off to Libya, just to cure my addiction."

"What did you end up doing there?" I asked as my eyes locked with his.

"I taught at the Fine Arts Faculty of Tripoli University," he said. And then he started to laugh.

"What's so funny?" I rejoined.

"On the first day of class, the guard would not let me in when I told him I was teaching. I was about twenty-six at the time, with a thick beard and a melancholy expression in my eyes. I must have seemed too young to be a professor. And so I climbed over the metal fence, severely slashing my hands. I went directly to the office of the University president, Mr. Ehsani – a tall and lanky man, whose back was slanted and who wobbled uneasily on an old wooden cane. His face, wide and white as a block of cement, was adorned with a mane of thick gray hair. A strange, uncertain smile seemed to be tattooed onto his irregularly curved lips. When I approached him, he stood still, head bowed. He quickly apologized and handed me an identity card and bandages for my cut. And so I taught the first day of class with my haphazardly bandaged hands."

"Then what happened?" Amina and I asked in unison.

"I taught the basics of sculpture and interior design for about one year, and founded the Department of Interior Design and the Department of Sculpture at the University. Alas, Qadhafi discovered my work and began to commission monuments through the University president. At least three times a day, I bumped into Mr. Ehsani who would invite me to drink tea with him. 'Wouldn't it be nice to sculpt a monument for the Leader?' he would ask, looking at me through his steady eyes and suspicious smile. I knew it was time to say farewell, but Mr. Ehsani would not grant me permission to leave the country, not even for a vacation. So I dispatched a message to my uncle Mohsen, who was in the United Arab Emirates at the time, beseeching him to send an urgent telegraph to Mr. Ehsani. When the telegraph arrived, he granted me five days to visit 'my ailing uncle in Italy.' I never returned. After a short stay in Italy, I went on to settle in the Netherlands for fourteen years."

For a moment he looked puzzled. He paused, and then his voice trailed off once more: "My life is a mysterious series of events. It was June 4 when I married my Jordanian girlfriend, when our daughter was born, when we divorced, and when I attained my Dutch citizenship."

"All on a June 4," I murmured to myself. I looked at him perplexed. That evening as we talked, I observed him closely. He was laughing hard, yet his hazel eyes were drenched with mournful tears. The small mole under his eyes glistened. His smile revealed a soul buried in sadness and suffering. I had never seen such an expression before. I thought about that look all through the cab ride home. Perhaps it was at that very moment that I made the conscientious decision to write a story about this enigmatic artist, whose vivid memories poured so generously from his lips. I am not sure. But before I knew it, I had fallen head over heals for him. I was breathing my story; the distance between reality and imagination faded away forever. His stories no longer dazzled me at an appointed time; they fluttered before me at the oddest moments. He constantly put my strength and commitment to the test.

It was not long before my agitated anchor settled in Damascus and we were living together. Just as I kissed him good night, memories came flooding back to him, and his lips surged with colorful and magical scenes of his childhood in Baghdad.

"It's late. Why don't you tell me these wonderful stories tomorrow morning?" I pleaded.

"No," he responded quickly, without even mulling over my request. "Perhaps I may not remember tomorrow. If you want to hear this story, you have to settle for now."

I soon learned that any protest was in vain. He won me over in spite of myself. I grabbed a piece of paper, and before I knew it, I was lost in the thickets of his village; I found exaltation under its tall palm trees and repose by the banks of the Tigris. I floated like a bird above the little boy he was, sustaining his vivid memories, his traumas and triumphs. I beheld his bewitchment when a paintbrush first touched his soft fingers, the dazzling moment when the lush thick red clay of the river banks of the Tigris melted within his hands and he transformed it into little spirits, animals, and enchanted cities. Before I knew it, it was no longer eleven in the evening, it was three or four a.m., and my storyteller was nowhere near wrapping up his tales. I fell asleep dreaming of tomorrow's magnificent images and colors, but the next day, he had often forgotten where he had left off. Or at times, he asked me to leave him in peace, for he was not interested in suffering those agonizing moments again.

Sometimes, on a night there was no story, I fell asleep by midnight, only to awaken around four in the morning, to the sounds of his fists pounding on the metal table in the kitchen. At first the reverberations of his monologues drifted like a shadowy mist into my dreams: "Why, my brothers, why? All those years, I fed you and our parents from my bread when I had none; I savored bitterness so that you may never experience the hunger and fear that hunted me down even in my sleep; and you repay me with blackmail and theft. Why?"

I often heard him mumbling madly to himself until I was suddenly startled out of my sleep. I opened the door and observed him, as he pressed his fists against the table. He had lit candles, and the shadows of his sculptures that filled the room danced around him and flickered on his face, in his soul. Like himself, his figures leaned toward one unstable point, but somehow managed to fool gravity by standing playfully on solid ground. I felt myself floating toward him as if carried by the shadows and kissed his forehead drenched in perspiration. I listened to his stories as he surrendered himself to the pain.

It seemed that an amazingly odd reversal of gender roles had occurred, and he was transformed into my Shahrazad. But while Shahrazad from *One Thousand and One Nights* told her enchanting tales as a means of deliverance, by inducing King Shahriyar's slumber, my Shahrazad told stories to escape life, to keep me by his side through the torment of the night. For it was during the night that the harrowing memories attacked him, leaving him bleeding in misery.

My pen and paper were ready as he summoned the mysteriously colored canvases of his memory. Some canvases were decked in bright hues, while others had grown dull and pale with time, beseeching me to dabble my own paintbrush within their faded contours. They wrapped themselves around me. At times they crushed me under their weight, at times they saved me from myself. As the portraits of his memories inhabited my very being, I no longer knew where his stories ended, and mine began; where his stories began and mine ended. I was not sure if the story I was writing fit into the genre of fiction, memoir, biography or any other literary form.

"Listen, Monkith, shall I read you what I have written thus far?"

I gathered my paper and read, poised for his assurance. He listened in silence, but then entreated me: "You are too overwhelmingly present in your narration. Let me speak, let me breath, let your characters converse for themselves. Allow my memories to dance without reserve. Let them love and hate, hurt and feel joy, let them live or end their lives if they so desire. Let them pursue their own steady stream. Don't stand in their way."

Sometimes, I gathered my sheets and ripped them apart, tears clogging my eyes: "But how do I keep myself from disappearing under your colossal canvases, their overwhelming thickness? My fear is that as I retrieve forgotten brushstrokes, my own very sense of self will fade. Will I recognize myself when I lay my pen to rest?"

"Well, perhaps that is another story."

A Room in Damascus

"A stranger with no path toward the homeland,
and unable to settle down in any other land."

Abu Hayan al-Tawhidi

It was a small room, about two-and-a-half by three meters –
hardly bigger than a prison cell – dark, humid, sad, and oppressive. You could tell from the stains traced by the humidity on the
walls that it had once been a bathroom. It had no windows, just
a door, a dilapidated wooden bed, a brown chair, and an old
chest of drawers.

The room opened directly onto the more spacious and
sparkling living quarters of the landlady, Umm Fadi – an old
woman, skinny and gnarled. Beneath her shiny forehead, two
huge black eyes peered out from bony sockets guarded by bushy
white eyebrows. Her snow-white hair, surprisingly thick for her
age, was bound into a tight chignon, and clasped by a mauve
headscarf, which came together in a bow above her head. Her
cheekbones were sunken, and she pursed her dry lips together in
a perpetually dissatisfied expression. She must have been ninety
years old. Along with forgetting her memories, she had forgotten how to smile.

The rooms formed a small ground floor apartment on
Damascus' Shah Bandar Square. Given the flat's prized location,
the enterprising proprietor had converted the bathroom into a
rental suitable for foreigners. Her first tenant was an impoverished young stranger, a handsome man with a small mole under
his hazel eyes. His laughter, though seldom heard, was refreshing and gentle. He had a melodious voice that echoed the rare
pride of a soul whose only reminder of its own existence were the
haunting memories of times long past but forever melded in the
core of his being.

Annoyances are adorned in many guises. His was gold-plated.
Umm Fadi hailed from a wealthy Damascene family. She
bedecked herself in scintillating jewelry: beaming yellow ear-
rings dangled from her lobes, loops of golden chains swung
across her chest, bangles of gold clutched her ankles and wrists

like angry snakes. When she shuffled about the apartment, pieces of gold fell to the floor. The new tenant heard the dull thud of her jewelry, mingling with her mad mutterings and cascading cough. He would pick up the errant adornments and return them to her. But unbeknownst to Umm Fadi, her four married sons and their families were prospective heirs thirsting for her death. Her sons had already stolen most of her property, squabbling among themselves, and now they vied greedily for what remained. The stranger noticed how every time her sons appeared her bangles were one by one replaced by fake jewelry.

Thankfully for her tenant, Umm Fadi rarely stayed at home, as she usually orbited between her sons' homes. But the eldest son's wife harbored an intense aversion to her, so one week a month, she was compelled to stay at home. Although she was not welcome in her eldest son's house, Abu Baha was still expected to fulfill his duties. Thus, he visited her every day during that week after the morning prayer, not just in order to deliver food, but also to check up on her health. He was a real estate agent, always devising schemes for extra money. His large beady green eyes were crossed. He was skinny with a large hump on his back, which he covered with tattered, second-hand clothes. For although he was affluent, he was the paragon of stinginess.

Once when he bumped into the tenant outside his bedroom, he gleamed, "Why don't you write a book about your life? I'll help you publish it, and we can share the profits evenly between us."

But the young man stammered, "I'm a sculptor, not a writer. Drafting my memoirs does not interest me."

As he opened the door and stepped into his room, Abu Baha grabbed his shoulder and responded with a slightly contorted smile, "Come on! It is just a matter of stringing a bunch of words together, and I'll take care of the business details."

As if mesmerized, the stranger whispered: " Words. They race wildly across my mind like a stampede of stallions. When I attempt to piece them together, as I put pen to paper, they gallop off in different directions. As a boy I used to sit down for hours to write, but now I do not know where to begin. Words trample across my mind creating wondrous images. I see them and I suffocate."

"Well, why don't you just ponder it," Abu Baha said as he tapped on the bedroom door. Then in an attempt to regain control of his mother's unruly tenant he added, "but in the meantime, please tidy your room? It can't be healthy sleeping on a pile of filth."

Once, as the young man lay in his room, his door was ajar. Scraps of conversation between the old woman and her eldest son drifted over to him. He overheard Abu Baha advising his mother: "My brothers are wretched. I am the one who thought of transforming the bathroom into a rental suite, and I am the only one who cares for this place and for you, for that matter. Come, let us go see a lawyer and you can give me power of attorney. We do not have to mention this to the others."

Umm Fadi just stared at him as he persisted: "My God, look at your unkempt tenant. Have you seen the squalor he languishes in? I am the only one who gives a damn about getting this place in order." A glimmer of triumph flickered in his eyes when he envisioned himself finally in control of her property.

In addition to delivering unwanted advice, he supplied his mother with Damascene delicacies. The intoxicating aromas of food permeated the apartment, and entwined themselves indelibly with the stranger's books, sketches, paintbrushes, his hair, and the tumultuous shadows of his heart. Sometimes, he opened the door of the magical box and stared at the bright red tomatoes, the yellow and green peppers, the zucchinis, the grape leaves, the eggplant stuffed with rice and meat, at the multicolored salads and yogurt dishes sprinkled with dry mint and finely cut garlic cloves, at the thin pancakes stuffed with cream. Occasionally, he reached his hand in to take a nibble. Usually though, he preferred to starve rather than plunder her food. Instead, he tried to conjure up fond childhood memories of his grandmother Fatema's wonderful cooking.

When Umm Fadi was not busy arraying herself in the ore of Nubia, she preferred to pester the stranger. He braced himself as best he could for the week she lingered at home, etching it in thick red ink in his calendar. When the fated week arrived, she turned his life into living irony.

She insisted that the apartment radiate cleanliness and order. Like a priestess anointing her temple, she shuffled around the flat splashing water on the walls and the tiles. The young man often struggled to keep his balance on the soapy surfaces. He might have forgiven her had she kept her eccentricities to herself, but alas, she showed no mercy. Once, having scraped together enough money, he bought a small Teflon pan. After frying his eggs, he washed the pan and left it by the sink to dry. He marveled at the sight of the pan's shiny black coating. But Umm Fadi was infuriated, believing that his frying had burnt the black surface. She scrubbed it so hard to remove the black coating that she rendered the pan sparkling silver – a beautiful, but worthless object.

Sadly enough, she treated her tenant as if he was at her beck and call. If she needed water, she expected him to fetch it for her. Worse still, he had no privacy, for he shared a latrine with her. In fact, one of the doors to the toilet opened directly onto his room. Umm Fadi never closed the door herself, expecting him to do the needful task. Given the weak state of her bladder, she seemed to be in a constant state of suspension between her bedroom and the latrine.

He did all he could to elude the eccentric old woman. During each week of the month that she whiled away at home, he arrived late at night and departed early in the morning. Sometimes, he avoided coming home altogether, preferring to sleep on a bench in Sepky Park. He endured the week of hyperbole with the comfort of knowing that she would be gone the following three weeks.

Although desperate to find more suitable lodgings, he knew this would be an impossible task. His true Iraqi passport had been revoked, so he now carried a fake one. It was the mid-1980s, and in order for an Iraqi to rent a room in Syria, he was required to procure official papers from the Iraqi Baath Party headquarters in Damascus. In the absence of these, the Syrian police was not authorized to register an Iraqi's name under a rental address.

But when he went to the Iraqi Baath office to fetch the papers, its director Hazem al-Qubaysi refused to help him.[1]

"Yes... Yes, I remember you," Hazem said, as he bitterly ran his eyes over the young man's tired, sallow face. After he sipped his coffee, he continued, "You are that good-for-nothing Communist who came to me a little more than a year ago after you finished your coursework at the University of Damascus."

"Yes," he replied impatiently, staring at the older man's piercing eyes. "I needed the necessary documentation from your office in order for the University to grant me my degree. Despite your initial pledge, you withheld it from me, and so I still do not carry proof of my graduation."

Hazem responded to the young man's candid words with his own startling frankness: "Well, I had heard about your involvement with the Communists, and did my best to expel you from the university and campus housing. Unfortunately, I was too late. You had already completed your studies and moved on to a new flat. So you see, I had to make you pay the price of your politics in whatever way I could later on."

"I am a nationalist, and just look at the way that you treat me. If you deal with me in this way, how do you handle despicable members of the Iraqi *mukhabarat*," he asked with sarcasm. For he had a sneaking suspicion that even though Hazen was affiliated with the Syrian Baath party and outwardly showed no loyalty to the Iraqi counterpart, he was indeed a true servant of Saddam Hussein.

Hazem laughed, "Well, members of the Iraqi *mukhabarat* are subject to their own special punishment when they pass my way." He yelled for his helper to bring him the papers he had asked for in the morning, and then he began searching for something on his desk.

As Hazem moved to pick up the telephone and make a call, the young man lost patience. His mood shifted from loquacious to a defiant terseness: "Listen. I do not want to waste my time. Will you or will you not grant me the papers I need in order to

---

[1] At the time, official relations between the Syrian and Iraqi governments had been severed. However, there was a branch of the Iraqi Baath Party in Syria, which on the face of it claimed to be loyal to Syria's Baathist government. The Syrian government discovered in the 90s, however, that it was actually associated with the Iraqi *mukhabarat*, Iraq's intelligence service. Director Hazem al-Qubaysi fled, first to England and then to Iraq.

register my name with a rental address?"

"I have to think about it," Hazem replied with an authoritative tone to remind him exactly whom he was talking to. With tightened lips, Hazem began sifting through the papers on his table, and the young man examined him in silence. He thought to himself that Hazem looked like an old shoe, worn by time, use, and conspiracy. A torn shoe bereaved of shoestrings, stitched back together randomly. You inspect it, and you cannot tell if it was once black or brown. As if to set himself apart from the Baath members in Iraq, Hazem shaved his mustache. The young man reflected that perhaps Hazem should grow a mustache in order to cover his haphazardly woven face. Regardless of his looks and his perfidy, he lamented that this man did indeed wield enormous clout in Syria.

As if reading these thoughts, Hazem lifted his face from his papers and declared, "No, I will not give you the documentation needed to register your name with the rental address." But then to emotionally torture the young man even further with empty promises he announced that if he stopped by in a week or so, perhaps he would provide him with the papers necessary for the university to accord his degree.

At this the young man rose from his chair, and left the building dejected. Fortunately, Umm Fadi neglected to ask him for the documentation. He desperately clung to his stroke of luck, living in perpetual fear that she might eventually come to her senses, and decide to get rid of her illegal tenant. With nowhere to go, he succumbed to her whims.

The old woman and her tenant lived in an uneasy relationship, sharing the bathroom, kitchen, veranda, and front door. Occasionally, a large and dirty rat, which appeared to harbor a personal grudge against them both, joined the household. No matter how much Umm Fadi sought to exterminate it, her efforts were in vain. She went so far as to bring a stray black cat home one day, but the enormous rat intimidated the cat.

It seemed as if the rat, sensing that it had gained the upper hand, cursed the young man. It soiled his dinner plates topped with dried bread and precious cubes of butter. Brazenly, it even climbed into his bed and dirtied his sheets. Each time he moved to pounce on it, the rat fled to safety. Sometimes it just crept in and stared at him. At times, the stranger envisioned the repugnant rodent saying, "You idiot! What the hell are you doing here?"

The young man tried to block out his nemesis by envisioning a secret world of his own making. On hot humid days of summer, he retreated into the sanctuary of his room, closing the door and blocking any hope of fresh air. The only source of ventilation was a small door between his room and Umm Fadi's, which deprived him of further privacy. One day, he decorated a big wooden block with clay and bronze and wedged it into the aperture. He carved the figure of a man climbing a broken ladder gasping to reach his destination, an old woman peering from behind thick bars, the face of a woman deformed by sorrow. But above the wooden frame with its horrifying images, loomed a gaping cavity through which slivers of light intruded from Umm Fadi's chambers and bounced off his humid walls. They evoked strangely shifting and lurid images throughout the night.

One of the stranger's main means of escape was to read. Once, he was completely gripped by Hesse's prose in *Steppenwolf*. All he could see were the words leaping off the page:

A heavy wave of anguish and darkness flooded my heart. Suddenly everything confronted me once more. Suddenly once more the sense of the last call of fate gripped my heart. Desperately I felt in my pocket for the little figures so that I might practice a little magic and rearrange the layout of the board. The figures were no longer there. Instead of them I pulled out a knife. In mortal dread I ran along the corridor, past every door. I stood opposite the gigantic mirror. I looked into it. In the mirror there stood a beautiful wolf as tall as myself. He stood still, glancing shyly from unquiet eyes. As he leered at me, his eyes blazed and he grinned a little so that his chops parted and showed his red tongue... [2]

As he absorbed these lines, he felt as if he was transfixed in a mystical corridor as well. His mind drifted toward trembling thoughts... Before he had managed to escape across the Iraqi border, the mysterious Bedouin at the checkpoint told him to

---

[2] Hermann Hesse, *Steppenwolf* (Henry Holt and Company: New York, 1963), 203-204

beware of Iraqi border guards and wolves:

"Shine your flashlight at the wolves to fend them off since they are afraid of light, and if you discern any Iraqi border guards approaching, fall on the sand so that they don't spot you."

How well he remembered his flight. He had lost all sense of time. His teeth chattered uncontrollably, and his ears were so frozen that they throbbed with pain. Only by exhaling into his cupped, cold hands and clasping them against his ears was he able to lessen the torment. It felt as if prickly iced needles had numbed his legs, but he did not know how to warm them. In a frightened trance, he quickened his pace. He began to run and perspire. To cool down again, he threw himself onto the ground, but in the frosty night air, the desert sand was as cold as ice. He wavered between feelings of unyielding chilliness and blazing heat, with terror his constant and loyal companion.

His eyes clutched the page, and he continued reading:

Again I looked into the mirror. I must have been mad. There was no wolf in the mirror, lolling his tongue in his maw. It was I, Harry. My face was gray, forsaken of all fancies, wearied by all vice, horribly pale. Still it was a human being, someone one could speak to.

"Harry," I said, "what are you doing there?"

"Nothing," said he in the mirror, "I am only waiting for death."

"Where is death then?"

"Coming," said the other...[3]

Bewildered, the stranger's head shot up from the page and he leapt to his feet. It was not the wolf's face in front of him, nor the face of the border guard, only the wrinkled visage of Umm Fadi squinted at him. Her quizzical gaze wore no trace of a smile. She was on her way to the toilet, and had stopped to check on him. As usual, she reprimanded him for the disorderly state of his room. He stopped reading, tossed his head back on the pillow, and surrendered his soul to the nightmares that he knew would inevitably ensue, if he should be lucky enough to conquer his chronic insomnia.

The stranger thought that if he did not die of provocation, his enfeebled soul would die of loneliness. He had received no news from his family in Iraq, and his friends were not allowed to visit him in Umm Fadi's presence. Worse, she forbade the drinking of *araq*.[4] It was not that she disapproved of it on religious grounds; she actually had no idea that *araq* contained alcohol. Rather, she frowned upon its pungent smell, which permeated the apartment. She, herself, preferred the odor of floor wax and household disinfectant to his mint-scenting alcohol. Her compromise was to permit him to bring home, unscented *araq*, which unfortunately did not exist.

Because he could not mask the fragrance, he could not drink *araq* on the days that she hovered vigilantly about the apartment. His sculptures were not welcome, either. The devout woman viewed them as impermissible idols, and thus, he had to work surreptitiously on his beloved art. Even when he was ill, he shoved his nose tight against the bed sheets so he would not have to endure her disapproval of his coughs and sniffles.

Despite Umm Fadi's wishes, his room remained in a state of chaos. It reeked of raw cigarette smoke and cheap spirits. It was filled with plastic cups rimmed with dry colors, paintbrushes, tubes of colors, polyester and clay sculptures, notes and sketches. One day when it became heaped with books and poems, including those of Saadi Yussef and Abdel Wahab al-Bayati, and tapes recording the poetry of Muzaffar al-Nuwwab, he had no choice but to place his polyester sculptures on the veranda. They now competed for space and attention with the clay flowerpots filled with roses, yellow jasmine, and geraniums that proudly lined the porch's spotless corners.

Aghast, Umm Fadi lost no time announcing that she would not tolerate the sight of those "idols" under her vigilant gaze. She resolutely demanded that he consign them to the anarchy of his room. Her spirits lifted noticeably, however, when he showed her a small clay portrait he had just quickly molded while she was pestering him. She screamed out in delight, "Well, you must be some sort of magician, young man."

"No, I have not done anything out of the ordinary. I have simply carved your portrait." His hands brushed over the features he

---

3 Hermann Hesse, *Steppenwolf*, pg. 204.

4 *Araq* is a strong colorless alcohol made of raisons and aniseed.

had sculpted moments earlier, and then he handed it to her.

"It does resemble me in the most alarming way, doesn't it? That must mean that it is simply a picture of me – not some forbidden idol," she proclaimed as she held it in her hands.

From that moment on, her disdain for his sculptures went up in smoke. Although she still would not allow his artwork to steal her geranium's thunder, she did grant him leave to keep the sculptures in his room if he so desired.

◆

Monkith Saaid was about twenty-four when he found himself back in Syria, the country of his university days, inhabiting this grim little room on Shah Bandar Square. He embarked on several projects in interior design, while working on a monument nearly five meters high. Despite the commission he earned for this sculpture, the young artist lived a pauper's life. On the verge of despair, however, he unexpectedly met an elderly gentleman somewhere in his sixties who needed a hotel decorator. Monkith agreed to take on the project, and they drew up a contract. He was given ten thousand Syrian pounds[5] in advance, and he began work in a large workshop the elderly gentleman owned. Moreover, with the down payment, Monkith bought some polyester and fiberglass, and set up a small polyester business in the workshop. With five employees working under his guidance, he was finally leaving his days of poverty in ex patria behind.

His penury may have been temporarily resolved, but the mid-1980s were trying times for most people in the region. The Iran-Iraq war raged on, with no sign of abating. He was not able to contact his parents, brothers, or sisters since all communications with Iraq had been severed from within Syria.

As he lay in bed, he stared at the light projected from Umm Fadi's room, which bounced off his walls, creating luminous canvases of death. His heart shrank with terror as he imagined cadaverous children, wounded or dead. Horrific scenes flitted before his eyes as he stared at the walls of crumbling paint. He pulled the thin sheets over his head so tightly that he could barely breathe. When he finally fell asleep, his fears hunted him down in his sullen slumber.

Even his evening sorties did not relieve him of his anxieties. One night, as he hobbled home along a dark, rubbish-heaped street, the scenes of war, death and decay, which he had seen reflected on his walls, leapt before him and struck him to his marrow. Not even a great quantity of booze could numb the pain. For a fleeting moment, he envisioned his mother and sisters in the company of harlots, clad in short skirts, garishly made up, panting huskily, crying. He wished to wipe away the black charcoal patches that smudged their tear-filled eyes. He longed to ask them why they were weeping, but they could not hear him. He ached to reach out to them, but they could not see him.

For a moment, he lost consciousness, but when he snapped out of his ambling nightmare and lifted his heavy lids, he realized he was staring at a forlorn woman, sobbing on the sidewalk. Her headscarf was ragged. Much of her hair dangled around her face and neck. Traces of a bright cranberry-red lipstick, encrusted at the corners of her mouth, smeared her lips. At the sound of his approaching footsteps, she panicked and stepped back. Just as she turned to run away, he cried out, "Please don't worry. Let me help you as if I were your own brother. I promise I don't want anything from you."

Something in his voice soothed her. She brushed the wisps out of her face and wiped the salty tears from her dark brown eyes. She lowered her face and began to whisper in a voice as soft as a gurgling waterpipe, "I am the widow and the mother of seven children. My children and I live with my mother and handicapped father. I've..." But then she lost her composure once more, and he could no longer discern the words, which emerged from between her steady sobs.

"It's okay, you can tell me. You have nothing to fear. I only wish to help you," he insisted as he approached her slowly.

Again a sense of calm overcame her, and she resumed telling

---

5 At that time every 30 Syrian liras (pounds) was the equivalent of one dollar.

her story, with her head still bowed down: "I've prostituted myself in order to feed my starving family. This evening, the men who fornicated with me hurled me out of their car without paying for my services."

At these last words, she wailed once more as she tossed her depleted purse on the ground. A gloomy sadness crept into Monkith's heart. All he could think was, What if this woman had been my mother or one of my sisters? What if they had been forced to sell their bodies in order to feed their families?

As the woman wept and flung herself on the ground, she grabbed her empty purse and cradled it close to her. Her frayed headscarf was now heaped haphazardly on the top of her head. Her thick black mascara smeared her cheeks. She rocked herself back and forth, humming: "Dear God have mercy on my home – on my poor mother, father, and children. Take me, but spare my children." Monkith dug into his pocket, and produced two thousand Syrian pounds. He knelt over and handed her the lump of bills.

"Take this, and go feed your family," he murmured as he helped her stand up again.

"God Almighty," she whispered, but then she remembered that she would probably be expected to return the favor in some way. "Please tell me, what can I do for you?" she pleaded, rubbing her arm across her running nose.

"Nothing," he said as he slipped the money into her pocket.

"May God reward you for your generosity," she whimpered. She did not turn to leave, but stood still, staring at her benefactor. Tears trickled down his cheeks as he bade farewell to her and resumed walking. When he turned around to check on her, he noticed that she stood transfixed gaping steadily at him. By now her tattered headscarf had fallen to the ground. He headed back to the Salihiya district so that if she pursued him she would not see where he lived. And then – once he was certain he was alone – he returned listlessly by another street to his small room.

Far from becoming an oubliette, his Damascus "prison cell" metamorphosed into a retreat for writers, artists, poets, journalists, and intellectuals – all friends from his university days. Throughout the three weeks that Umm Fadi was absent, friends gathered there nightly. He only had one comfortable brown chair, so he bought small folding stools and set them around his table. Before the ineluctable bouts of boozing began, each guest showed his regard for the other by offering him to sit on the brown chair, the most comfortable seat in the room. And then when the "gentleman" who had the honor of resting his buttocks on the brown "throne" rose to use the bathroom, everyone else stood up as if in mock salute and rotated one chair. This ceremony of courtesy continued around the clock until, by the end of the evening, everyone had had a chance to sit on the best seat in the house.

Evenings in his cramped chambers were laden with political and cultural discussions. They spoke of the raging Iran-Iraq war and their personal sorrows. Monkith transformed books into drums he tapped on, as his close friend, writer Abdullah Saqi, sang dolorous Iraqi hymns with his enchanting voice. They told jokes and burst out laughing, but their eyes were filled with tears. Many were young men, whose sharp twists of fate had placed them on the path of alcoholism.

Once at the end of an evening, Monkith and Abdullah made a pact that they would both try to stop drinking. Abdullah always used to stop over at the liquor shop for a shot of *araq*. But the next day, Abdullah arrived ecstatic: "You will never believe what happened to me! I left my apartment today and spent an entire day without drinking a single drop! Can you believe my willpower?"

"What a show of true willpower!" Monkith and the others chimed in as they beat their hands against the books and sang.

"Well, my friend," said Monkith, "I think this calls for a celebration," and he popped open a bottle of *araq*.

Everyone joined in laughing, singing, and clinking their glasses as they celebrated Abdullah's amazing feat.

His friends lit cigarettes, and before long, thick plumes of smoke billowed through the room. As usual, the haze in the room became unbearable.

"Damn you, can't you open a window," the guests cursed their host in unison.

"As you can see, this room possesses no window that I may open," Monkith yelled at them.

But they did not stop complaining. One day, he grew weary of his friends' reproaches. He had an idea. That afternoon, he bought some wood, glass, paper, and curtains. He made a large rectangular wooden frame; he drew a large rectangle on the wall and painted it black. He placed a rectangular glass over the black, and then he hung the wooden frame over it. He outlined the frame with wooden mullions, cranberry colored curtains, and a rose-colored sash. The following evening, when friends launched into their usual gripes about the likelihood of asphyxiation in the room, he flung the window open. Everyone was relieved, yet surprised. "Good God – Why didn't you open the window before?" they chimed. The *trompe l'oeil* was a huge success. And thus persisted many late night revelries where this Damascene intelligentsia poured out its heart, sang, and tapped its fingers on books. Monkith, in turn, entertained his friends with vivid memories of his childhood in Baghdad.

Shahrazad spoke. And the window was always open...

An Enchanted Village

"Farce without end? My innocence would make me weep. Life is a farce we all have to lead."

Arthur Rimbaud, *A Season in Hell*, 1873.

I was born behind a half-opened door on August 18, 1959 in Griyat, a small village in northern Baghdad, to Nuriya Jawwad al-Jaboori and Naji Saaid al-Azawi. My mother rose to use the bathroom, and as she began to pass the door, she gave birth. The delivery was fairly simple and painless. My birth occurred during the month of Safer based on the Arab lunar calendar. The saying goes that any male child born in this month will be afflicted with bad fortune, and so the elders of the family must sacrifice a rooster, in order to ward off bad luck. But my family forgot to make the necessary offering.

◆

Folklore and legend were all the rage in Griyat, a picturesque village that wore the Tigris River as a glittering necklace around its long, slender nape. Only one small opening of the river's waters connected the small, independent and predominantly Shii populated village to reality; A'dhamiyyah, the Sunni Muslim district in the center of Baghdad. The river cleaved Baghdad's throbbing heart, separating A'dhamiyyah in the north from the Shii Kazamiyyah region on the other bank.

The verdant Griyat was known as the region where the Abbasid Caliph Harun al-Rashid[6] spent his vacations. It was cool in the summer, mild in the winter – a perfect place to escape the hustle and bustle of the city. The caliph began construction on a beautiful castle where he intended to pass his summer vacations. Alas, he died before the fortress was finished, but his son Shams completed it, and spent his holidays in the area. It was in this picturesque village where Monkith Saaid – whose full name read Monkith Naji al-Azawi – was raised in a typically middle-class Iraqi family. He was the eldest

---

[6] Ruled 786-809 A.D.

son in a family of seven children. His birth was followed by that of four sisters – Manal, Ibtihal, Iqbal, and Amal – and two brothers – Muhammad and Ahmad.

In Griyat, the four seasons – ever distinct yet enigmatically entwined – aroused Monkith's senses. When he closed his eyes, it was only the rustling of the sacred palm trees, which tricked him into thinking that the seasons were unchanging. For the palm trees stood tall and green throughout the year. They were like a mother to the inhabitants of Griyat, nourishing them and sheltering them from the remorseless glare of the sun. Villagers climbed their supple branches, slept under their blissful shade, and delighted in their juicy dates. They cut the trees' fronds and fashioned wicker tables, chairs, and sofas out of them. Out of the palm's straw, they created hats, purses, and belts. In order to ensure that young shoots would sprout, villagers carefully trimmed certain fronds each year.

By April, the palm trees began to radiate with the buds of newly formed dates, and by the sweltering summer months of July and August, magnificent clusters of dates of various hues and flavors adorned their delicate branches. Monkith threw pebbles at the branches of the smaller trees, which hung low, so that dates tumbled to the ground and he could taste the summer's munificence. When he had satiated his appetite on all that the lower branches had to offer, he climbed higher and began to toss more clusters to his friends on the ground. Having severed all the dangling looms, Monkith jumped to the ground and scrambled to his feet. He collected the dates in the folds of his thin white *galabia*,[7] only to return home with deep maroon stains. The spanking that would inevitably follow was well worth a taste of the first seasonal offerings.

When he and the other children had reaped the harvest of the smaller palm trees, they searched for the bounty of mightier palm trees. In Griyat, there was one about fifty meters high called *Al-Aytah*.[8] It swayed back and forth as the frisky wind whistled through its fronds, yet it stood impervious even during the most trying seasons of the year. The villagers believed that *jin*, or spirits, inhabited it. Parents warned their children neither to approach nor climb this palm tree, particularly at night. Playing on the children's fantasies had the hidden benefit of preventing any nocturnal injuries sustained while climbing.

Very few dared approach *Al-Aytah*. But there was a woman named Fakhriah who remained undaunted. She was tall and thin, with a thick black mustache coating her parched upper lip. She had married, but was later divorced on account of her bristling masculinity. She climbed to the top of *Al-Aytah* every evening, and, like a nightingale, sang the most celestial hymns. She infused Griyat with her melodious voice. The lyrics that flowed from her hirsute lips touched on compassion and bitterness, blessings and misfortune. From her treetop vantage, she searched for Monkith and the other children to toss them the first savory dates of the season. Nothing would make Fakhriah happier than sensing the children's delight when they sank their milky white teeth into the saccharine treats. Despite his parents' repeated warnings, Monkith was not afraid. He often climbed *Al-Aytah*, searching for Fakhriah. He dreamed of flying with her to the top of the branches, discovering the tastes of new and unknown dates.

In addition to savoring ripe dates, Monkith relied on other senses to identify the tumbling of the months. Spring brought the honeyed scent of flowers to Griyat. The air was imbued with a delicious perfume of white jasmine and orange blossoms, which his sisters wove into bracelets, necklaces, and anklets. At first, the orange blossoms resembled flowers, but once they pollinated, they took the form of small oranges. Those that fell to the ground had a sour taste, which mingled with the earth, exuding a pleasing scent. The oranges that clung to the tree ripened into a wonderfully sweet fruit.

The red anemone, whose five petals were a deep blood red, was born in the spring. According to Sumerian mythology,

---

7 This is a traditional Arab dress comprised of a long, loose shirt that reaches the feet.

8 *Al-Aytah* means "the shout." It is the name used to designate all exceptionally large palm trees.

Tamuz – the handsome god of fertility – was in love with Ishtar[9] – the goddess of love. They fled from Mesopotamia to prevent the other gods from marrying off Ishtar to a deity of their own choosing. As a result, the gods killed Tamuz, and forced Ishtar to return to Iraq. Later, they regretted that they had killed the beautiful god of fertility and flagellated themselves to atone for his death. According to this legend, which fascinated Monkith, from the blood of the martyr Tamuz grew millions of red anemones.

In the spring the Tigris swelled and became reckless, and legend had it that the waters churned with the thick red blood of Tamuz. For when the mountain snow melted, the Tigris flooded its banks and deposited rich red clay. Monkith loved to run his hands through the moist sedimentation, and for him this was the seasons' most precious gift to the people of Griyat. He waited all year impatiently for the river waters to recede and then he raced to his grandmother Fatema's house by the Tigris, where he lost himself by the riverbanks.

Art was born for him the day his small feet first sank into the moistness and the smell of the earth and churning water filled his nostrils. His long, nimble fingers dug into the mud and wove the carpet of shapeless red clay into cities and houses larger than himself, elephants, dogs, imagined spirits and animals, all with their own mysterious stories. Gentle and delicate with his hands, he became one with the clay. When he returned home from his grandmother's, at the sight of his soiled clothes and body covered in a film of dirt, his mother spanked him and warned: "You just wait and see what happens when you play with that filthy clay again. It seethes with dangerous bacteria and carries the blood of Tamuz. It will seep through your skin and cause all sorts of unimaginable and incurable diseases. The infection will start between your fingers and crawl like angry red ants across your skin."

"But I love playing with the clay. Nothing will stop me!" he cried out between sobs as she slapped him again and again. Then she paused, squinted her eyes and spat out: "Your whole body will sprout purple blisters, even your eyes. If you play there tomorrow, you shall see. And your father shall slap you even harder than me. Do you understand me, son?"

But he was determined. He discovered a bottle of penicillin in his father's medicine cabinets and rubbed it on his fingers before falling asleep. He dreamed of the new creatures and cities of clay he would create, how their colors would transform under the mystical reflections of the sun at different times of the day. Every day he was drawn to this imaginary and solitary world, which he forbade anyone else to enter. Sometimes at the end of the day, he would destroy the cities he had erected so that other children would not have the joy of doing so, and the next day he would build anew.

"Good heavens! Just look at yourself! You always make a mess of yourself when you're out to play," his mother screamed. Knowing that this would not hinder him from wandering off, she tried to frighten him: "And anyway, you are too young – it is far too dangerous to frolic by the Tigris on your own."

But he always trailed off to the Tigris, which never ceased to fascinate him. In the spring, his hands also became stained with bright colors as he painted and traded eggs with his friends, which they then threw into the Tigris. Shii Muslims borrowed this Christian custom. It was held that if the water was sacred, so were all the objects thrown into it. Indeed, if a Quran or a Bible was torn or damaged, Monkith watched the villagers throw the scriptures into the water. And each time a baby was born, his mother flung the umbilical cord into the Tigris to receive blessings.

There was a saying in Iraq that the nature of the Tigris changed according to the time of day. The river was thought to succumb to mood swings, much like a woman. In fact, many Iraqi girls were named after it. In any given season, the Tigris borrowed its color from the reflections of the rising sun. Its hue was deepest in the summer, when the sun was at its zenith, and the currents were still. At noon, the hot river sparkled like a sheet of dancing white diamonds. When the sun set, the Tigris donned a royal mantle of purple and crimson red. In the evening, the

---

9 Tamuz and Ishtar roughly correspond to Adonis and Venus in Greek mythology.

calm waters mirrored Kazamiyyah, the Shii village, on the opposite bank. Monkith found the reflections to be particularly arresting at night. For the holy shrine of Musa Ibn Ja'afar, lit in the evenings, was visible from the banks of the Tigris.

If Monkith smelled spring in Griyat's orange blossoms, he relished summer in the popular fried fish *mazgoof*. The saying went that the Tigris was like a lady in the summer, gentle and well mannered. On warm summer evenings, he and his family engaged in the favorite Baghdadi pastime of strolling along the river's peaceful banks and savoring the tasty fish at the numerous open-air restaurants. The fishermen worked overtime to haul in great quantities of fish and fry them in shallow pits along the shore. They used special wood, from mulberry trees, for fuel. It imparted a distinct flavor to the frying fish, and it produced a pure yellow fire with no trace of smoke. Monkith and his family wandered past restaurants and observed the hapless fish as they darted around in large tubs of water, each harnessed to a string. A finger was pointed, a string was pulled, and a fish began to fry.

During the months of June through September, it was not uncommon for Griyat's inhabitants to sleep under mosquito nets on their rooftops. The children especially loved nodding off in the open air. Many of the roofs lay close to each other, separated only by a small wall, over which adults and children climbed to reach their neighbors' terraces. Often, grandmothers visited and the children gathered around them and reveled in their charming stories.

In the early fall, everyone descended from their rooftops and moved back inside. Little by little, the leaves of the orange and lemon trees began to fall, and it did not take long before the bitter cold of winter descended upon Griyat. When rough and abrasive rains pelted the small village, the streets and pathways turned into murky puddles. At times, electricity went out. In the autumn and winter, the air grew chilly and the Tigris mad. It lost its warmth and overflowed its banks once more. Still, the trees remained pregnant with oranges, lemons and *raranj*, a wild fruit with a bitter taste. With the leaves of the palm trees still luscious, the locale seemed like a verdant oasis abloom in the desert of winter.

Charming Griyat was no ordinary village, but an enclave steeped in religious and cultural traditions. Life seemed to be a story flowing from the pages of *One Thousand and One Nights*, a place where imagination unexpectedly melted into reality. Love died and was born again. Madness burst forth and would then be extinguished for a time. The heart throbbed with life and then slowed its palpitation until it reached its final rest. Here there was no life, and yet it was the center of life. Honor faded and honor lived in it. Piety bloomed rosy flowers in a field of blasphemy. Legends of this village perished and then were born again.

There was the infamous tale of Sheikh Taha, tall and gaunt, with a sparkling white *galabia*. As a child Monkith could not recall the distance between the legends he was being told and his own dreams. Legend had it that the Sheikh went swimming in the Tigris one day. As he waded along the riverbanks, he caught sight of a dark-colored *jinnee* with the head of a fish and long, curly brown hair, which touched the ground and wrapped itself around his enormous ankles. He had small silver fins and lush green seaweed clung to his body. This strange creature beckoned Sheikh Taha to the depths of the river and handed him a magical red potion, permitting him to breathe under water and flourish among his people.

The reflection of the sun brought a majestic rainbow of colors to the depths of the sea, which fashioned the rippling walls of the houses. Some walls turned purple, and others were hues of orange, yellow, and green. According to the time of day, the shades changed from darker to lighter tints. Precious gems lined the earth's surface, and mermaids with long flowing hair drifted through the ruffling water.

At first, the gold, the pearls, and the beautiful nymphs below the multicolored surface dazzled Sheikh Taha. But then his eyes fell on a girl named Sheriah as she floated by him in a long white gown. When she glanced at him with her wide, beatific smile, he fell in love with her instantly. Sheriah's thick, curly black hair grew until it touched her feet. Her eyes were as green as emeralds. Purple lights from the reflection of the sun danced on her large pupils, and she wore a string of purple pearls around her nape. Although he was an outsider, when he asked for Sheriah's hand in marriage, her parents accepted him as if he were their own son. The engagement party was filled with dancing and laughter and the wedding date was set for several months later.

Sheikh Taha happily shared in the river people's extraordinary life; a life without any fear or sadness, only trust. And love. After a while, though, he observed disturbing occurrences. When a baby was born, the river people cried, and when a person died, they celebrated. They beat the drums and sang. Oh, how he yearned to know why. A few days before his wedding, he asked and the river people explained that when a person passed away, he rejoined God. But when a baby was born he was penetrating a world far removed from God.

But Sheikh Taha could not envision a life in which he would rejoice at the loss of Sheriah or their future offspring. He knew he could feel only sadness if they were lifted from this world, despite what the river people said. When he argued with them and questioned their beliefs, the river people banished him from their kingdom. Back among his own kith, he cried inconsolably for his lover. For the rest of his life, he waited for her along the banks of the Tigris. He built a small, dismal hut and lived by the water, with his pet snakes and rats, scaring children and adults alike with his mad ramblings.

Monkith used to search for him along the Tigris and split his sandwich with him. "I brought you a sandwich, do you like liver?" he asked.

Sheikh Taha took the sandwich and they ate in silence. Monkith watched as the toothless old man sucked his sandwich, not batting an eyelid. The Sheikh was always silent, and except for an occasional bout of mad mutterings, he never uttered a word. He squat on his heels and stared out to the river. Monkith told him of his own adventures, and the old man seemed to listen attentively.

Over time, Monkith no longer found Sheikh Taha by the river. When he told his parents and neighbors, they suspected that the Sheikh might have died. Monkith's father, Naji, took matters into his own hands and knocked on the door of Sheikh Taha's rundown old hut. When no one answered, he called for his neighbor Mehdi. The two men pounded down the corrugated door and found the Sheikh dead on his bed. His two pet snakes wrapped around him. Stealthy, scurrying rats had infested his filthy room. Under the dead man's head, the men found thirty thousand dinars,[10] money the Sheikh had accumulated to pay for the river bride's dowry. Sheikh Taha's family used the money for his burial, and distributed the rest to his heirs.

The night the Sheikh died, I dreamed that I searched frantically for the strange jinnee that had waded along the Tigris. I found him and he offered me a sip from the magical potion so that I would be able to descend to the greenish purple depths of the sea just like Sheikh Taha. The magnificent colored candles at the bottom that danced with the water ripples thrilled me. But there was a storm and the colors of the depths whirled and entwined themselves together into a thick purplish black. I heard yelling above. I was called from above, but was frozen. I woke up screaming. My father grabbed my hand and told me it was time to get up, it was time for Friday prayer. I felt so sad to leave the miraculous colors of the underworld. I did not wish to open my eyes and return to my reality, a reality that had ostracized this Sheikh and turned him into a madman.

My father, a Shii Muslim, made the Haj, or pilgrimmage, to Mecca when he was twenty-six years old. Upon his return, as was the custom, he was bestowed the respectful title 'Hajj Naji' or more simply, 'the Hajj.' After his pilgrimage, he became increasingly devout. The impression he left on his neighbors and relatives became important to him. The first question he asked me in the morning was: 'Did you pray?' I would say that I had not and he would strike me with his heavy hand. Soon thereafter, I learned to go through the motions of praying, but these gestures felt empty to me. I closed my eyes and cursed my father's hand, which had left its bitter imprints on my body. I cursed the Prophet Muhammad for requiring prayer five times a day.

I saw religion as a weapon my father hurled against his children, and it felt like no one bore the brunt more than I did. Although in certain respects, I enjoyed more freedom than my sisters, my status as eldest son curbed my movements. His expectations of me were oppressive. For my father believed that if you raised your eldest son well, then all the other children would follow in his path. But if you were lax with your eldest son, your other children would also suffer. To my father, the behavior of his eldest son – who rebelled

---

[10] At the time every one Iraqi dinar was about $3.30. 20 dirhams equaled 1 dinar. 1 dirham equaled 50 feles (cents).

against all forms of authority – was nothing less than a personal affront.

Thus as a child, I created an imaginary world that no one else was able to enter, a space all my own. For I found in Baghdad a society that combined the best and the worst that life had to offer. The strength of religion and political ideology was often confining, yet the beauty and richness of nature, mythology, colors and tunes, made Baghdad magical, like a haven for the curious. It was like living in heaven and hell at the same time.

The Ascent of the Baath

It was 1958, the year before Monkith's birth, and the end of the Monarchy that the British had imposed. General 'Abd al-Karim Qasim – with the help of General 'Abd al-Salam 'Arif – had led the successful overthrow of King Faisal, and presided over the revolutionary government of July 1958. The king met the brutal fate of all deposed Iraqi monarchs: his hands were tied to the back of a vehicle and he was dragged to death. Only a few years earlier, it would have been a cart; but on that day, it was a car. Never mind. A stern and inhumane tradition was observed chapter and verse.

General 'Abd al-Karim Qasim was now in the vulnerable position of being the virtual head of state, with 'Arif as his second hand man. From the beginning, Iraqis adored their simple leader, Qasim, who never married, but instead devoted himself entirely to his nation. He lived the life of a pauper. He did not even own a house, but rented a small room in the Defense Ministry instead. He owned just a bed and one set of military clothes. In 1959, owing to 'Arif's treachery, however, the then obscure Baath party was able to entrust an alarmingly cruel and ambitious young fellow by the name of Saddam Hussein with the task of assassinating Qasim and pitch forking the Baath into office. The destitute Saddam, from the impoverished village of Tikrit to the north of Baghdad, got only so far as to shoot Qasim in the leg before fleeing for his life – first to Syria, and then on to Egypt. Five years later, however, the Baath staged a successful coup and seized the reigns of power. The people may have adored Qasim, but he was a naïve leader who underestimated the complexities of politics. He was duly executed. Upon his death, his men found no more than three dinars in the pockets of the bullet-ridden corpse.

Yet most Iraqis did not believe that their beloved 'Abd al-Karim Qasim had been killed. Even those who witnessed his assassination on television continued to deny the fact. They watched how his own treacherous soldiers from the Ministry of Defense surrounded him, and how he resisted, heroically returning fire. Finally, one soldier managed to approach him, put a bullet through his head, and spat on him.

Still no one accepted his death, and Iraqis created legends concerning his whereabouts for years to come. Some recounted stories of how they saw Qasim's face etched in the beautiful full moon. Others said that he had traveled to Iran and would soon return. There were those who merely said that he had vanished temporarily.

Monkith was just five years old when the Baath staged its February 8, 1963 coup. As a child, he heard tales of the courage of Qasim's loyalists. For Iraqis did not simply lie low and play dead to the Baath party coup. The Kazamiyyah region of Baghdad, a Communist party stronghold, put up a fierce resistance. The area fell after three days when Saad Matruk, the leader of the uprising, surrendered. To show that it meant business, the Baath shot him point-blank in front of a wall and a crowd of spectators.

Ibrahim Hariri, a Communist writer of short stories who was to become a close friend of Monkith's, spent more his life inside Iraqi prisons than out of them, owing to his political affiliations. Years later, in exile, he described to Monkith how he and his fellow comrades had participated in the protests of Kazamiyyah:

Dauntless, we rolled forward with guns blazing. Tanks festooned with posters of Qasim approached us. But that was only a feint. As I approached one of the armored vehicles, it started shooting at me. Only one of us carried a gun of any consequence; the rest just carried brandished pistols. How many comrades were massacred in the Kazamiyyah resistance these days!

I hid behind a barricade and aimed at a tank. Unfortunately the pistol did not work. Our resistance lasted from Friday through Sunday. But after three days Kazamiyyah surrendered. Many on our side were killed. I saw a man who had been shot lying on the ground and someone - not a doctor - was trying to extract the bullet with a razor. I fled. Salam Adil, Secretary General of the party and an important leader of the resistance, escaped unscathed. But after a few months, he too was killed.

There was much treachery. Informers told the Baathi leaders where people were hiding out. I was held in one prison for forty days and then transferred to another fortress. One of my jailers told me that the prison guards had buried alive everyone who had been removed from the first prison. But for some reason, I was not killed. My name was on the death list, but then it was erased. I did not ask why, but I felt that I had been granted another life!

Chaos was the norm after the Baath gradually seized the reigns of power in the period between February and November 1963. However, the regime of General Abd al-Salam 'Arif – who had previously betrayed Qasim and helped the Baath depose him – soon sidelined the Baathists. 'Arif may have been a strong military officer, but he was a weak politician. As a result, the task of ensuring peaceful coexistence between the junta and the intelligentsia fell to his prime minister 'Abd al-Rahman al-Bazzaz, a liberal intellectual. Shortly thereafter, deputies of Iraq's parliamentary body, the Majlis, reached an agreement to halt the collective persecution of Communists.

Under 'Arif's regime, the round up, imprisonment, and execution of individual Communist party members continued unabated. Monkith's father, a government employee who had joined the Communists, was jailed for about one year. Monkith's cousin Ali Hadi al-Jaber, graduate of the University of Chicago, professor, and fifteen-year veteran of a Swedish company, was also imprisoned several years in a row for being a Communist. Monkith's uncle Haydar was killed on account of his left-wing affiliations.

When his father was incarcerated, it fell upon his pregnant mother, Nuriya, to support him and his younger sisters Manal and Ibtihal. Nuriya became a seamstress, and ran her business from the home of her mother-in-law, Habooba. Although, in keeping with a firmly rooted cultural practice, Nuriya lived with her husband's family, she was too proud to accept financial help from then. She sewed dresses to earn money to feed her children. In fact, all of Habooba's sons and their families led separate lives under her roof. The women cooked together in a kitchen submerged in silence; and then ate their meals in different quarters of the house.

Not long after his father's imprisonment, Monkith, his sisters, and their mother visited him in prison. For the first time Monkith beheld his father's softness and vulnerability. Naji appeared behind the window in his pajamas. He was unshaven, his hair was disheveled, and his eyes were misty. Nuriya had just given birth to a new baby girl named Iqbal. She held her up to the pane of glass to take a closer look. Tears welled in Naji's eyes and his eyebrows quivered as he stared at his daughter's unreachable tiny hands.

How he longed to feel their softness. Perhaps it was this sudden emergence of life that triggered it, but once he was released, he immediately turned his Communist zeal towards religion. It was after his discharge from prison that he made his pilgrimage to Mecca. He continued to work as a low-ranking government employee until, a few years later he was purged from his job. Forced into early retirement, he decided to open a small shop that sold construction materials.

In the meantime, Abd al-Salam 'Arif met an unfortunate end in April 1966 when he hopped on a plane that crashed under mysterious circumstances. Some caustic tongues poignantly observed that 'Arif had gone up as meat and come down as charcoal. It was not until July 1968, that a different faction within the Baath staged a second coup d'état. President Abd al-Rahman 'Arif, the handpicked younger brother of Abd al-Salam 'Arif, went into exile in Turkey, and Ahmad Hassan al-Bakr took power. Although Bakr may have held the title of President of Iraq from 1968 to 1979, Saddam Hussein, his vice president, stood behind the scenes and pulled the strings.

Recalled Monkith:

I remember the day of the revolution in the summer of '68 vividly. It was July 17th. Although it was only seven o'clock in the morning, it was a sticky summer day. I was perched next to the door that opened on to the parlor, gaping at the veranda and the garden. My mother, who always woke up early to buy bread and prepare breakfast, was planting a small palm tree in the garden. Umm Hassan, our neighbor who was a fortune-teller, came over. She announced that there had been another revolution. This hardly came as a shock since we Iraqis were used to coup d'états by now.

My family turned on the radio to hear 'Bayan Raghme Wahed' (Communiqué Number One), a phrase that came to be used on broadcast channels to signal the announcement of yet another putsch. A joke circulated among us that anyone who wanted to attain power had only to wake up at four in the morning, slip into his military boots and occupy the radio station. Despite the frequency of such political upheaval, we were all still curious to see how events would unfold. At the time, Saddam, the new vice president, was young, handsome, and virtually unknown outside the inner circles of the Baath party. Those who did know something about him knew that he enjoyed a reputation for cruelty. Iraqis affiliated with the Baath, however, supported him unflinchingly.

For as long as one week after the coup, Iraqis had no idea who had really risen to power. Aware of the poor reputation that it enjoyed throughout the county, the Baath scrupulously withheld news of its take-over. The tidings could not be kept secret forever and once word trickled out, the party leadership – in an effort to win over the people – liberated some political prisoners and paid them compensation. On the surface, the early years of Baath rule were times of relatively enlightened politics in Iraq. The party organized the National Front as the umbrella organization that contained the various fractious parties representing Communists, Shiis, Sunnis, and Kurds. At the time, several tolerant and progressively minded advisors counseled the party leadership. In later years, they were eliminated one after another.

In the early 1970s, the Baath orchestrated a nationalist cult around Adnan al-Qaysi, an Iraqi wrestler residing in the United States, in order to distract the people from politics. The party wooed him back to Iraq and showcased his fame as part of a nationalist exhibition. The nation followed each wrestling match with bated breath on television. The handsome pugilist would step into the ring amidst the bombastic fanfare and hoarse screams of the spectators clamoring for another victory. Monkith gazed as he flexed his artificially copious muscles, and began to stare mercilessly into the eyes of his competitor, John Ferari, who had been jetted in from America just for the occasion. John Ferari, America's famous wrestling champion, sturdy as a heavy oak tree and more than two meters tall, with long brown strands of oily and unkempt hair that formed a wholly unappetizing mullet, stood snorting fiercely at his nemesis while sweat trickled down his heaving body. Both strutted around the ring with puffed up chests like two cocks readying for the showdown. They flexed their taut bodies in a show of vainglorious display. Monkith's family along with the nation at large, ohhh-ed as John Ferari threw Qaysi on the ground, and ahhh-ed when Qaysi stood up, knocked Ferari over, and kept him effortlessly supine and squeamish on the ground with the tip of his fiercely bulging, shiny elbow. The audience was aghast and erupted in exuberant cries of exultation as Qaysi stood once again triumphant.

For the Baath, the 1970s were also a golden age of economic growth. In large part, this was due to the nationalization of the oil industry. Until then, foreign companies owned fifty-one per cent of the joint ventures set up in Iraq. However, the Baath party, under the command of President Bakr, rewrote the rules of the game. Iraq now owned one hundred percent of the oil companies.

Monkith was thirteen years old at the time of nationalization. His cousin, Ali Hadi Jaber, was an oil expert, who had been imprisoned under the regime of 'Arif for being a Communist. After his release, he proposed nationalization to Bakr, who readily agreed to it. For although Jaber had attended an American university, he was opposed to foreign control of Iraqi resources. Nationalization of one of the world's most sought-after commodities brought about a veritable bonanza.[11] As Monkith entered his adolescent years, Iraq could count itself among the richest countries in the developing world, both in terms of industry and agriculture. Every middle-class family possessed a car and enjoyed a healthy income, while unemployment was low. Many vacationed in Europe. Saddam Hussein, then still vice president, observed that Iraqis threw away more food than they ate. On a more ominous note, in one interview after another, he vowed that in the future he would make Iraqis pay for their profligacy.

Increasingly, from the mid-1970s onward, the Baath searched for more sophisticated ways to contain the population. Clearly Qaysi's acrobatics could not keep Iraqis perpetually quiescent. Officers of the *mukhabarat*, Iraq's dreaded security force, were sent abroad to learn from their counterparts in East Germany. And so the *mukhabarat*, thoroughly refined its repertoire of ruthlessness, seeking to implant fear forever in the hearts of the populace by honing a society of blood, death, and murder. The secret service was later credited with having created the enigmatic figure of the axe-man Abu Tabar whom the regime held responsible for the shower of red pellots, which induced the death of famous doctors, engineers, and Communists across the country. The Baath showed daily television footage of corpses, sliced dead by the elusive Abu Tabar. The terrified people watched the bloody scenes of the latest murders of the mystery axe-man, as if they were episodes of a heated television serial. Not surprisingly, very few Iraqis ventured out on the streets after nine in the evening. When Monkith returned home late in the evening from his grandmother Fatema's home, his father pulled him in the house and slapped him hard: "God curse you, son, you could have been killed by Abu Tabar! You should not be in the streets after nine! Why do you torment me in this way?"

Before long, the *mukhabarat* had succeeded in creating a society stalked by its own shadow, and spies were planted in every household. And then one day, a spokesman for the Baath appeared on television, trumpeting the capture of Abu Tabar. The authorities had dragged a young man aged thirty before the television camera who confessed to the murders he had allegedly committed. In great detail, he described each crime. He later disappeared from public view, and rumors had it that the *mukhabarat* had bribed the young man to make a confession. The Baath had supposedly promised to send him to Germany as a millionaire, but after the confession, he was found dead together with the rest of his family.

---

[11] Between 1970 and 1979 Iraqi per capita income rose from approximately $4,500 to more than $8,000 in constant 1987 dollars.

Two Grandmothers from Baghdad

The night she passed away, I dreamed I was lying in a deep pit. My family cried above. I howled, but my sobs could not reach their ears. The gravedigger threw dirt into the chasm until I could no longer fully discern the sky. I could only see patches of blue surrounded by spots of dark brown mud, as if there were blue stars in the dark of the night. Suddenly all the blue faded and I only beheld brown above. My breath failed me. I could no longer shriek. As I opened my mouth, it filled with brown clay. And then I felt a hand searching for me. I imagined myself being lifted high above and soon I was looking down on the abyss and the mourners below. I soared higher into the milky white clouds until I could distinguish neither my family's tear-filled faces, nor apprehend their screams of sorrow.

An olive-skinned woman with long flowing jet-black hair held my hand and together we rested on a patch of soft white fluff. It was only when she took out her little treasure chest and began polishing the items of silverware it held one by one that I recognized she was my grandmother Habooba. Not the Habooba veiled in black who I had known all my life, but a comely woman clad in a satiny white gown. She smiled at me and handed me a piece of silverware so I could help her. I felt at peace, but suddenly began to cry. I yearned for my mother and my other grandmother Fatema. I bellowed, and I could no longer discern the stunning woman. She faded away behind fluffy white curtains. I could barely breathe when I woke up panting in the darkness.

Monkith's paternal grandmother, whom everyone used to call Habooba (sweetie) or Haboobti (my sweetie), struck him as a strange woman. She took showers with the door flung wide open, so that he was able to examine the contours of her body minutely while she splashed – eyes closed – water over her head to rinse off the soapsuds. The tattoo that slithered across her body captivated Monkith. The flowery green pattern crept from the tip of her toes, up her legs, over her stomach, and across her sagging breasts. He later learned that Habooba had tattooed her body to arouse her husbands' desire; a common practice among women of wealthy families.

Habooba regaled Monkith with stories of her childhood. She pulled him close to her and said: "My dear father was a wealthy businessman who was engaged in commerce with Iran. On the day of my birth, he was in Tehran. He called my mother and named me 'Shah Zanan.'"

"Shah Zanan," Monkith whispered, trying to articulate the foreign name. "What does it mean?"

"It is a Persian name designating 'the most beautiful of beauties,' and I was called Sheznah, which is the Arabic version of that name," Habooba said, her eyes sparkling with delight.

Monkith scrutinized Habooba's heavily wrinkled face for traces of her former glory. He stirred to ask her something else, but she hushed him and continued in a slightly more conspiratorial tone: "Well, as I neared my teenage years, it became clear that I was living up to my name. I soon became the object of desire for those men who had the privilege of entering our household and seeing me. One after another they asked my father for my hand in marriage only to be flatly rejected. My father was determined that I was too special to be given away to the first suitors, and I placed my trust in his wisdom."

She paused for a moment and smiled. Monkith lay mesmerized next to her. As she grew silent, he was stirred. "When did your father decide you should get married?" he asked with impatience.

A sweet note of justified pride crept into her voice as she continued: "My father's favorite older brother used to visit our household frequently – he, too, was a wealthy man of commerce. As he sat with my father, I used to serve them tea and sweets as I did with all our guests. My uncle soon took a special liking to me. He saw me as a polite and well-mannered little beauty. He asked my father if he would be willing to offer my hand in marriage to his favorite son, Saaid – a tall and dashing businessman. At first my father feinted refusal, but then he happily accepted. At the time, I was a little over thirteen and Saaid was eighteen."

"What was your marriage like?" Monkith interrupted impetuously.

Habooba sighed as she wandered down the narrow alleys of her memories and continued: "I had not seen my cousin for several years, but I felt so much excitement on the day of the wedding. I was seated on a chair perched high against the wall and everyone observed me closely. I had a cold and kept sniffling, but my mother handed me a handkerchief and told me to gently brush it against my running nose. During the ceremony Saaid and I barely spoke – But I noticed that he had kind eyes and was very handsome. I think I fell in love with him the first instant I beheld him, and on our wedding night, when I lifted my veil, my astonishing beauty enchanted him. So it was love at first sight for both of us."

She paused for a moment. Her eyes were hazed and she tried to rise from her seat.

"Wait, Habooba. Please tell me more. What happened after your marriage?" Monkith asked as he tugged at her arm so she could not rise.

"Every day our love grew deeper than the sea and vaster than the sky. Before neighbors or relatives even had a chance to interfere and tell us it was important to give birth to a son, I was pregnant and expecting a son. Indeed God had blessed me with an amazing fertility, which brought us one son after another. And this is how your father and all your uncles were born."

"What was my grandfather like?" Monkith asked

Habooba smiled as she enthralled him with stories of the grandfather he never knew: "Saaid, your grandfather, followed in his father and father-in-law's footsteps. He engaged in trade between Iraq and Saudi Arabia and became a wealthy man of commerce. But," and for a moment, she drifted off into her own secret world, "I was devastated when he was captured during World War I and held as a prisoner of war for fourteen years in 'Chan wa Machan.'"

Monkith mulled over the name of the place "Chan wa Machan," but could not locate it on any of the imaginary maps he was so fond of browsing as a young boy.

"Habooba. Please don't stop. What happened to him in prison?" Monkith implored her to tell him more.

But Hahaooba was deep in thought. Frustrated, Monkith started shaking her. Once she returned from her reverie, she resumed the thread of her tale – but ignored her grandson's specific question: "Of course, many suitors flirted with me while my husband was in prison, but I remained faithful. I refused to believe their empty prattle of how Saaid had died in captivity."

"Was he really dead, or did he escape 'Chan wa Machan?'" Monkith asked, only later realizing that this was Habooba's skewed pronunciation of China and Japan.

Tears filled her eyes, and she refused to dwell on details of her husband's homecoming – despite her grandson's insistence. Nonetheless, she briefly narrated how he eventually returned by foot, tired and haggard, and died a few days later. And how during that brief interlude, he and Habooba managed to conceive their last son, whom she named Kafeeh, which is Arabic for "enough now!"

Habooba's only remaining possession of her husband was a colorful treasure chest, decorated with a dainty floral design. Spoons, plates, and other precious Chinese *objets d'art* filled the trousseau. How proud she was of that box, and with what gusto she showed it to everyone! She opened the box and delved into its contents like a newlywed bride marveling at her wedding trousseaux. Monkith, Manal, Ibtihal, and their cousins would sit next to her silently as she carefully removed each piece of silverware and polished it. She would pass around the sparkling cutlery, but only allowed her grandchildren to admire it for a split second before she snapped it away and confined it to its safety once more. Every day she counted her spoils to make sure that none had disappeared. None of the children dared approach the box when she was not in her room – she had scared them into thinking that an enormous *jinnee* with huge green wings inhabited the receptacle and protected her husband's soul. Every now and then Monkith nestled up to the box, hoping to catch a glimpse of the strange *jinnee*. But he was too afraid to rattle his grandfather's guardian spirit.

Habooba dressed in black for as long as Monkith could remember. Indeed, after her husband's death, she remained loyal and dignified in her grief. She recounted: "In accordance with tradition, I trailed my husband's cortège back to the house for a final farewell. A group of male friends and relatives placed the coffin halfway through the front door of the house – with half the coffin inside the house and the other outside; this signified the combination of the world that the dead man knew while he was alive and the unknown world he was now entering."

Habooba described how the men elevated the coffin into the air three times, before carrying it to Najaf, an important holy city where Shiis bury their loved ones. As the men raised the coffin in the air, mourners proclaimed what a great man Saaid had been. Many of the women ululated and cried: "May God have mercy on him." The third time the men lifted the casket, they suspended the coffin in mid-air, so that the distressed Habooba could slip underneath it. According to tradition, if the widow passed under her husband's coffin, she could not leave the house for forty days. Not all women followed this strict custom, but since greater grieving was seen as socially reputable, Habooba was proud to say that she had. She recounted her sacrifices many times to Monkith and her other grandchildren, who listened in astonishment.

Having one been a great beauty, the widowed Habooba was extremely jealous of all her sons' wives, but none more so than Monkith's mother, who had the misfortune of being exceptionally beautiful. The tension between the two women arose even before Monkith was born. Much of it dated back to a severe rainstorm that disrupted the house's plumbing and knocked out electricity. Habooba, who wielded absolute power in the household, ordered Nuriya to fetch water from the Tigris. The obedient daughter-in-law, who happened to be in her eighth month of pregnancy, grabbed her jug and soldiered out into the storm. Suddenly, she slid near the bank of the Tigris. The heavy clay jug brimming with water slammed against her stomach. By the time she had managed to drag herself home, the baby was lifeless, a stillborn that bled out of her.

From then on, Nuriya – albeit never in the presence of her husband – insisted that her mother-in-law had aborted her firstborn son. The strain, which had merely irritated their relationship up until then, now blossomed into a full-fledged animosity between the two women. Habooba told her son that his wife would stealthily slip out of the house the moment he left for work, only to return shortly before he was due back. At times, he was inclined to believe her, and he fought with his slandered wife. But in the end, after consultation with friends and neighbors, he always discovered his wife's innocence and begged for her forgiveness.

Unable to compete with her daughters-in-law for her sons' affection, Habooba feigned an illness that put her on death's door. Abu Karim, the local medical expert, attended to her on a weekly basis. He was a popular, rotund, and above all jovial man. Not only was he plump, but he also sported an astonishingly short bull's neck, whose fleshy folds wrapped themselves like a wreath around his obesely beaming Buddha face. He arrived, always full of jokes, with a knack for making people laugh. Only too well aware that Habooba was not dying, he filled his syringe with water and injected it into her flabby buttocks in order to give her the impression that her worries were being taken seriously. The shots worked veritable miracles. Every time the ailing Habooba received an injection, she would heave an audible sigh of relief. Each time the "doctor" left she announced that he had once again saved her from death.

One day, Abu Karim found his patient in a particularly sorry state. Habooba lay on her bed moaning, one hand clamped to her forehead and the other gripping her stomach as if convulsed by pain. Monkith sat in the corner of her room on her treasure box, awaiting the weekly ritual with an air of paramount indifference. The "doctor" offered Habooba a glass of date juice, and then administered the shot of mineral water. Out of the blue, however, Abu Karim abandoned his usual routine to give the family a "tragic" piece of news: there was absolutely nothing wrong with the patient. Everyone was astonished and stared at Habooba in disbelief.

Abu Karim, confident that he had the full attention of the family, declared authoritatively: "It seems our Habooba desperately needs a husband. If your family can find a sixty-year-old man for Habooba to marry, all her problems – as well as yours – will most definitely be solved!"

At this, Monkith noticed his parents, uncles, and aunts breathe a sigh of relief and struggle to suppress their laughter.

"Why, the little devil – why didn't we think of this before?" Kafeeh said as he nudged Naji and winked at Habooba.

But Habooba would hear none of it. With unexpected passion suddenly displayed by a dying woman, she protested that she would never marry another. "What dried cow's dung! I will remain married to Saaid until the day I die!" she screeched, zeroing in on the hapless Abu Karim, whose Buddha-like composure suddenly disappeared between the trembling folds of his quaking bull's neck. "I've had enough of this rot. I am dying. Kafeeh!" she snapped, appropriately punctuating her peroration with the wonted invocation of her youngest son's name.

As she threw a pillow on the ground, the room grew stiff with silence. But they would not give up on the idea, as they were happy to hear that there was a possibility for the ordeal of Habooba's hypochondria to be over. Monkith noticed how his parents, uncles and their wives frantically whispered among themselves about a possible suitor, but alas, none could be found.

"What about Hajj Abbas? He's a widower, and all his children are abroad. He's looking to remarry!" Monkith's Uncle Hamid declared.

"But Hajj Abbas is only fifty years old. Habooba is sixty. So it would never work out," Naji said with frustration.

"And besides, Hajj Abbas is the paragon of stinginess! But what ever happened to Abu Ismael? I don't think he ever got remarried!" Majid gleamed.

"I heard that he traveled to Najaf, and in any case, he cannot be more than forty-five years old. Too young for our Habooba," Kafeeh said sadly.

Monkith – cool as a cucumber – decided to apply his budding knowledge of mathematics to the escalating situation. Seeing how eagerly his family responded to Abu Karim's proposal, he ventured to offer a solution.

"I have an idea," he cried out into the frustrated chatter. "If you can't find a sixty-year-old man, you don't have to give up. Why don't you search for two thirty-year-olds instead? Thirty plus thirty equals sixty!"

At this, the room erupted into a laughter, which washed away the tension engulfing them like a heavy rain after a severe dust storm. Even Habooba smiled. Ultimately, though, there was no point trying to reason with her. She refused to remarry. Eternally devoted to her deceased husband, she remained a prickly thorn in her family's side until the day she died.

Although Monkith regarded Habooba as a brusque woman, he was nevertheless drawn to her world. Her room was a warm, dark, and mystical abode. He visited her every day. While he completed his homework, she poured him a light tea called

Shay al-Aroos[12] from a samovar. He felt at ease in Habooba's room and spent hours speaking with her on many subjects. One winter afternoon, Monkith, still excited from his teacher's history lesson that day, exclaimed: "Oh, Haboobti, how great we Arabs are – we are so mighty! We even reached China. Oh, how I wish the Arab race will always stay mighty!"

But Habooba did not believe the Arabs were a vigorous race. With an amazed laugh, she replied: "How can this be so? We Arabs of Mesopotamia had been vanquished by the Sunni Muslim Turks and absorbed by the Ottoman Empire, which imposed a harsh rule on us! Oh my son, the Turks need one thousand years at least to become *jehash*.[13] But these same ignorant Turks were able to capture and rule over us for five hundred years. So tell me, son, how many years do you think we Arabs need to become Turks, and then *jehash*, and then finally human beings?"

Habooba held Monkith, his sisters, and their cousins spellbound with all kinds of wonderful stories from *One Thousand and One Nights* and all the other splendid fables born of Baghdad. On summer nights, she climbed with the children to the rooftop. Under a dusky sky, the children gathered around the old woman to listen to her vivid tales.

In the manner of Shahrazad, she spoke: "Once upon a time there was a handsome king who entered one of the large vaulted rooms in his castle and scattered his magical seeds across the mosaic covering the floor. That evening a young maiden with a moonlit face and long, jet-black hair entered the room, and soon she was expecting a child."

The children huddled together in silent anticipation of what would happen next, but Monkith could not hold still, "Why is she awaiting his child? How did this happen?"

Ibtihal's big brown eyes opened wide in astonishment and

---

[12] This means "the tea of a newlywed bride." It consists of three-quarters of hot water and some sugar, topped off with a sprinkling of ground tea leaves.

[13] A *jehash* or a jennet is a female donkey that is the offspring of a male horse and a female ass, and thought to be very stupid.

Manal began to giggle, while Habooba blushed profusely. In the manner of other adults, when telling stories, she used the metaphor of scattered seeds to avoid explaining the lovemaking ritual between men and women. She asked Monkith to please hush, but he could not overcome his curiosity.

"Did the princess stay with him in the evening?" he persisted.

Habooba coughed, trying to drown out the question with a feigned fit of asthma. "Please, son, let me continue."

But Monkith fired so many questions at her on that night and on many others that she started to use an Arab proverb to describe the curious youth: "He who digs a well with a needle and searches for the father of the bastard child." The other children kept quiet, but Monkith persisted even when she reprimanded him.

When she delved into her stories, she entranced Monkith, his sisters, and cousins. Every night she wove her tale but rarely brought it to a conclusion, continuing her narration the following evening in the manner of Shahrazad. One story Monkith vividly remembered:

"Once upon a time, a young woman approached a midwife and told her that a pregnant woman was nearing her confinement and desperately needed help giving birth. The midwife agreed to accompany the woman to her village. Entering the expecting mother's home through a strange round door, the midwife found several cats, one of which was giving birth, sprawled over the floor. The midwife was thoroughly miffed at having been made to believe that she was going to deliver a fellow woman's child, but she applied herself to the task anyway, since she had already made the long journey to the remote village. After the kitten was born, as a token of gratitude, the young woman draped a garland of onions over the midwife's cloth veil, which she wore under her black *abaya*.[14] The midwife, irritated by the odor of the onions, turned the cloth over like a bib. The moment she left the house, she threw away the wreath. But once she returned home, she noticed that one piece of onion still clung to her veil, and it was made of gold. She tried frantically to locate the cats' door again, but when she returned, it had disappeared."

Habooba may have filled her grandson's ears with fairytales, but she made life impossible for Monkith's mother. When he was seven years old, his parents decided to move into their own home, several minutes from Habooba's dominion. But it was not long before he found his way back to her house. He did not always miss his eccentric grandmother. Indeed there were times he was happy to be far away. Yet he somehow found himself drawn back into her enchanting world.

If Monkith visited Habooba's on Thursdays, he and his cousins accompanied her to the religious shrine of Sheikh Shibli whom the villagers in Griyat revered as a holy man and whose shrine they would flock to for picnics on Thursdays and Fridays. The "pilgrimage" usually ended at a small clearing surrounded by trees, which was supposedly the spot where the Sheikh was buried. Villagers decked the ground with candles and draped the surrounding trees with colorful handkerchiefs with which they hoped to satisfy the holy man and win his grace. The rainbow of brightly colored cloths flittering in the wind enchanted Monkith. While his cousins and neighbors ran around and frolicked, Monkith gazed at the marvelous colors dangling above him, his imagination spinning with run-away images and stories – one piece of cloth looked like a two-headed water buffalo with purple legs, a melting candle below resembled a one-eyed lion, several sly swallows building their nests, and a small red donkey taking a nap under the golden sunlight.

As many false alarms Habooba may have had, she did eventually reach the end of her path. Soon, she went blind. It was the nine-year-old Monkith's responsibility, as the eldest grandson in the family, to take her by the hand when she went out for walks. For two years, Monkith was at her beck and call. He forfeited much of the freedom he had enjoyed playing with his own friends in order to take care of his increasingly morose grandmother. Often, when he slipped out of the house to play, his father spotted him and told him Habooba needed someone to accompany her to the market. She grew irritated when Monkith

---

[14] This is an all-concealing woman's cloak worn loosely over the body.

asked her to tell him a story. The only sounds that now surged from her mouth were bitter complaints that no one was taking care of her and fulfilling their responsibilities – most of all him.

When Habooba fell ill, she refused to see a doctor and preferred to lie in bed, claiming she was awaiting death. For some time, no one believed her. All her life, she had ranted and raved about dying. But, as it eventually became clear to the family that she might really be passing away, they placed her mattress on the floor. Observing a hallowed family tradition, they invited a poet to try to prevent the ailing Habooba, through words, from succumbing. Her daughters-in-law dipped their hands in a glass of water, and sprinkled it into Habooba's mouth. In keeping with their duty, they wailed loudly, but if the truth were told, the passing of this difficult matriarch was something of a relief. The requisite period of mourning persisted in this way for several days as Habooba succumbed to the frosty anticipation of imminent death. Each woman competed with the other for the loudest wails and most ear-shattering screams. And yet each was equally careful not to let any gesture betray a hovering sensation of inner anticipation for the moment that Habooba would draw her terminal breath.

The day she passed away was a strange one for Monkith. Habooba's brain hemorrhaged. Blood spilled out from her mouth, drenching her pillow and sheets. She lay in bed motionless, with her eyes wide open. A frighteningly strange expression fluttered on her wan face. The scent of death entwined with the perfume of camphor, which the women of the household sprinkled over the corpse. The men and women shuffled around the room, and Uncle Kafeeh opened the window to let in some fresh air. Monkith's father paced up and down the room, trying to regain his composure. The eleven-year-old Monkith sat on Habooba's treasure box in the corner of the room, quietly observing everything in a state of stupor, unable to sort out his own feelings.

The family placed Habooba's body in a wooden box about two meters long. Several men raised her coffin into the air, suspended half inside, half outside the front door. They lifted Habooba three times to say farewell. Then they fastened her coffin on the top of a car and commenced their journey to Najaf where they intended to lay her next to her beloved husband, Saaid. Nuriya and Naji did not wish for their children to be prematurely exposed to funeral mourning, but in the confusion, no one noticed that Monkith had come along for the long ride.

Once they arrived in Najaf, Monkith shuffled into a room unnoticed by the heavyhearted women. He watched as they laid her corpse down and washed it with mineral water and dappled it with camphor, which was thought to be an everlasting perfume. Next, they dipped cotton into a bowl of camphor-scented essence and stuffed the buds in all the openings of her body. Then, they clad her in a pure white satin dress and wrapped white cotton sheets around her whole body before placing her in a long rectangular case. Monkith began to analyze the composition of colors. He realized that white was a cold color that kept away the sun. But then again, he concluded, Habooba would not need the sun's warmth anymore. Those who mourned Habooba wore black, because they were still alive and wished to attract the sun.

Soon thereafter, the men arrived and carried the coffin to a pit. The family lifted Habooba's covered corpse out of the casket and laid her in the dirt. In accordance with Islamic belief, Habooba was not buried in a coffin, as it is believed that at birth the body rises up from earth and at death it is sent back to the earth. The men laid Habooba on her right-hand side,[15] while gathering closely around the pit. The women assembled around them. As was customary, the gravedigger took a piece of dirt and threw it on Habooba, uttering the ritualized invocation: "And such is the life of us mortals on earth. We emerge from earth and to earth we return." As the gravedigger continued to toss dirt on her, Monkith slowly left the women's section and inched closer

---

[15] The right-hand side is considered sacred in Islam, for it is promised that on the Day of Judgment, God will place the book, where the good and bad deeds are written, in the individual's right hand. Also, in traditional Islamic belief it is said that the good deeds are inscribed on the right shoulder, while the bad deeds are on the left-hand side.

to Habooba's grave. He watched as the gravedigger flung dirt until no trace of her remained exposed. He listened to the women as they pierced his ears with their dutiful screams of exasperation. Unnerved, he searched for his father who was choking on his tears. It must have been then that Naji noticed his son's presence. "My God, what on earth are you doing here, Monkith? Off you go to your mother, we're leaving soon. Don't you dare leave her side," he yelled.

Initially, Monkith felt only relief at having been discharged from a cumbersome duty following Habooba's death. He did not shed a single tear, but a strange sense of loss was with him nonetheless. That evening when they returned home from Najaf, he sought solice in his room. He secretly turned the volume of the radio so low that his father would not make out any of the "unlawful tunes" he had prohibited in his home due to his own strict interpretation of Islam. "How many times have I told you that listening to music is a sin," his father had often said as he smacked his ear. But now Monkith searched for any song by Abd al-Halim Hafez, his favorite singer from Egypt, and found one, which reminded him, he could not exactly explain why, of Habooba.

Oh, my dear heart,
We meet together for tortuous pain.
A meeting always enveloped in deep pain.
Don't lay still and don't fall asleep,
Oh, my dear heart.

It would take many years before Monkith realized just how much this woman had given him after all. Through the act of storytelling, she had fired his imagination. She had spun a web of legends around him, tales that touched the hidden depths of his own burgeoning creativity.

◆

Monkith's relationship with his maternal grandmother, the sweet and gentle Fatema, stood in stark contrast to that with the domineering Habooba. Monkith found Fatema, a fair-skinned woman with clear green eyes and Persian roots, to be stunning.

She accentuated her beauty by dressing in hues of dark green with white or black stripes. Whenever Monkith saw Fatema, whom he affectionately called *Jedeyti*, my grandma, his chest swelled with happy feelings. He loved to nestle his cheeks against her neck, for he loved the way she smelled. As he held her unwashed headscarf close to his nose at night, he was lulled into peaceful sleep.

Chocolate from Fatema's hands tasted sweeter than anything he would eat for the rest of his life. When he stayed with her, he woke up in the middle of the night with strange cravings, sometimes for bread and sugar, yogurt, even fish. Oh, how he longed for Fatema to feed him from her gentle hands and tell him delicious tales! His favorite was the story of the paper fish. With Monkith snuggled close to her, she began:

"Once there was a family that lived near the Tigris. It was a tradition in the household – passed down by generations – to have fish every Friday for lunch."

"*Jedeyti*," Monkith interrupted, "my parents also prepare fish every Friday."

"Yes, my son, given the proximity to the Tigris, many Baghdadi families abide by this tradition."

"Where does the tradition come from?" he asked as he cuddled closer to her and smelled her neck.

"It may have been influenced by the Christian practice of abstaining from red meat on Fridays," Fatema said as she caressed her grandson's forehead. As Monkith's eyelids began to close, she continued:

"One night, one of the sons woke up crying – just like you sometimes do," she said as she nudged Monkith, who opened his eyes and smiled. "Exhausted by a long day's work, the boy's father hurried to his room and asked him what was wrong."

"Choking on his sobs, the little boy gulped, 'Father, please do not be upset with me. I am craving fish tonight and cannot fall asleep.'"

Fatema looked down at her drowsy grandson and continued: "'Good Heavens, son, it is two in the morning. Where on earth are we supposed to get fish at this ungodly hour? Why didn't you finish your dinner earlier?' He paused. Exasperated, he added, 'I mean, you left your whole plate untouched!' He rose to turn off the light once more shaking his head in disbelief."

"But the boy began to sob again and rubbed his aching stomach with his hand. Eventually, his mother also woke to the sound of weeping. She, too, entered her son's room to see what was wrong. As he cried, his father lifted him from the bed and carried him to the kitchen. His mother placed him on his chair and nestled close to him. His weary, bleary-eyed father suddenly had an idea. He ripped a piece of paper from the boy's notebook and drew a picture of a fish on it – a bright green fish with yellow fins and eyes. Then his mother offered him a piece of bread left over from dinner. Suddenly mollified, the boy dipped the bread onto the paper fish and swirled it around and around in creased rotations. He savored each morsel of bread as it touched his lips. By the time he had gnawed away at the crust, he was full, and his father and mother tucked him into bed. He fell sound asleep the moment his cheeks pressed against the pillow. But his mother and father were not able to sleep that night because of the piercing smell of the fish, which permeated all the corners of the house."

Fatema was an exceptionally kind, patient, and pure woman. She hailed from a propertied, upper-class family, but her brothers eventually usurped all of the inheritance. She spoke Arabic, English, and some Persian, and was an indefatigable model of tolerance towards her husband, Jawwad al-Salman. They married when she was almost twelve, and he was sixteen. He had spotted her one day walking with her mother, and fell in love with her almost instantly. Immediately he sent his father and older brother Hamood to ask for her hand in marriage. Although they were not paternal cousins (the preferable match) Fatema's parents readily agreed to the marriage. They had already given their eldest daughter in marriage to a first cousin, and only trouble had arisen. Their son-in-law beat their daughter, and the sharp screams, which emerged from their villa, brought scandal to the family.

Although Fatema's parents welcomed Jawwad into their family and the conjugal celebration was a joyous one, the wedding night proved traumatic for Fatema. Scared of the new husband she barely knew, she was uncomfortable with intimacy. When they were alone in the bridal chamber, Jawwad lifted her wedding veil and quietly observed his trembling bride. She seemed more radiant than the first day he had glimpsed her strolling with her mother. Her long brown hair framed an oval face, out of which peered astonishing green eyes, like distant valleys whose hues changed at different times of the day.

Without uttering a word, his hands caressed her rosy cheeks and played with her wavy hair. She began to cry as he drew her closer to his chest. He wiped the tears from her eyes, kissed her soft forehead, and pulled away, whispering that there was no rush and that he would wait until she was comfortable. It was only after a week of Jawwad's gentleness that the young couple was able to consummate their marriage, and soon a deep friendship blossomed between them.

Yet the first years of marriage were marked with hardship. Fatema's young, prepubescent body was not able to endure the pains of pregnancy. Each time she became pregnant, after several months, she had a painful miscarriage, and Jawwad was fearful that she would bleed to death. After losing a child four times, her mother took her to a doctor – a distant cousin on her father's side – who lived around the corner. He examined Fatema and announced to her mother: "It seems that Fatema's small frame is still not ready for childbearing. Please be patient." And then he turned to Fatema and said: "May God be with you my child."

Finally it seemed that luck had arisen for Fatema and Jawwad. At age sixteen, after six miscarriages, she carried her baby through nine months of pregnancy. With the arrival of the first warm breezes of spring and in the presence of the midwife, her mother, and husband, Fatema gave birth to a beautiful boy – round and strong, with milky white skin and bright blue eyes. He always seemed to giggle, and he slept peacefully through the long hours of the night. Fatema and Jawwad named him Anwar – meaning "brightness and light." In thanks, on the day of Anwar's birth, Jawwad went to the butcher and purchased a fat rooster – a symbol of masculinity – which he slaughtered, then distributed the meat to the poor. Relatives came from far and wide to greet the happy parents and behold the new infant who had miraculously entered the world.

Alas, on Anwar's eighth day, he died of a mysterious illness – and Fatema insisted that some evil eye had struck the happy child tearing him away from her. Within a year, though, she was pregnant again, and for the next decade of her life she gave birth to one girl after the other. "Don't worry, God will bless you with a boy next time," neighbors and relatives would whisper softly. As much as Jawwad hoped for a son to carry his name, and as much as he cursed his fate, it was only after a series of eight girls – Fakhriah, Saniya, Badriyah, Layla, Annissa, Nuriya, Maysun, and Sadiyeh – that his two sons – Mohsin and Annisse, finally tumbled into the world. During the first several years of her sons' childhood Fatema dressed them in unbecoming, tattered shirts and pants, old shoes either too big or small, so that no evil eye would endanger them and lift her husband's pride and honor from the world.

Monkith's grandfather Jawwad came from a propertied family controlling vast tracts of land. Having inherited money both from their parents as well as paternal uncles, he and his older brother Hamood lived off the income, which their family's holdings yielded. But one day, tragedy struck the household – Hamood became gravely ill. A German doctor performed an operation, but the surgery ended in failure. Still, the doctor said, "Just hand over a bit more money for his treatment and he'll get better." It was a lie. Within three days, Hamood was dead and the doctor had fled. And so Jawwad al-Salman had now become the family's sole heir. No matter how fast he spent money, there were always more reserves to draw on. His *abaya* was made of the finest silk, just like the gowns of Saudi Arabian sheikhs. The proverb "Fire can't eat his money" seemed to epitomize his spendthrift behavior, and not surprisingly, the local inhabitants used to deploy the epithet in the same breath as his very name.

Figures of religious authority felt uneasy toward Jawwad, for he had discarded standardized and ritualistic forms of prayer, preferring instead to deal with God as though he were his best friend. From the moment of his spiritual awakening in his mid-forties, he never set foot in a mosque again. He dissuaded his friends from making the pilgrimage to Mecca, saying that before the pilgrimage a person was pure, but upon his return he would begin to gossip and bother those around him – like a dull knife, which could barely cut, transformed into a sharp, blazing knife.

Jawwad was a stern man who struck fear and awe in those around him; especially those who dared try to contradict him. Brimming with pride, he declared that he would prepare himself fully, and even wear his clean white shoes, when he confronted his enemy. In the firm belief that it was beneath his dignity, he never laughed. Indeed Monkith was afraid of his tall, dark, and temperamental grandfather.

Yet as much as the fiery Jawwad struck fear in the hearts of men, he made many a woman's heart flutter. A dashingly handsome womanizer, he lavished his inheritance munificently on multiple mistresses. And he didn't have the least qualms about speaking openly about his countless amorous exploits. However, it was Fatema whom Monkith's grandfather truly loved. At meals Fatema always served her husband the choicest food. She peeled his fruit and fed him as if he were her baby. He told his grandson how much he revered Fatema, but he never did so in front of her. Monkith thought it strange, not to mention slightly ridiculous, that his grandfather considered it a weakness for a man to profess his love for a woman.

When Monkith stayed with his maternal grandparents, he slept in Fatema's room. When he grew older, Fatema gave him his own room on the top floor. As the eldest grandson, he often received certain honors as well as responsibilities. Before and after a meal, a specially designed and relatively large copper basin was placed next to his grandparents' seats. It had a perforated surface and a soap dish. It fell to Monkith to pour water from a pitcher slowly into the basin, so that his grandparents could wash their hands before eating. They would gurgle and rinse their mouths before spitting salivated foam into the basin. After dinner, Monkith helped his grandparents fill their plates with dates and fruits, plucked from the luscious garden below.

No doubt, Monkith found relief from his parents' rigid authority in Fatema's garden along the Tigris. There, he discovered a way of temporarily satisfying his insatiable curiosity regarding the process of creation. Unable to climb the tree that held the birds' nests, he rigged a mirror to a pole and hoisted it up through the branches. He held the reflecting surface at an angle, and watched the young birds hatch, fascinated by the energy of the little lives that burst from their shells. There, in his grandmother's own paradise, he listened to the wind ruffling through the palm trees, which were pregnant and heavy with dates. There, he breathed the scent of the earth covered with white razeghi flowers, and remembered the taste of the fruits he had eaten at dinner the night before. There, he laid his head back and gazed at the reflections of the sun flickering on the Tigris before napping off in the open air.

Some Thursday evenings, Monkith accompanied Fatema and the rest of his family on a river outing. Many Baghdadi families, whatever their religious affiliation, made these quasi-pilgrimages. Those who wished to ask the Christian St. Marjorius for a wish carried the thick triangular end of a palm tree branch with them. They cut their offerings in the shape of a boat and poked small holes into it before lining it with candle wax. Then, they dropped a film of dirt onto the wax, and struck the candles upright onto the sticky surface together with pieces of "os," a tree renowned for its special scent. Next, they sent the makeshift offering adrift, joining the fleet of other lit boats bobbing up and down on the Tigris. And so with Fatema he would experience the magic of the river, of wood and running water, of new and intoxicating scents.

It was from Fatema's garden along the banks of the Tigris, that he molded cities out of the red clay. Yet these timeless waters, known as the cradle of life, also harbored death. For the river's ferocious eddies had claimed the lives of many children. Fatema often spoke of these dangers to prevent Monkith from putting his life in harms way near the river, though she was no more successful than his mother.

"Don't you remember the story of the three little doves?" Fatema whispered to him.

"No," he replied as he nestled close to her.

And so Fatema whispered gently: "Their grandmother beseeched the three little doves not to leave their nest. The first one tried to fly, and fell. The second one sought to help him and he also plummeted. The third one followed suit. In the end, a ravenous cat gobbled them up for lunch. So you see what happens to children who do not obey their grandmother? Please, Monkith, do not play by the Tigris alone again," she said as she caressed his forehead.

And when animal fables did not work, Fatema told him the legend of a *jinnee* named al-Salooeh, an old lady with long lavender hair and the body of a fish, who inhabited the depths of the Tigris and grabbed hapless children at the banks. Yet, if the child kissed her breast and drank her milk, al-Salooeh spared his life and adopted him. However, if the child did not suck her breast, she dragged him down to his watery grave.

By the time Monkith reached the age of six, he still did not know how to swim, although he constantly wandered off to the Tigris. So his grandparents decided to take matters into their own hands. They asked their son, Mohsen, to teach his nephew how to swim. Every day, uncle and pupil ambled to the Tigris for the lesson. Uncle Mohsen's teaching method consisted of lifting his nephew high in the air, smashing him into the water, and watching him flail.

Monkith eventually concluded that if he was going to learn how to swim, he had to do it on his own. Everyday, during the afternoon nap, he snuck out of the house for a couple of hours and headed down to the Tigris to practice his strokes. At first with slow, faltering steps he tread though the water. It splashed against his legs as he surged forward, wading into ever deeper waters. When the river enveloped him to his waist, he threw himself on his back and began to kick with his legs. He stroked the water with his hands, and gradually shed his fear, drifting further and further into the pleasant ripples.

The day finally arrived when Monkith's skills were put to the test. Uncle Mohsen, hoping to embarrass the lad in front of his friends, threw his nephew into the tide. Instead of floundering as expected, Monkith's head bobbed instantly to the surface and he began to swim. All the friends who had gathered around them poked fun at Uncle Mohsen. The gentle Fatema looked on, smiling at Monkith's triumph and beaming with pride.

Once Monkith learned to navigate the Tigris, he headed to the river to swim every day. Fatema and Jawwad, frightened by their grandson's increasingly daring escapades, prohibited

Monkith from swimming, and devised a way to figure out if he was obeying them. They stamped Jawwad's name with ink on Monkith's arm. If it was found to have faded, it meant that he had gone swimming.

Not to be outwitted, the precocious boy discovered that if he rubbed oil on his arm, the stamp would not vanish when it was soaked. And so every night, when Fatema and Jawwad lifted the sleeve of the sleeping child, they found the stamp intact. Monkith fooled his grandfather and even Fatema. He had used his wits to outsmart his elders, leaving him free to discover life on his own terms.

The Winged Bull

Its graceful hooves firmly cleaved the dusty ground while it spread its long, delicate wings with utmost confidence to soar freely into the sky. It sported both the brawny body of a bull, as well as a subtly molded man's face, with smiling lips, and a round chin cupped by a long, delicately chiseled beard with wheel-cut facets. It was a creature some five meters high, and my whole being merely reached up to the bull's foot. I stretched out my hand to touch it. The bewitching moment stayed with me forever.

That morning, my mother dressed me in green, as there was a fieldtrip to the museum in Babylon for the preschool – those in the group of four-year-olds were supposed to dress in green, while five-year-olds had to don red. Once we arrived at school, all of us children gathered to mount the buses along with the six accompanying teachers. The bus ride seemed interminable, as none of us had any idea of where we were headed. I was so excited that I left at home my backpack and egg and tomato sandwich, which my mother had prepared for me that morning. This was my first school fieldtrip, and I had no idea what to expect.

A couple of hours passed before we arrived in Babylon. All of us children scrambled out of the bus, pushing and tripping over each other. When we arrived at the museum, a mad swirl of greens and reds tangoed with each other like uncontrollably dynamic brushstrokes on a canvas. We heard the teachers barking out our names and ordering us to hold hands. Then we were to meet our group leader who stood in the garden under a massive stone sculpture of the famous winged bull, which was enclosed by metal chains. I believe I experienced the first shock of my life at that very moment. I beheld what resembled a gigantic jinnee from One Thousand and One Nights just like the one that my grandmother Habooba had described to me. How I longed to tell her about it when I went home that day! I could barely touch the foot of the magnificent sculpture. All the other children tried to crawl under the metal bars, until the teachers yelled at them. But I climbed the metal fence and just stood dumbstruck in silence. I stretched my hands out to finger the bull's muscular curvatures, and as my increasingly agitated hands stroked its massive, solid calves, I wondered not only what kind of creature this was but also how it was constructed. Most of the other children had scurried off into other directions, but I stood still, fixed in awe. I fancied myself sitting on its back, holding onto its soft wings, ascending the houses and gardens and floating above the majestic Tigris.

Then, in a trance, I sauntered off to see the other monuments. I soon stumbled upon another massive monument of a lion with a sculpted human form lying on the ground directly underneath it. My teacher, Abu Salah, and another tourist stood beside it, and my teacher informed me that the name of this sculpture was 'the Lion of Babylon.'

'Why is there a lifeless human form nestled underneath the lion's body? Is the lion eating it?' I asked both of them.

The shifty-eyed tourist did not look me in the face as he moved to speak. He seemed to slur his syllables as if was searching for an impromptu answer himself at that very moment: 'No, the lion is not devouring the man. The man hurt his sister and so God punished and disfigured him and transformed him into a lion.'

My teacher, an impatient sort of character who possessed social airs about him, brusquely responded, 'No. This sculpture symbolizes the power of Babylon. This lion can kill anything that seeks to challenge the strength of Babylon. And so, yes, it is about to gobble up the figure underneath it.'

The embarrassed tourist nodded distractedly, and moved on to the next sculpture. And I felt satisfied by the second explanation, which highlighted the glory of Babylon, and made me feel as if I was a part of an important and timeless civilization. I stood staring at its splendor for a few moments, but felt drawn toward the monument of the Winged Bull once more. I stood in front of it. I marveled at the way the sun caressed each part of its body, creating luminous shadows on the ground.

I stroked the bull's graceful hooves once again, and felt my own insignificance in the face of such genius. It was yet inconceivable to me how human hands could have hewed such a magnificent sculpture. That year, I had begun making clay cities by the Tigris. I insisted on playing with the moist sedimentation despite the spanking I knew I would incur from my mother when I returned home with my clothes, hair, and face streaked with mud. And now, as I stood before the Winged Bull, it slowly dawned on me just how little I had yet accomplished in my own life. But I persisted, because the act of artistic creation was almost like a Winged Bull in me, a powerful force that could not be denied.

A Pair of Faded Yellow Sandals

As he waded through the riverbanks, he peered down at his feet. His yellow sandals sparkled in the pure water below. The sand ran through his tanned toes, and collected underneath his soles in slippery dampness. The sandals, whose straps were torn and pinned back together, were far too small. His toes stretched out and touched the moist ground below. One sandal slipped off his foot and he ran after it. Having caught it, he kneeled down and shed his other sandal, slid them through the water, lovingly brushing off all the sand and cleansing them. He wore them again and shuffled back home. As his dusty sandals flapped under his feet, he ignored the harsh stares of Habooba.

This was the year his father was imprisoned. The Azawi family still lived in Habooba's home, and his pregnant mother, Nuriya, was busy working as a seamstress to support Monkith, Manal, and Ibtihal. She accepted aid from no one, least of all from her meddling mother-in-law.

Habooba glanced at her grandson's faded yellow sandals, and glared at Nuriya: "Don't you think it is high time you bought your son another pair of sandals? Just look at his protruding toes. What will the neighbors think when they see him? My son is a respectable man, and his son must bear his image."

Tears streamed down Nuriya's tired face, but she did not bother responding. In any case, she knew better than to ask her son to throw away the torn and faded sandals he adored. A week earlier she had bought him a new pair of bright blue sandals, but he hid his yellow sandals under his pillow as usual, and cried throughout the night, refusing to part with them.

"Very well then, there will come a day, very soon, when he just won't be able to wear those sandals. Let's just leave him alone for now," his mother whispered to her sister Layla when they met the next day to help their mother Fatema prepare lunch. Layla squatted on the floor and sorted chickpeas and lentils as Nuriya hid her face in her hands and lamented her eldest son's stubborn behavior.

Monkith knew that no one understood his bond with his sandals. They were his "loyal friends". He walked with them very carefully, and when he dashed about, he felt they were like wings. Often, he climbed over fences and snuck into neighboring gardens to pick oranges. He relished the adrenaline rush and the subsequent satisfaction of getting away scot free, time and again. He knew his sandals would help him escape. But at times, when he sprinted, they let him down and ripped apart. When he returned home, he fastened the straps to the sole with a safety pin. He believed that they would always accompany him on his adventures.

One day his sandals carried him to the house of his neighbor Osama. His mother had gone to have tea with Osama's mother, Umm Jalil. The two boys played on the garden swing while the women drank tea. But instead of swinging back and forth on its creaking hinges, they climbed to the top of the bars and hung like monkeys from their arms and legs. As Monkith dangled, one of his yellow sandals fell to the ground. He glimpsed down at his shoe and began to climb down carefully. When he jumped to the ground, Osama's big brown dog barked and then bit Monkith's arm. He cried and then bit the dog's back to defend himself. Then he fainted.

The two mothers came rushing outside when they heard the ruckus and quickly called for Osama's older brother Jalil to take him to the hospital. Monkith was scared and his nose tingled, as the doctor pricked him with fourteen shots onto his stomach. He searched in desperation for his yellow sandals, but they were nowhere to be found. Instead his wandering eyes chanced upon a pair of bright blue sandals sitting on the table beside him. Monkith began to scream inarticulate words, as his mother caressed him and said that in just a few minutes the pain would subside and he could go home.

Aunt Sadiyeh's Wedding Preparations

It was 1986 in Damascus. I called my cousin Naïm, who had just moved to Germany, to wish him a Happy New Year. I asked about all my friends and relatives in Griyat – my parents, my sister Amal, my sister Manal and her husband Hussein, my Aunt Sadiyeh... Aunt Sadiyeh? She had recently passed away consumed by grief after she had lost both her sons in the Iran-Iraq war. I hung up the phone, full of sadness. My thoughts drifted back to memories of my childhood in Baghdad – to the day of Aunt Sadiyeh's wedding preparations twenty-two years earlier.

◆

The wonderful scent of cardamom and the stifling heat of the sauna. Loud breathing, laughter, singing, and screams. Women belonged to a secret, mysterious world, and this, the day of Aunt Sadiyeh's wedding preparations, was one of the rare opportunities for allowing Monkith to drift into it. He was six years old. No longer a child, not yet an adult. The feeling that he did not belong to either group permitted him to wander from one sphere to the other. Each side regarded him as an imposter. Yet the ambiguity of his position offered unforeseen chances.

This particular Thursday morning, whispering and excitement filled the Azawi household. Monkith did not know what to make of it. On any other morning, his mother dressed him, bathed him, and shuffled him off to school. Yet, this morning, she ignored him completely. She placed the one-year-old Iqbal in the care of her sister Layla, dressed the younger girls Manal and Ibtihal, and immersed herself in the preparation of a few snacks before grabbing her childrens' hands and shepherding them along the Tigris to the house of her parents, Fatema and Jawwad. Monkith's aunts Annissa, Badriyah, Maysun, and Grandma Fatema's sister, Zahrah, were already gathered there by the time they arrived. They, too, had prepared food. They picked a colorful assortment of fruits from the garden, and packed them into plastic bags.

Monkith soon found out that they were about to embark on an excursion to the *hamam*, or public bath, in the region of

Kazamiyyah as was customary for future brides like Aunt Sadiyeh – and other female relatives – prior to a wedding. There, they would sing and laugh while washing themselves, removing their excess body hair, and indulging in massages. A small ferryboat was set to carry the group of women from A'dhamiyyah to Kazamiyyah, the two halves of the throbbing heart of Baghdad cleaved by the Tigris.

Monkith accompanied his mother and aunts, all clad in black *abayas*, on their walk towards the river. His younger sisters Manal, Ibtihal, and Iqbal stayed behind with Fatema and Layla. The family was full of other male children, but he was the eldest, and thus the only one who had been chosen to chaperon the group. As they ambled towards the landing where the boat driver already awaited them, Aunt Sadiyeh entertained him with a famous story about the Abbasid Caliph Harun al-Rashid. How prophetic her story turned out to be in light of the events that were about to unfold for Monkith on that same day!

Aunt Sadiyeh began: "An uncouth Bedouin once approached the Caliph Harun al-Rashid in order to pay him a compliment. The swashbuckling Bedouin declared at the top of his hoarse voice, 'It is as if you're a dog watching over the faithful. You're like a donkey carrying the weight of all the suffering.' The caliph initially took offense by what he took to be a supreme insult. But then, he thought twice. He realized that the Bedouin, who spoke in the unrefined tongue of the nomads, had probably meant well. So rather than punish the man, the caliph installed him in a castle along the Tigris to see whether his surroundings could permanently transform his manners. One month later, the Caliph Harun al-Rashid approached the Bedouin again. He asked him if he had anything new to say. This time – his heart beating with delight – the Bedouin responded in poetic language, 'The eyes of the gazelle lie in Rasafa (A'dhamiyyah) and in Karakh (Kazamiyyah). It is beauty that transported me from what I knew and what I know now.'"

Many questions weighed on his mind, but when Aunt Sadiyeh had finished her story, they had reached the wharf. As he and his aunts boarded, Aunt Sadiyeh squeezed his hand to signal that he was to sit still and behave himself. In fact, because of their need to project modest behavior, none of the women dared utter a word in the elderly oarsman's presence. His aunts were anxious about the upcoming day, for this was the first visit to the public bath for most of them, including his mother. They sat in silence. All that reached Monkith's ears was the swish of the oars sinking into the water. In the languid stream of the idle midday current, he beheld the majestic palm trees that lined both riverbanks, the calm waters, the balmy sky. It was a pleasant winter day, mild, and the sun stroked their skins while the air remained chilly.

Monkith ignored the awkward hush that blanketed the group, and shuffled noisily about the boat. He dangled his hand in the water, delighting in the soft waves that crested under his fingers. As the boatman raised his oars, he yelled at him to pull his hand out of the water because he was unwittingly changing the coarse of their tiny vessel. Monkith, however, persisted despite the stern glances of his mother.

Finally, the oars stopped their circular motion. The women climbed out of the boat one by one, and threaded their way through the winding streets and alleys in the direction of the *souq*.[16] The smell of spices, mixed pickles, candles, incense, laughter, and music filled the air. The group of black-clad women continued through narrow passageways until they reached an obscure entrance. This was the gateway to the public bath *Hamam Haydar*.

The nervous women passed together through the tacky red curtain, which served as the door, and carefully stepped down a flight of three slippery stairs. Inside sat a chubby black matron, somewhere in her early forties, wearing a tattered *abaya* that must have seen better days. She slowly hoisted herself up from the reed mat on which she had squatted as the women entered, wheezing considerably before she had piled her roles of fat into the erect posture in which she was able to parade the sheer volume of her unmitigated corpulence with an air that betrayed no strange amount of pride. Monkith, for his part, instantly disliked her. Her body emitted an unsettling odor, which seemed to trail off as

---

[16] Market

she moved about. It was the smell of stale sweat mingled with the damp earth. She squinted at him and the ladies through closely-knit brows and with no glimmer of a smile. There was something both disquieting and pathetic about her. To his young eyes, she appeared as if she had never smiled in her life.

The keeper of the door expectorated a bolus of phlegm onto the dusty ground and scrutinized Monkith with thinly veiled contempt, before addressing his mother in a coarse voice: "Access denied!"

The women stared at her in dumbstruck silence as she continued: "There is something in the boy's flirtatious eyes, which signals that he's no longer at an age when he may enter the women's section. He must enter on the other side – the men's bath." She looked down at Monkith and then shoved him aside with her strong, chubby hands whose fingers were adorned with flamboyant gold rings.

"Please, my son is far too young to brave the men's public bath on his own," Nuriya insisted as she held her son close to her.

"The answer is no. No means no!" the doorkeeper snorted with irritation and began to walk away. There was a malicious twinkle in her eye.

"But this is our first time to the public bath! How were we supposed to know? We have made the trip all the way from A'dhamiyyah to Kazamiyyah, please just this once," Aunt Badriyah pleaded as she grabbed Nuriya's hand to help calm her nerves. Tall and tenacious, there was a marked authority and confidence in Badriyah's being. The other women knew that if anyone could convince the hamam guard it was Badriyah.

The tenacious doorkeeper glared angrily at Monkith again, but then yielded. Spying Badriyah's bags filled with oranges, though, she did not consider herself defeated. She beamed triumphantly and instructed her: "I would wait until after the hamam to eat those. The acidity of the oranges joined with the heat and commotion of the sauna will make you feel nausea!"

As they passed through the portal, Monkith's head spun. For a moment, enveloped by the heavy steam, he felt as if he had arrived at the Day of Judgment and he began to tremble. A large stained glass opening on the ceiling sprinkled in hues of green, red, turquoise, and for the first time he witnessed what could only be called "colorful air." He stood still; he thought he was dreaming. A rush of surreal colors and perfumes mingled with the echo of the dripping water and the oppressive heat of the sauna. The colored silhouettes of nude women enthralled him. He watched as they paraded behind the misty vapors – flitting away like butterflies as quickly as they had appeared out of the fog. When he recovered from his original fear, he thought he had entered a marvelous world, and his mother lured him to penetrate it ever more deeply.

The prude women in his family wrapped themselves in towels and entered a special separate chamber they had reserved. He noticed that his married aunts wore nothing, while his unmarried aunts Maysun, Annissa, and Sadiyeh still wore their underwear, which he too was required to wear. The thick gold bracelets, which wrapped around the slender ankles of Aunt Zahrah fascinated him. And for the first time he noticed that his Aunt Layla's eyes were turquoise, the same color as the marble-shaped lights above the ceiling. As the women began to bathe and talk, he wiggled away from his mother's side, and began to explore some of the other rooms.

From afar, the silhouettes and voices of the women faded into one another and he was unable to make out the individual forms. Screams of delight and song filled the air. As he drew nearer, he noticed how some women coyly covered their private parts, while others strutted confidently. He noticed that most women squatting on the ground had a silver mirror, an amber-scented cream, a *kiseh*,[17] a *lifeh*,[18] a wooden comb, and some cardamom soap. The soap, which filled the air and lined the floor with thick and sparkling suds, intrigued him. And yet, the suffocating steam that wafted in misty phantoms through the *hamam* frightened him. He longed to speak to the women and ask them if he could look at his reflection in their mirror and

---

[17] This is a rough sponge used to rub off dead skin.
[18] This is a soft sponge used to rub soap on the body.

play with their soap, but they cast him away and yelled for his mother to retrieve him.

"My God, son, if you don't sit still, I will slap you," yelled Nuriya, suddenly yanking her son and forcing him to plop down next to her so she could shampoo his hair and properly soap his body. He screamed as she clamped his head between her knees. Her hands clutched his hair like talons. She rubbed the soap over his face; his eyes burned from the aggressive suds, which managed to ooze into his tightly closed lids. He held his hands tightly over his eyes as she poured a suffocating stream of warm water over his face and body.

With his sparkling clean body, he shed his sandals, romped through the soapsuds of his shampoo, and relished the sound of the splashing water. With his toes he traced marvelous images of the women surrounding him in the soft suds and watched as their features elongated and then faded into the steady stream of running water. He glanced at Aunt Maysun, the most over-weight of his aunts, whose layers of stomach skin rippled like the waves of an ocean. He drew her body with its thick flesh and watched as the soap suds of his design disappeared under a stream of fresh water. He arched his back in sheer satisfaction, and after a few minutes he set off again to examine each room with insatiable curiosity.

In one crowded room, his eyes spotted an obese red-haired woman, whose thick folds of flesh on her shoulders nestled her neck. Her face was the color of a sun-baked brick. She sat on the ground with her legs spread out wide. A green flowery tattoo design wrapped itself around her sagging breasts and slithered down her stretched-out stomach, which reached the ground. One by one, she took her kiseh and rubbed it over each woman's body to peel off the dead skin, and then washed her with the lifeh. Some women preferred to clean themselves, while others argued among themselves about who would be next with the professional. At the moment, there was a chubby dark-skinned woman – with a face as wide as a cooking pan – lying on her back. The obese red-haired woman rubbed the torn black kiseh aggressively over her skin. With one plump hand planted tightly on the woman's enormous breast as if she were grabbing an orange off a tree, the corpulent women moved up and down the woman's arm and lower torso, and slithered the *kiseh* under her underwear to catch the forgotten dead skin. Her large, dropped bosom brushed against the woman's dark body. As the woman's skin piled with spots of thick, long black dirt, the huge woman plunged a blue saucer into a tub of water and poured it over her neck, arms, and torso. A stream of water filled with thick black lines flowed across the floor, and the corpulent woman turned her client over on her stomach and continued. Once the obese woman had completed her task, she sponged and then massaged the sparkling clean body, while the other women sang. As the chubby woman stood up, a young girl – whose skinny brown body looked like a dried date – rose and plopped herself in front of the red-haired woman with the *kiseh*.

Monkith wandered into another corner where women were applying a product called *Dawa al-Hammam* on their excess body hair. A few minutes later, the women rubbed it off with water. They appeared like a team of plucked partridges. Their hairless bodies now appeared soft and shiny, while the floor was filled with their drifting, runaway hair. The combination of the dead skin, loose hair, and running water created a slippery humidity on the ground, and Monkith searched for his sandals. As he knelt down to put them on, he saw one woman with milky white skin grapple her sagging breasts and the flabby roll of flesh around her waist, and burst out into a contagious hilarious laughter. The women began touching each other, whispering and teasing about the fun they would have that very evening. With unashamed mirth, a few women mimed how they would lie with their husbands in a snug embrace that evening. The others roared with laughter. Monkith approached them and longed to ask if he could feel the liquid they had rubbed on their skin and if he could touch their newly-spruced arms – but they chased him from one corner to the next. "Out of here! Quick, you piece of dried-up camel dung!" they screamed as they shook with inner laughter. He was considered an intruder, a stranger in this world of women.

Cast out of that room, he returned to the sauna. He opened the door and observed how the women in the sauna perspired profusely and breathed deeply. He was overwhelmed by the small shiny pellets of sweat, which studded the women's glistening bodies like the sheet of diamonds that covered the Tigris on a hot summer day. The doorkeeper sauntered casually into the sweltering room. In a hoarsely abrasive voice, which brooked no dissent, she huskily reminded the women not to eat oranges in the *hamam*. Monkith watched as the perspiring women sat on the ground and snacked on grape leaves instead. But he could not eat anything. His stomach became queasy from sensory overload.

"Close the door, you good-for-nothing! You are letting out all the steam," screamed a decrepit old woman with an intricate henna design covering her wrinkled breasts and shoulders. The flabby, loose skin at her center hung low like an old goatskin bag. Dumbfound, he stared at the creased woman and quickly shut the door behind him.

Finally, he could contain his amazement no longer. Hiding behind a pillar of mist, he beheld a slender, pale-skinned girl with soft, jet-black hair stretching down all the way to her firm and shapely buttocks. His eyes wandered over her wan skin and he noticed how her hair had been plucked from every part of her body. He inched closer. Her breasts, a milky off-white, dangled from her chest like ripe oranges swaying in Griyat's balmy summer breeze. He noticed how, at first faintly but ever more strongly, her bosom began to heave as she hummed the long-forgotten memory of an old lullaby in absentminded oblivion. How her lackadaisical voice enchanted him. His eyes fell on her maroon nipples atop a field of milky goose bumps, which stood at attention as if the hidden rigor of the song demanded the minstrel's corporeal attention. Lost in thought, the nymph plaited the long, curly strands of her damp hair. Oh, how he longed to touch her soft mounds, finger them, feel their consistency, mold them, and remake them in his mental image. Monkith stepped closer. He observed the moist, curly, black triangle dancing above her pubis and was struck by how much rubbery, brown folds between her legs reminded him of sugary ripe dates in the autumn. Feverishly, Monkith gasped for air. Salty pearls percolated down his torso. As if in a trance, he took one more step toward the singing siren. He stared sheepishly at her beguiling face until he slipped and fell. If only she had not attempted to help him get up. He reached up to touch the tender skin at her very center. She began to screech at the top of her lungs: "May a fever strike you. May the flees of a thousand camels infest your armpits!" Her hand descended in a stinging slap. The *hamam* instantly filled with hoarse shouts and cries of indignation: "Get out, I tell you! Damn you, you insolent little bastard!" The doorkeeper appeared and jerked him by the ear, "I told you this would happen. Go, put on your clothes you filthy-minded fish and haul your shameful posterior over to me!"

Before she could abscond with Monkith, though, Nuriya grabbed him and spanked him. In a voice that burnt him like hot coals, she screamed, "Monkith, I forbid you to stir. Otherwise, I shall tell your father what happened, and you know what that means!"

Nuriya quickly dressed her banished son and sent him to sit next to the entrance with the keeper of the gate, while she and her sisters finished washing up and preparing for the wedding. It seemed like interminable hours that he stood there whiling away in the dull corner with his thwarted yearnings. The crestfallen Monkith heard his mother and aunts singing as they bathed the young bride behind the thick, colorful curtains of mist. As more veiled women approached the door of the *hamam* and spoke to the foulmouthed matron, he wondered what they would later look like before they were swallowed up by the steam and soft melodies. Forbidden images of milky-white round spheres soaring in the wind, heaving bosoms, endless strands of waving hair loomed before him. Drowned in the faint lullaby he had heard moments earlier, he gazed at the women with his reddened eyes. The stern matron looked down at him suspiciously and slapped his face, instantly awakening him from his reverie.

When his mother and aunts dressed again, they paid the doorkeeper and Monkith sighed with relief that he could now rejoin his family. As the cluster of women left the *hamam*, the furious woman warned Nuriya not to bring her "little devil" again. This was the last time that Monkith was at an age where he could wander freely into the forbidden realm of women; his surroundings and actions had thrust him into manhood.

As they walked out the door, Nuriya grabbed her son's hand: "Can't I take you anywhere without you causing a public scandal? What did you think you were doing by touching that girl?"

"I swear, I did not mean to. I slid on the soap suds and I grabbed on to her to keep from falling," he insisted disingenuously.

"Well in any case, this is the last time you can come – we are not allowed to bring you anymore." In fact, it was the last time she herself set foot in the *hamam* again.

As they wended their way through the narrow winding streets of the *souq*, he heard the women whisper and giggle about what had happened. The traumatized Monkith did not understand why his mother glanced at him so harshly and clasped his hand so tightly, but at the same time, she secretly laughed about the blunder with his aunts. As they drifted through the narrow streets, the smells of the pickled lemons and spices, the strange sounds and music, no longer touched his senses. He felt strangely anaesthetized. The vehement intrusiveness of the images and colors he had beheld hours before still engrossed him. That evening, he caught a cold and could not eat his dinner. He slipped into bed with an empty stomach and had an impossible time falling asleep. When his eyelids finally snuck over his tired eyes, the darkness of the night's canvas was thickened with milky-white spheres whirling through the wind, endless maroon dots, long, curly black strands that spun around in circles. There were black triangles and thin brown folds waving underneath him. A flowery tattoo design with sinuous branches darting off in all directions enwrapped itself around his small body. As he struggled to escape its grasp, he searched for the face of the pale-skinned girl but she hid behind a misty curtain. He could hear her lush lullaby drifting toward him and enveloping him in its moistness.

A Forbidden Glance

Every evening for months on end, it was the same rather mysterious ritual in their new home, a few miles away from Habooba's villa, where they had previously lodged. Every night, Nuriya would beseech a recalcitrant Monkith and an equally stubborn Manal to rinse the dirt off their faces before climbing into bed. Meanwhile, she would feed Ibtihal and Iqbal. A brooding Naji would hide away in his room, and start mouthing foul expletives to himself if the children did not comply with their mother. Yet strangely for someone so obsessed with facial cleanliness, Monkith noticed how his mother would often smear garish colors in her face after rinsing it repeatedly during daylight hours. After she tucked the children into bed in the room they shared, Nuriya slipped into bed with Iqbal. A few moments later, when the house had settled into sleep, Naji began coughing like a sick sheep. Nuriya kissed Iqbal, rose from her bed, and checked on the slumbering children. Then she tiptoed carefully into her husband's room. All the lights were switched off and the house fell silent. Monkith drifted in and out of sleep as he waited for her to return to the room he shared with his sisters, but most often he was fast asleep before she ever did.

One winter evening, Monkith decided that he needed to unravel the mysterious goings-on. That evening, he squinted at his mother out of the corner of his eye, as she applied *kohl* and a gaudy cherry-red lipstick in the bathroom and then shuffled her children off to bed. This time he complied without protest. He immediately turned off the lights and closed his eyes. He listened as she crawled into bed with Iqbal, rose to the sound of her husband's crackling coughs, and routinely inspected his sisters before she peered down at him and embraced him. This time he did not open his eyes and say good night. A strange stillness filled the house. The night was impenetrably dark. A few moments later, he made out her footsteps from the creaking wood panels lining the floor as she penetrated her husband's room and furtively shut the door behind her.

Monkith groped his way past his sisters' beds, tiptoed out of his room like a thieving servant, and stood silently outside his father's door, peeping through the small crack of the door very carefully. It was a freezing cold night. He did not wear his slippers, so they would not make noise as he walked. As he stood transfixed in the corridor, his bare feet rubbed against the cold wooden floor sending shivers throughout his body. He barely breathed and he could hear the sound of his heartbeat skipping. He spotted a glimpse of his father lying in bed, while his mother ambled aimlessly around the room brushing her hair. She looked startlingly beautiful. An expression he had not seen before sparkled in her eyes. Then she approached the bed, shed her nightgown and completely nude, she crawled into the bed underneath her husband. The now familiar body of his mother seemed somehow alien, as if her small, modest frame was invaded by some startling *jinnee*. His spirits flagged as his mother's body disappeared under that of his father who bore down on her face with his. His father's backside was thin, but solid as an iron beam. It seemed as if he were crushing her, and Monkith was terrified when he heard his father's strange sighs and cries, which overpowered his mother's stiff silence. He could not understand why his father was hurting his mother; he could not fathom her stoic compliance. He felt hatred for his father, sadness for his mother.

He felt like an impotent and passive participant in their bestial enactment. He could barely move; the sonance of his heart beating stung his ears. He urinated on himself, and then he stumbled down the stairs and fled into the bathroom. His stomach ached as he spat into the toilet and threw up. Salty, gushing tear drops spilled all over his grimaced face, distorted in agony and his mother rushed out of the room to see what was the matter. In the background, he heard his father screaming that he wished for all the children to be in bed at this time of night.

When his mother found him, he looked up at her with tears in his gloomy eyes. It seemed to be the same Nuriya who occupied his mother's thin frame, but somehow she seemed different. Monkith was so disappointed in her and did not know how to express it. Nuriya left the bathroom confused, ordering him to return to his bed before his father came and spanked him.

The next day he could barely speak to his parents. The image of his mother's purity had suddenly, irretrievably, faded away like a shriveled, dry artichoke. His father seemed to be a hostile stranger, the sound of his stiff breathing felt wretched to his ears. That evening, despite his mother's insistence that the children change for bed, Monkith refused and instead took the bright red balls from Manal's juggling set, climbed down the stairs, and began to perform. As he juggled for his cheering sisters, he purposely threw one ball against the living room window. The glass shattered, and his parents came running into the room. His father grabbed him and slapped his face so hard it began to bleed. But it did not matter to Monkith. From that day onward, he did all he could to make sure his parents were never alone. He monitored them, especially at night. He felt tired and moody, as he hovered between his room and the bathroom in the evenings to soothe his mysterious nocturnal stomach pains. No one fathomed what was wrong with him; he invented all sorts of stories to explain his repeated bouts of vomiting.

The Grape Vine

The grape vine, which clung to the trellis directly under Monkith's balcony, was Naji al-Azawi's greatest pride. He brought all sorts of fruits and colored grapes from the market to the house, but the bright violet grapes, which hung over the trellis, were out of bounds. Every morning before setting off, he admired the bright violet clusters, whose leaves ruffled over his head.

One day he caught Monkith reaching for a grape, and he struck his hand with a wooden spoon. "Haven't I told you time and again, these grapes are off limits?! I fetched grapes from the market yesterday, please eat those and when they are finished I'll buy some more," his father said tersely.

"But I just want to taste one of these, dad, just one," pleaded Monkith, fully aware that his father's strictures were increasingly losing their sway over him.

"No, not these!" Naji responded with another whap of his wooden spoon, and Monkith ran screaming into the house. From the balcony above, he solemnly observed his father as he caressed the beautiful clusters before departing.

There has got to be some way that I can savor those grapes without his finding out, he thought to himself as he stared at the fabulous, forbidden fruits. Deep in thought, he sat down to play with his large assortment of marbles – many of which he had won from the other boys in school. He dumped out the contents of a thick woolen sock, and out rolled marbles of different colors and sizes. He smiled as he dug into his pocket and added a newly won large green one to his collection. He loved looking at their bright colors, examining their different shades and contours. He watched them as they rolled on the floor and faded into each other's shades. As the marbles' slippery texture rubbed against the palm of his hand, he wondered if he would ever be able to feel the softness of a bright violet grape that decked his father's vine; if he would ever be able to watch as its lively color merged into his assortment of marbles.

At last he hatched a clever ruse. He returned his colorful treasures into the woolen sock, afraid of his father's puritanical dislike of any form of amusement. He descended into the garden and searched all the trees for a small branch he could cut off, and then he taped a razor to the end of the stick. He severed another branch and attached a paper bag to it. Once his father had left, he stole into the garden and squatted under the trellis. He marveled at the magnificent violet clusters, through which the rays of the sun were kaleidoscopically refracted. He hoisted both sticks simultaneously. While he cut the grapes with one stick, he placed the paper bag directly underneath it. He felt elated as the grapes tumbled into the bag one by one. Then he slipped into his room and hid the stick in his cabinets, which he locked with a set of keys that he buried in a secret garden cache so that his sisters would not stumble upon them when they played in the room. He stared at the ripe burgundy clusters. He cut off a grape, felt its texture in his hands, let it roll next to a small red marble, and then tossed it in his mouth. Full of disgust, he expectorated a toxic mush of purple pulp across the floor. The grapes his father brought from the market were much more juicy and sweet. Angrily, he squished the grapes into a soggy napkin and threw them away.

Now, every day when his father left the house, he neatly cut down a few more clusters, which he slung across the garden walls into Umm Hassan's garden or tossed in the trash. It took a few days for Naji to realize that somehow the grapes were making a mysterious exit, but he could not figure out how or why, for they were so neatly severed from the vine. In frustration he watched as they vanished until little by little no more bright purple bunches hovered over his head as he left the house in the morning.

"By God, I have a feeling I know who the culprit is," screamed Naji, who began to harbor suspicions. "Monkith, where are you?" he shrieked as he climbed up the stairs to his son's bedroom. He poked about Monkith's room in search of some evidence of misdemeanor. He found none, but by chance he stumbled upon the bulging sock filled with marbles. Marbles in hand, he descended into the garden in a rage, as if a wasp had just stung him. He yanked Monkith by the ear, and pulled him into the bathroom. He slammed the door and began yelling, veins bulging out of his forehead like pus-infested pimples about to pop at any moment: "Curse you, boy, is this the example you want to set for your younger sisters?"

Naji did not wait for his errant son's response, but began to hit him aimlessly. His face brimming with incandescent scorn and disgust, he grabbed the sock and emptied the marbles down the old-fashioned latrine – a large pit in the ground with a foothold on each side for squatting. Tears welled up in Monkith's eyes as Naji gloated at him in hollow triumph. Monkith flung himself to the ground and wept uncontrollably, refusing to leave his room for days.

Rasool

There is a story told of a mysterious man who arrived from the south of Iraq to live in Griyat. His name was Rasool. He was prematurely bald with a high fore-head that cradled thick eyebrows, which provided shade over two large black eyes as dark as coffee beans. A natural purple line outlined his eyelids like kohl and his black lashes were so thick and long that they curled over several times. He wore a white turban and resembled a Sheikh. Rumor had it that he had killed a man in his village in the south, and thus escaped to Griyat. No one knew whether the rumors were founded, but over time the inhabitants grew fond of the older man. He opened a popular café that specialized in mazgoof. Starting from five every afternoon his café was filled with regulars. It became a hub for the local poets to meet, a place where people spent hours writing, talking, or just staring into space.

Over time, a rumor spread that a young stranger was desperately searching for Rasool. Apparently, he wished to unearth everything about Rasool – what he did, where he lived, where he worked. These rumors eventually faded, and were thought to be the product of an overly productive imagination.

One summer, a few years later, an orphan, also named Rasool, arrived in the village. He was a short, stout, bowlegged young man with silver eyes. Every evening he sipped his tea at the older Rasool's café. It did not take long for the loyal client to befriend his older namesake. He evinced a strong interest to learn everything about the elderly man. The two Rasools spent many tireless hours together, and the older Rasool regarded the fatherless young man as his own son. Every evening he yearned for his visit. Everyone grew accustomed to young Rasool lingering longer than all the other clients.

One summer afternoon, young Rasool strolled along the Tigris feverish. He carried a white satin cloth, which was wrapped around a long, slender object. His silver eyes shimmered and he could barely see in front of him. Monkith's Aunt Badriyah spotted him on her way home from the market. She said he was drool-ing, and it seemed as if he was muttering to himself that it was time to avenge his father's death. She called out to him, but he could not hear her. He stumbled along the banks of the Tigris. He fell and rolled around in the water holding on tightly to the long object enshrouded in white satin. Badriyah followed the hap-less man, fearful the river would pull him further in. When she saw the drenched and disheveled man leave the water and enter Rasool's café as usual, she breathed a sigh of relief and set off to her home.

That evening, while families strolled along the Tigris, the piercing sound of gunshots tore through the languid air. The stunned inhabitants saw a Jeep speed away from Rasool's café. A group of men and women rushed into his shop. The sound of shrill screams pierced the sky. They found the body of the older Rasool – riddled with bullets on the floor of his shop. He was delirious and muttering madly to himself as he passed from this realm into the next.

In pain, the old Rasool raised his arms and whispered, 'He told me that his name is Rasool, and that he has come to avenge his father's death.' He began to whimper something else in pain, until he gasped his last breath.

Later, stories spread that the younger Rasool had been the subject of all the gossip, and that he had been the one trying to trace his older namesake for years. Rumor had it that the older Rasool had killed the father of the younger Rasool. The latter's mother had been pregnant at the time of her husband's murder. She gave birth to her son on the day that his father died, and she named him Rasool. Throughout his childhood, she told him that he had been named after the man who slay his father, and that one day it would be his responsibility to avenge his father's death. When Rasool turned sixteen, his mother appeared before him in her simple white wedding gown, holding a long rifle. Her long curly black tresses dangled over her shoulders and covered one of her golden eyes. She removed the smooth satin covering of her dress and wrapped it around the rifle

'My son, it is now time. You must search for the man who lifted your father's soul from this earth. It is your duty.' She handed her son her deceased husband's rifle, and then she fainted and never woke up.

The Movie-Teller

One pleasant spring day, Monkith knocked at the corrugated garden gate, from which the pastel blue paint was flaking off, and sounded its bell, but no one answered. He rang repeatedly. He scuttled up the creaky wooden gate, and peered onto the dust-coated slanted veranda. There was a telling silence. Neither his friend Hatem nor the other eight children who usually played in the small garden surrounded by crumbling walls were to be seen. Monkith felt there was something amiss and kept buzzing, but after a few minutes he despaired, jumped down, and turned to leave.

"Hey, wait," yelled a voice he barely recognized from behind the wall. "I am coming." One of the Hatem's eight brothers opened the door and gaped down at Monkith. Monkith knew some of them, but he had never spoken to this brother, whose bright red face filled with sores looked like the inside of a pomegranate. The tepid spring breeze ran through his wavy brown hair.

"I'm going to play a game of *Udah* and *Bolbol*[19] with some boys down the street," Monkith said, staring at the older boy with resolute eyes. "I've come to see if Hatem wants to join my team. Is he home?"

"Well, yes, he is, but he is actually tied up at the moment," Hatem's brother said evasively. As he spoke it seemed his face grew redder. Monkith gave him a quizzical stare, so his interlocutor added by way of explanation, "It is his turn to be the movie-teller today." He scrutinized the seven-year-old boy carefully, and then hastened to add: "You must be Monkith; I think you live right down the street from us, don't you? Well, why don't you come in, you might enjoy this. Come. My name is Latif," he said, giving Monkith a friendly slap on the back. "We'll let you in for free this time." Monkith quickly forgot the game of *Udah* and *Bolbol*, and willingly followed Latif down a dark, narrow corridor leading to a new adventure.

---

[19] This is a game similar to baseball, except that the boys bat sticks rather than balls.

Hatem's eight siblings ranged from five to sixteen years of age, and their father sold pickled spices on the street corners of the market. They lived in utter squalor. Unable to afford cinema tickets, let alone enjoy toys, they devised a plan to escape the deadening days of monotony. Every week, they pooled their meager allowances, so that at least one of the brothers would be able to go to the popular local cinema in A'dhamiyyah, which screened a new European or Arab film every week. The money could be stretched to allow the week's spectator to buy some sodas and snacks as well. There was one important rule, however. The week's designated moviegoer had to describe the film in all its intricate details to his other siblings. This weekly treat became a ritual for them, a colorful interval in the interminably drab stretch of a wretched childhood.

Latif led Monkith down a gloomy corridor, which opened onto a small, stuffy room. There were no windows in this room, which had been constructed in the garden and attached to the house. The paint on the walls was peeling and the broken white tiles had grown yellow with filth. An odd assortment of musty mattresses and sheets were stacked against the wall. Torn magazine portraits of Egyptian singers Abdel Halim Hafez and Umm Kulthum were tacked haphazardly on the wall. Although the brothers had dimmed the lights, Monkith could discern his friend Hatem sitting on a dilapidated wooden chair at the center of the room. A group of boys of all sizes were squatting on the floor grouped around him. Utter silence engulfed the room. Latif and Monkith tiptoed in and found a seat among the others, who had been waiting impatiently for Latif to return. When all were settled, Hatem, who was perched on the chair, closed his clear blue eyes. He lowered his head, then lifted it again and emitted a soft hum. It grew increasingly more sonorous, filled with more and more timbre. The boys on the floor began to breathe more deeply. Monkith sat still, but struggled to keep his seat, as those around him pushed and shoved so that they could inch closer to Hatem.

The movie-teller's blue eyes widened. His hands and legs moved with impassioned fury as he introduced the Egyptian movie *Nagam fi Hayati* (*Melodies in My Life*) and sketched the open-

ing in all its details – the music that played, the colors, the characters. "On the screen appear the names of the actors one by
one... singer Farid Al-Attrash... the handsome Hussein Fahmy...
and the stunning Mervat Amin... The intense sounds of the *ud*
drifted through the air. Hanan, played by Mervat Amin, is a
young woman about eighteen years old. She strolls down a narrow hallway. She has thick long brown chestnut colored hair and
skin as white as the moon. 'Congratulations! Congratulations!'
students exclaim as she passes by. She has just graduated from
Cairo University with a B.A. in philosophy." Hatem mimicked
her facial expression, the way she tosses her head as she walks
with pride.

   "Hanan enters a room where Mamdouh, played by Farid al-
Attrash, is seated and playing the *ud*. He is an older man with
white sideburns and dyed black hair. His eyebrows are as sharp
as a sword, his face white and triangular. He is wearing a dark
blue and white checkered shirt and blue pants. His eyes are on
his *ud*. The music grows more intense as Hanan watches
Mamdouh. Hanan's father, a short and stubby man, enters and
also observes Mamdouh."

   The room was choked with silence as Hatem continued:
"Hanan and her father invite Mamdouh to a fancy restaurant
that evening in honor of her successful graduation, and during
the meal Hanan talks about how she wishes to visit her mother
who has remarried in Lebanon. As her father and Mamdouh try
to persuade her not to go, there is a belly dancer performing. She
is chubby and has long brown hair and milky white skin. She is
wearing a black corset and long black skirt with slits, and she
waves around a long yellow silk scarf. She rubs her hands
through her hair. She shakes her behind, at the moment that
Hanan's father nods his head in agreement that his daughter
travel to see her mother and stepfather."

   Hatem paused for a moment and observed his curious audience. No one stirred as they waited for him to continue his narration. As he bowed down his head and caught his breath, all
eyes were on him. The breathing in the room grew louder as his
audience lost patience with his silence. He lifted his head again
and spoke in a solemn tone, "Hanan is reading a magazine on

the plane and daydreaming." In imitation of Hanan, Hatem stared out into space and smiled as he whispered: "Flashbacks. The blue sea. She is meeting her lover in Lebanon... She is wearing a pretty red shirt and black pants, her hair is dancing with the wind. She and her handsome lover Mohsen – her stepbrother – sit on the rocks by the beach. They talk about how long they have known each other, how long they have loved each other. He brushes his hands through her thick brown hair, under her chin. He kisses her lips. Soft music plays in the background..."

Hatem stopped and searched for the images. The steady breathing of his audience seemed to stand still in anticipation of his next words: "Again we return to Hanan sitting on the plane. She is gazing into space, pining away for her lover... And then another flashback. She and her lover walk on the beach and kiss. She is wearing a short summer dress. Her legs are long and thin. The steady sound of the clear blue water... Waves..." Hatem flapped his hands up and down and murmured the swirling sound of the waves breaking.

"She has now arrived in Lebanon," Hatem announced abruptly. "Her mother and stepfather greet her at the airport. But her lover is not there. He has another appointment... But from her bedroom window that day Hanan hears Mohsen whistling and calling up to her. She runs out into the street to greet him... Soft music in the background. She climbs on the motorcycle with her lover. Her arms around his waist. The wind blows through her hair, ruffles her blouse." Hatem hooted to imitate the whistling wind. He rose from his chair and twirled around and around in a circle like a whirling dervish. Dizzy, he plopped back on the chair and resumed his narrative in a more serious tone. "But that afternoon he tells her he wishes to emigrate to Brazil and she is not happy," Hatem whispered, tears rolling from his eyes. He wiped his eyes and muttered gently: "Her mother notices her depression and writes to Hanan's father informing him that his daughter is having a romantic crisis, in love with a man who does not deserve her. A loser. Hanan's father reads the letter to Mamdouh, who is shocked that Hanan is in love with someone else. He offers to go to Lebanon to help out Hanan, and her father readily agrees."

Hatem's voice grew more intense as he followed the thread of his narration: "Hanan is in the ocean swimming with Mohsen. He tries to touch her, but she says that it is over between them as long as he insists on leaving her and traveling to Brazil... Later she is wearing a black shirt with a small yellow flower in the front. She hears that Mamdouh has arrived and is so excited to see him. Hanan's mother and stepfather throw a party for Mamdouh. The colors are intense, the music thrilling. There is singing and dancing." Hatem rose from his seat and began to imitate the jubilant movement he witnessed on the big screen. After a few moments, his audience ordered him to continue his story. He plopped himself back on his seat and resumed: "Hanan is wearing a short white summer dress with a black silk scarf wrapped around her waist. Her breasts are showing from through her dress. Mamdouh, who is wearing a black shirt with white collars, begins to sing. Hatem repeated the song in a voice that sounded severely out of tune:

I love you.
So please love me too.
Love is legitimate.
I have loved you for a long time.
Oh, my sweet jasmine,
Pity this tender heart.
Spare me.
I love you.
So please love me too.
Oh, gazelle of the valley,
Hide me in your heart
I love you. So please love me too.

"Oh, come on, Hatem! Please get back to the story. Don't leave us hanging," Latif yelled at the top of his lungs.

Hatem ignored his brother and rose from his seat again, smashing his hands together and wiggling his behind as he spoke: "Mamdouh claps his hand and Hanan dances around him, waving her black scarf in the air. Blue waves roll in the background. Mohsen sits in the corner and watches angrily. Hanan tosses her black scarf over to Mohsen as she passes him, and he pushes it aside."

"The dawn of another day," Hatem whispered solemnly as he took his seat once more. "Hanan's mother confides to Mamdouh that she is worried about a heartbroken Hanan. Mamdouh offers to hire Hanan to help organize his paperwork, so he can keep watch over her. And so Hanan is now working for Mamdouh. One day as she leaves his office, Mohsen stops by in his motorcycle and asks what she is doing at Mamdouh's. She leans against a car. Her low-cut summer dress shows the crevice of her large, round breasts. Her full arms are exposed. She tells Mohsen she has nothing to do with him anymore so long as he is traveling to Brazil, and she tries to ascend the car to leave. But Mohsen grabs her arm. He looks her in the eyes, and smiles, saying that he has decided not to travel to Brazil. At this, she giggles and hops on his motorcycle. She places her arms around him and holds him very tight. The wind blows through their hair as they drive through the woods. They run laughing through the woods and throw themselves on the ground. They grow quiet and look each other in the eyes. As he approaches Hanan, Mohsen notices that she looks more sublime than ever, nestled on the lush green grass. The reflections of the sun dance on her face and in her dazzling hazel eyes. She peers up at him. She places her hands on his knees. He slips closer and touches her shoulders; his lips kiss her neck and glide slowly toward her mouth. They begin to kiss on the lips ever more fervently. They fall on the ground. He is on top of her and leaves brush against her hair. The trees above shelter them, the music is intense."

The breathing in the room grew frenetic as Hatem described her long tresses of thick brown hair, her moist red lips, her soft legs, her neck smooth and white, and their sighs as they embraced and caressed each other. No one stirred, their foreheads beaded with perspiration, their bodies quivered. A foul whiff filled the room. As Monkith twitched, he noticed Latif drooling absentmindedly, while another brother licked his lips as he pictured the kiss. Suddenly the room erupted in laughter when Latif pointed to his younger brother Amer who had an unanticipated erection, which he forgot to hide in front of the others since he was so wrapped up in Hatem's description. A startled Monkith watched Amer place his hand on his crotch and giggle with embarrassment along with the others. Although he too burst into laughter, Monkith had no idea what had happened between the lovers. So many questions stirred in Monkith's head as the movie-teller's voice drummed on...

"Hanan is worried, but Mohsen holds her in his arms and tells her not to worry – he will marry her immediately. But Mohsen does not keep his promise and travels to Brazil. Hanan is devastated. A couple months later Hanan feels dizzy, and Mamdouh makes an appointment for her at a hospital where she learns that she is pregnant. Mamdouh loves her even after he discovers that she is expecting the child of the handsome Mohsen. He runs to her apartment to make sure she is okay, and witnesses her suicide attempt. Mamdouh picks her up from the floor where she was inhaling the oven gas, and nurtures her. Mamdouh tells her he will marry her to prevent a scandal and that he shall raise her child as his own. He promises her that if she ever desires her freedom from him, he will grant it to her. No one else shall know their secret, he says as Hanan lays her head on his hands and cries in gratitude... They hastily marry and seven months later "their son" is born... But years later, Mohsen returns penniless from Brazil. He asks his father about Hanan, who says that she is happily married to Mamdouh. But when Mohsen sees Hanan, although she rejects him, he is convinced that she is still in love with him and that her son is also his. Mohsen swears that he will fight for her love, although both Hanan and his own father tell him to leave her alone..."

The breathing in the room halted as each member of the audience felt the suspense of Mohsen's return. Would Hanan reconcile with him or remain faithful to Mamdouh who had saved her life and had loved her and her son throughout the years? Hatem peered over his audience. Tears flowed from his eyes as he drew closer to the conclusion. Although out of breath, he quickly resumed his narration: "Mamdouh notices Hanan's sadness and confusion. He overhears Hanan telling Mohsen that she and Mamdouh share a feeling on a different level than love: fidelity. When Mohsen says that he knows that she still loves him, she does not deny it, but she declares that Mamdouh saved her life and that she must remain loyal to him... Tears fill

Mamdouh's eyes as he leaves the house, realizing that he will have to set Hanan free. In concert, he sings as Hanan watches him on the television and cries."

Although Monkith and the rest of the audience were tense with excitement, they sat quietly through the song that Hatem sang for them in imitation of Mamdouh:

I am your prisoner.
I have no one else.
I am your prisoner.
You perplex me.
I only have you.
Since the first day, oh, my tyrant,
You kept me from tasting sleep.
I tried to forget you,
But I lost my heart to you.
I obey your desires.
But you only love my tears.
I hope my night becomes longer,
Oh, my love...
Oh, my love...
But you love someone else.
Your tears are dear to me because I only have you.
Oh, light of my eyes,
Our life is filled with empty dreams.
I shall accept what you impose on me...

Hatem continued the story for his tear-jerked audience: "When Mamdouh closes his song, he wipes the tears from his eyes. Meanwhile Hanan weeps on her couch... That evening as Hanan and her son sleep, Mamdouh writes a letter telling "his son" that he has to leave, since he does not wish to keep him from knowing his true father... that he knows that one day he will understand that Mamdouh left him because he loved him with all his heart. And he tells Hanan that she is young, that it is time for her to live with the man that she truly loves. But he tells her he shall never forget their beautiful life together and that she will always be the most beautiful melody in his life... Hanan reads the letter the next day and smiles... In the next scene there is an airplane taking off for Cairo... the final scene – Hanan and Mohsen stroll on the beach cheek to cheek."

Fancying himself an actor taking a bow, Hatem closed his eyes and lowered his face. He hummed the same melody with which he had opened his story, and no one in the room moved. Monkith began to twitch in his seat. He was shocked that Hanan had left Mamdouh for the treacherous and lazy Mohsen. "That is a strange and unbelievable ending!" Monkith blurted out. There was a buz in the room as all the boys argued among themselves about whether Hanan should have mended ties with Mohsen. The "movie" had ended, but its vivid sounds, colors, and smells blotted out everything else for days after as Monkith mused on what he had heard and felt. He went over and over the story again in his head to see if he could convince himself that it made sense for Hanan to resume her love with Mohsen. But he could not.

The movie-telling became the talk of the neighborhood, and soon other children flocked to the entertainment. Monkith continued to attend, but after that first time, along with the others in the audience, he paid for his seat. The cinematographic narratives were well worth the price, though, since the way in which the story was told was always more intricate than the original movie itself. After all, the movie-teller's colorful imagination seeped into the plot of the actual movie.

The Donkey Deal

She stood whimpering feebly in pain. A thick crimson fluid streamed from her posterior as she fell to the ground with a loud thump. A stout Bedouin with a high forehead and pointed black eyebrows approached her with soft steps. He lifted her up, after wrapping a rope around her harness. As he stroked her head, he shepherded her to the base of a palm tree that sprouted two trunks, forming a snug v-shaped fissure. He ushered her head into the cleft, and stood before her on the other side of the tree. He comforted her as best as he could while her tears flowed, and she moaned in deep discomfort. With diffident grace, she remained standing. Before long, a black lump began to ooze out from between her legs, and then a small head came into the light. Within moments, a baby donkey, covered in slime, had tumbled to the ground.

The mother turned around and licked the blood and fluids that clung to her baby's fur. After a few minutes, the donkey struggled to stand, but lacking a sense of balance, it soon fell. Again, it attempted a few feeble steps. All the while, the doting mother licked her newborn as it sucked her milk. Soon, as if jubilant, the calf practiced traipsing. It even aspired to quicken its pace into a run.

The seven-year-old Monkith, observing this miracle from up in a mulberry tree at the Bedouin camp, gazed longingly at the joyful baby donkey:

"You're happy now," he thought to himself. "But soon humans will burden your back with their loads, you'll be forced to carry great weights. I will try to protect you from perpetual drudgery."

He was lost in thoughts, but from afar, he caught sight of his father returning home from the café. Without a moment's hesitation, he jumped down and hurried home to the safety of his room, where he busied himself with his math homework. As he worked with the numbers, his mind drifted off to the baby donkey, and before long, he had unwittingly transformed the numbers on the paper in front of him into baby donkeys of all colors, shapes, and sizes; taking their first steps and jumping happily in the air. His yellow pencil touched the paper. Two zeros formed a pair of eyes framed with the circular number five as a head connected to a long neck comprised of number one, which sat on the curvy number four. A red pen united the number three with its soft arches to the circular number five, and stretched the two shapes together – and out tumbled a baby donkey.

The next day, Monkith set out to the Bedouin camp to check on the newborn donkey. By now, the frisky youngster had learned to move on its own. It leaped up and down. After witnessing its birth and its first movements outside its mother's womb, Monkith spiritually adopted this donkey. He was determined to follow its progress and shield it from all harm. And so every day he lingered near the Bedouins' camp. In his eagerness for the donkey's well-being, he brought the donkey bread, but the Bedouins told him that this was not healthy for the animal. They handed Monkith some grass instead and allowed him to feed the donkey with it.

◆

As a child there was no animal that Monkith loved more than donkeys. He would wait for the donkeys as they were sent back and forth from the farms and to the markets, hauling okras and tomatoes in the summer, and oranges in the winter. Monkith noticed with a wry smile playing on his lips that all the humans who usually considered donkeys to be stupid beasts of burden failed to notice that they were in fact smart enough to remember a trail after being led down it only once.

He loved to wait by the side of the field for a donkey to pass, where he would then hop on its back. Whenever the donkey reached its destination, he slid off. And when his beloved mule turned around, he rode it back to where it had started. Before long, he learned how to order the donkey to slow down or to quicken its pace. Unlike other children, he harbored no anxieties at all that the creatures would kick or bite. The donkeys somehow sensed his gentle nature and returned his affection. Needless to say, it became his dream to buy a donkey and embark on his own adventures.

Whenever Bedouins came into Griyat to sell their goods, Monkith fluttered around them. He frolicked with the donkeys and camels that lugged their loads of milk and cheese from house to house in the wintertime. Sometimes, when he played with the Bedouin children rolled up in filthy rags, some of the neighborhood children grew angry with him.

"You fool!" one boy cried out. "Bedouins are flea-ridden riff-raff, stinking away to glory all the way from here to the putrid gates of hell!"

But the Bedouins' lifestyle intrigued Monkith:

"Go to hell, you nitwit! I adore playing with them," he replied with a defiant grin. His thoughts wandered off... They inhabit the most interesting tents made of palm trees, he marveled to himself. How I wish I could live in one myself one day!

Among the Bedouins was a teenage boy named Jassem. Jassem had dark leathery skin, a flat face, and short, cropped hair. He wore a stained yellow *galabia*. The teenager with a silvery glint in his eyes soon noticed Monkith's obsession with the baby donkey whose birth he had witnessed. He broached Monkith one day, as if he had read his thoughts and said, "Hey, why don't you just fork over some money and buy the beast? It will finally give you some peace of mind!"

"I would love to, but for how much?" Monkith replied perhaps just a bit too eagerly.

Jassem feigned a vacuous expression with his eyes. The only hint of motion on his face was the toothpick protruding from his fleshy lips. It yo-yoed up and down in response to the whimsical play of his casually lolling tongue, which licked his yellowish teeth eaten away with decay.

"Three dirhams." Jassem suddenly retorted with aplomb and walked away pretending he had to tend to other responsibilities.

"But I only have two dirhams and twenty-five felas!" Monkith hastily shouted after him. "Come on, why don't you give me a discount. I promise I will take good care of it," he pleaded.

Jassem lackadaisically turned around, raised his arched eyebrows in an expression of supreme ennui and feigned a thoroughly disinterested refusal. "Sorry kid, there's no way in hell that I can sell you this beast for less than three dirhams." He paused and noticed how Monkith's eyes fell to the ground. "Hey, my family is already losing by selling it to you at that price. My parents will probably kill me when they find out. I am only doing this because I know how much you adore this donkey," he suddenly spurted out.

"Come on. I don't have any more money, and there is no one who will care for this donkey the way I will. I promise," Monkith insisted. Frustrated, he stomped his feet and turned to walk away.

At this, Jassem relented, and held out his hand to strike a deal. A smile shone on Monkith's triumphant face. He dug his hands in his pockets and handed the money over to Jassem. So excited that he forgot to say good-bye to Jassem, he set out on the back of his donkey. He dreamed of all the things he would experience with his new pet, and how as best friends they would never part.

"Tomorrow we'll go to school. You'll meet my friends. I'll take you to my grandparents' home by the Tigris; you will marvel at all the fruits in their lush garden. You'll meet my grandfather Jawwad – revered by everyone in Griyat as the most famous fishermen in Baghdad. Mind you, he only tasted fish once in his life and almost choked to death on a bone when he was six years old. He never ate fish again, but he always enjoys fishing. He loves watching others – particularly me – savoring his catch. And I will build you a beautiful house by the Tigris. You can rest there while I build cities of clay. Ha ! Just imagine the comfortable stable I'll build for you. Don't worry; I'll never let the other children smash it into pieces, ever. I promise, you'll be safe with me. Oh, here we are, we're home."

As he approached the front of his house, his pregnant mother peered out of the living room window. All she could see through the trees was her son, suspended high above the ground, floating at a leisurely pace through the garden.

"Oh, my God," she cried out, drawing a deep breath as if she was counting to ten in the futile hope of regaining her composure. "What is that silly good-for-nothing up to now?"

She watched as the tree began to shake mysteriously. She was taken completely aback, for she could not see the donkey munching its leaves from the other side. Nuriya abandoned her cleaning, ran as quickly across the room as her heavy body would permit her, and flung the door wide open. Monkith stood facing her with a happy grin plastered all over his face. He tried what any well-meaning child would have done with a new friend: he began to enter the house with the donkey.

"Hello, mamma, this is my new friend. He has come to live with us," Monkith beamed from ear to ear.

"Ah! Good God! Ashes on my head! May you bury me alive and throw lice in my grave!" Nuriya shrieked thoroughly revolted. She began pounding her wrists against her head screaming inarticulate curses. Manal, Ibtihal, and Iqbal, who had been playing with their juggling set, came scurrying into the room. Manal and Ibtihal noticed the donkey and began to giggle, but two-year-old Iqbal began to cry at the sight of her mother who was caught up in a frenzy. Monkith stood still staring at his mother and sisters in disbelief. He dared not enter the house, but planted himself buy the door. He caressed his donkey's head and whispered to it that it was safe, all the while watching his mother closely.

When Manal carried Iqbal over to her mother, Nuriya threw herself down on the couch to regain her nerve. In her seventh month of pregnancy, she began to feel convulsions in her swollen stomach. Now even the shocked Iqbal began to chuckle at her eccentric brother's blunder. At the sound of the laughter, Nuriya recovered from her shock, but to keep herself from joining in the mirth, she grabbed Monkith, and then her hand descended with a good thwack.

"Don't you ever bring this braying bastard back to our house. Do you hear me? If your father ever finds out, he will wring the last drop of lunacy out of your twisted mind. Now, scram and return this donkey immediately to its filthy owner." Still fuming, she decided to take out her wrath on the dirty tiles and resumed scrubbing the floor with a vengeance, treading hurriedly over the water she had so carefully poured just moments before she beheld her son floating in the air.

Monkith was crestfallen. Heavy tears fell from his large hazel eyes and clung like dew drops to his thick black lashes. "Please, mamma, let me keep it to ride to school, even if only for one day!" Monkith importuned, but Nuriya ignored him. "Only once, only one day. Please," he begged pulling her skirt as his sisters stood clapping and rooting for him. To distract their mother, Manal began juggling as Ibtihal, who held Iqbal, began dancing around and around in circles until she became dizzy with excitement.

But Nuriya stood her ground. "Monkith," she hissed, as if her patience was about to snap. He looked up at her in dismay. In as calm a voice as she could muster, she continued, "I do not want to argue. Return this donkey to its original owner before your father comes home and spanks the wits out of you." She pushed him aside to continue shining the floor. But Monkith refused to accept the sudden chance of fortune.

"Please mamma, just one day," he said stomping his feet in defiant protest. Water splashed in his mother's face as his feet touched the ground in a resounding thud.

"Go now, or I will summon your father this very moment," she hollered in a tone of exhausted patience giving way to full fury, as she turned an ominous shade of purple. Monkith, knowing full well what lay in store for him, relented.

Outside he stroked his pet. "It is no use arguing with her, dear donkey, she will not yield. She will call for my father and he'll spank both of us. He'll hit you so hard, that you'll bleed forever," Monkith whispered to the donkey as he caressed its snout and they set off to find Jassem.

Jassem already spied Monkith returning to the Bedouin camp from afar. As, indeed, he had expected him to all along. With a shrewd eye for business, he had foreseen the outcome of the transaction.

"Hey, you're back again. What do you want now?" he asked with a twisted smile.

"Jassem, you will never believe it. My mother is forcing me to return the donkey to you. She won't even let me keep it for one day. I'm so sorry." Tears welled in his eyes as he let go of his donkey.

"Well, okay, I can take possession of the donkey again, but I can't give you a refund. I've already handed the money to my father," said Jassem in a serious tone, which feigned disappointment.

Monkith had lost his fortune, but he did not care. He was only able to think of the unfulfilled dreams he had hoped to share with his new friend. Tears rolled down his cheeks as he parted with the donkey: "Dear donkey, don't be afraid. I will come by every day to visit you. That will never change. I promise."

That night he refused to sleep in his parent's home, but stayed with his grandmother Fatema instead. He complained bitterly to her about his mother, about how he bought a pet donkey, but his mother did not let him keep it for just one day to ride to school, and how this was his dream, which his mother had stolen from him. His grief was boundless, but the incident of the donkey deal only provoked laughter in the family for many years to come.

The Pigeon Keeper

"Come, come, little bird. You can trust me!"

One cold winter afternoon, a pigeon with soft, dangling white and gray rear feathers and a long white neck with black polka dots, walked languidly on the edge of the dusty rooftop. Intent on capturing it, Monkith climbed a ladder to the second level of the rooftop. Once there, he followed the pigeon, which bobbed slowly up and down, until he was able to reach out with his hand and hold it fast. The pigeon squirmed in his hands, but within moments grew listless.

The next day he visited his uncle Hamid's small shop around the corner and borrowed some broken wood, a hammer, and rusty nails. With the door of his room locked, he constructed a small wooden home for his pigeon so that none of the stray cats would pounce on it. He installed the birdhouse on the second level of the rooftop, far away from his father's prying eyes. He watched as his new pet spread its faded gray wings and flew away, to return a few moments later to its home filled with birdseeds.

Monkith felt that they were close friends, and he shared his deepest secrets with it as he scattered seeds. He confided in the little bird about the new marbles he was collecting after his father had dumped the contents of the bulging wool sock down the toilet – how he had just traded a slippery purple marble for a bright green one with yellow stripes! He emptied out his new marble collection for the bird to see, and imagined that it clapped its wings in approval of his cleverness. Red, blue, purple marbles rolled across the bumpy surface of the rooftop, and Monkith ran after them in all directions.

Once when he was in the living room teaching his sister Ibtihal how to play tricks with her jump rope he noticed the pigeon, pecking its beak on the window, as if it was saluting him and telling him how alone it felt on the roof.

"I need to bring you a friend, little one, so that when I am at school or doing my homework, you won't feel so lonely," Monkith whispered to the pigeon as it fluttered before him only to flee at the sound of Naji's voice: "Monkith! I have told you a million times not to play jump rope in the house. You good-for-nothing! You loser! When do you plan on listening to me?"

The next day Monkith set off for Kazamiyyah to see an old vendor named Chakouz, who was frightfully obese. He sported large, loose yellow teeth, and was known for his moodiness, flaring temper, and rigid prices. One of his eyes was a bulging green, while the other – as if to make up for the protrusion – was blind, with white mucus oozing out of his lashes. His right leg had been amputated, and soiled clothes covered the rest of his deformed body. He limped around on a long red cane for support. He was a horrific sight, but Monkith did not mind. All that mattered to him was that this man sold birds. Despite his astronomical prices and his principled refusal to bargain, his selection was, without doubt, the best in town.

Monkith walked toward the infamous small shop on the side of the road. He pushed away the flies as he quietly opened the dilapidated wooden door. A horrible pungent smell of pigeon filth enveloped him as his eyes searched for Chakouz, who had fallen asleep in the corner. On the table next to the old man was a broken earthenware vase with large red artificial flowers with torn petals. Despite the shop's sodden state and the dust falling over his head, Monkith inched closer. At the sound of Monkith's approaching footsteps, Chakouz was suddenly startled out of his sleep, and poised to fling his cane at the intruder.

"Wait sir, I have come to inquire about your pigeons. I currently have one pigeon and want to buy a companion for it," Monkith proudly declared.

The old man, still half-asleep on his chair, scrutinized the serious eyes of his young customer, and then snapped: "Okay, now listen to me, kid, if you have the requisite bundles of cash on you, choose any fluffy fella you fancy. By God, what the hell are you waiting for you somber-eyed turtle? You're looking at me as if I've cheated you out of your father's inheritance or something!"

Undaunted, Monkith responded, "Well, I'd like to buy a companion for my pigeon, but I'm not sure whether it is male or female. How can I tell the difference?"

Taken aback by Monkith's equanimity, Chakouz figured that the young lad was serious, and warmed to him. He stretched out his arms, rose from the chair, and asked, "Well, tell me, then, does it make any sounds or is it silent?"

Monkith hooted in response: "Bullabaloo, bullabaloo…"

"Well then, your pigeon is male. For female pigeons are silent as a grave," said Chakouz proud to show off his knowledge.

"In that case, I'd like a female bird. Could you show me your selection?" Monkith asked, smiling pensively and marveling as he waved away a fleet of mosquitoes.

"How much do you have on you? Give me an idea and I'll let you know which sassy lady you can afford." Chakouz hobbled closer to Monkith, grabbed his arm with his chubby hands, and led him to the cages.

"I have one and a half dirhams." He dug into his pockets and handed the coins to Chakouz.

"One and a half dirhams," Chakouz repeated to himself pensively as his eyes roamed around the shop." Let me see what this can buy you. Oh, yes, one and a half dirhams will get you any of the pigeons in this corner here." He pointed to the cage hanging on the right hand side of the wall whose paint ran down in streaks and was cracking due to the humidity. The gray-colored ceiling above was festooned with spiders' webs.

Monkith spotted a white Damascene pigeon of surpassing beauty. He looked with wonder at her long lush white rear feathers, which fanned out as if she were a peacock, proudly strutting about. He adored the way she pranced ever so gently, like a pampered princess. He handed over one and a half dirhams to Chakouz, who then placed the pigeon into an old plastic bag, which he sealed with tape. He poked two small breathing holes in the bag and then handed it over to Monkith.

"Now, scram kid, and don't come crying to me like a sobbing mama's boy if your filthy bird gets lost. Whatever happens, I sure as hell am not going to give you a refund, understood?" Chakouz hissed, as his mood shifted suddenly from admiration to impatience and then to unbridled anger. He whacked Monkith's back with his cane, and slammed the door behind him with a loud bang.

Monkith thought he was dreaming. He held his white pigeon in his arms, gently so that the bag would not ruffle its delicate feathers. As he walked serenely on, he imagined the pretty chicks that would hatch after crossing his male pigeon with this Damascene beauty. He remembered what his friend, Osama, told him the day he had seen a sparrow seated high in the air above him on the electric cable wires. As the bird froze, another one mounted it. It seemed as if the prostrate bird was lifeless.

"For goodness' sake, why is that sparrow hurting the other one so much?" Monkith asked.

Osama laughed. "No, don't worry. The male bird is not hurting the other one when it bounces up and down on it. My brother Jalil told me that this is how birds make more eggs that will hatch into chicks. You know what I mean," he said as he gaped at Monkith's troubled eyes. "They're doing it!"

Once he had discovered where chicks come from, every time he saw different birds, Monkith imagined what they would look like after crossbreeding. Now he wondered what this pigeon's long confident rear feathers would look like when crossbred with the male's downward slanted feathers. He envisioned the dazzling offspring, which would be born. All sorts of birds of all forms and faces whirled around him as he set off for home – blue and red striped with thick yellow feathers, white with purple wings, crimson red with large black eyes. His agitated mind set them loose, and he soared with the fantastic winged creatures above his neighborhood and school. They flew higher and higher and the clouds were now within his reach. He reached out to touch a soft purple patch and it melted between his fingers.

That afternoon when his father was not paying attention, Monkith crept up to the rooftop with his new purchase. "Well, my dear friend," he whispered to his pigeon, "you will never imagine the surprise I have for you. You now have a female companion. You won't feel abandoned anymore." After dinner, Monkith was seized with an idea. He searched the bathroom trashcan for his father's tossed away razor. He tiptoed barefoot into the kitchen and searched for a piece of soap. In his excitement he ignored the coldness of the tiles, which brushed against his naked feet. He rubbed the block of pale yellow soap in his hands and against his nose. Its edges were moist from recent use and emitted a strong putrid odor far removed from the familiar scent of the clay by the riverbanks. He hid the soap and razor in the towel in the bathroom, and that night after his sisters had fallen fast asleep and his mother had crawled out of Iqbal's bed to join her husband, he descended the stairs and dashed into the bathroom, shutting the door behind him. The stiff silence deafened his ears. He unwrapped the towel, and took out his new treasures. The overused razor rubbed against the soap's sticky surface and peeled off the moist edges. He cut deeper and carved a wing inlaid with sinuous designs. Beads of sweat fell down his forehead as he set his ears on the alert for any unexpected movement in the house. He tore deeper still. A second wing emerged and then two feet. And wide eyes...

For a few weeks, Monkith climbed to the rooftop every day after school and watched his pigeons as they flew into the distance, to the horizon, vanishing point before swooping back down to the safety of their home. It was as if they always sensed when Monkith was about to bring them seeds; they flew over his shoulders and fluttered with excitement when they saw him approaching. Out of the clay he collected at the Tigris, he molded small plates for their seeds. And in the evenings, he covered their cage with a blanket for their safety, and when the night air grew chilly he ignited small fires for them.

But then one afternoon, Monkith's father spied his son with the birds on the rooftop. Naji – whose face contorted with seething rage – secretly slithered behind Monkith and lost no time in administering a stinging slap to his face and back.

"I don't understand, what have I done wrong?" Monkith screamed out in pain as his father's strong hand pulled his ear.

"Why do you disobey me this way? Why can't you live up to my expectations, you good-for-nothing, huh?" He spluttered with anger as he struck his son aimlessly left, right, and center, while drops of sweat fell randomly from the bulging veins on his boiling red bull's face. Naji cuffed his son in a tightened grip and shook him all the while yelling:

"You insolent dimwit! Haven't you learned that pigeon keepers have a vile reputation?! Why do you think that Hajj Abbas and the other neighbors keep on saying that if you spend time with your pigeon on the rooftop, you are nothing but a deprived pervert ogling at the ladies in the gardens below, huh?!" He spat on the ground punctuating his remark with saliva. "A rotten lot, they are, those pigeon keepers! Inveterate liars, the whole lot of them! Stealing others' birds and then denying it. Why do you think that even courts do not accept their testimonies? Pah! Pigeon owners are no more reliable than gypsies. If you want to curse someone, you have only to call him a pigeon keeper! Do you understand me, son? Why do you want to sully my good name and provoke such a scandal, huh?"

Monkith looked up at his scowling father. Tears filled his eyes. His shoulders hurt from his father's iron-fisted grip. His whole body burned in pain. But his desolation benumbed any other sensation.

"Well, do you understand me, you silly nitwit?" his father yelled and shook him again.

"Yes, I do," he screamed. "I promise I'll never do this again."

"Good, now hand over these birds. You will never see them again, is that clear?" Naji trumpeted, pushing his son aside.

Monkith nodded his head in brooding silence. But as a seven-year-old, he could not truly fathom his father's words. He watched as his father released the two birds into the air. He envied them as they flew away into freedom. He felt a rush of relief, though, when the birds returned a few minutes later.

"Well, I see," Naji muttered through gritted teeth while look-ing his son up and down with a thinly veiled contempt. "It seems you have already trained your pigeons to come back to you."

Monkith watched as his father grabbed the two birds by the legs, squeezed them brutally, and descended the stairs. From the rooftop, his eyes followed his father as he left the house with a bag, marching steadily toward some unknown destination. Naji returned hours later, glowing with delight. That evening, he proudly declared at the dinner table that he had given the two birds to Hajj Abbas to have them butchered. Monkith fell into a deep depression. Resentment began to fester.

A Faithful Pet Nightingale

It was a breezy autumn day, and the eight-year-old Monkith sat on the veranda with Manal and his mother who was breast-feeding her infant Amal. They watched his father wield a fly swatter. The older man approached Monkith and whispered, "My goodness, I think I see a little fly on your cheeks, son."

Using a fly swatter, he slapped him on both the right and left cheeks. Monkith's tender flesh flamed red from the sharp sting. Little squared shapes from the swat formed on his face. Monkith's fingers touched his skin, and he could feel the bloody red squares forming like broken windows.

"Why, father? Why have you done this?" Monkith cried.

"Don't talk back to me, I told you that there was a fly on your cheek," he replied angrily, as Manal looked down in silence. Cradling Amal in her arms, his mother cried, but said nothing. Monkith burst into tears, and ran to the bathroom to behold the horrid sight. Embarrassed by his cranberry red cheeks, he held his head high and determined that he would not go out and play with his friends until his face was back to normal. Just as his autumnal wounds began to heal, winter led the way for new chances.

One day, on his way to school, he spotted a wounded black and white nightingale by the roadside. A newly recovered Monkith decided to adopt it and nurse it back to health. He carried the bird home, washed its wounds, and soon it regained health. He called his new friend "my little *bolbol*"[20] and let his sisters pet its soft fur. But it did not take long for Nuriya and Naji to become irritated with the attention Monkith lavished on his new pet rather than on his homework. Naji searched for his belt to strike his son, but Nuriya convinced her husband that she could find a clever scheme to get rid of it.

One day, as his Nuriya was rocking Amal to sleep, she told Monkith, "If the bird truly loves you, it will fly back to you even if you set it free."

---

[20] Nightingale

Never one to shy away from a challenge, he decided to test his mother's hypothesis. "Well, let's go into the living room, and I'll let my *bolbol* out of its cage." Monkith watched in suspense until his bird loyally returned.

"It only hurried back to you because it was in the house," his mother explained nonplussed as she burped her daughter. "The true test would be to release the bird in the garden, where it could soar to freedom in the soft blue sky," his mother chimed.

"I am sure it will return to me even if I let it free outside," he stubbornly insisted. Monkith carried the cage into the garden and set his feathered friend free. It spread its wings, and rose higher and higher into the sky, before alighting on one of the tallest trees in the garden. Complacently, the bird gazed down upon him. Monkith glimpsed up at his bird, grief-stricken.

After surveying the garden from its lofty perch, the nightingale set out to explore the world beyond the garden walls. When Monkith could barely discern his pet, he began to cry. Five minutes later, however, his bird was back in sight. It settled on one of the lower branches of a tree and glanced at Monkith. Monkith was thrilled, and placed the cage on the ground beside him. He opened the door and held his breath.

"Okay, my little *bolbol*, come back home. I promise you that you are safe with me," he whispered tenderly to his friend. Faithfully, the bird flew into its cage.

From that day onward, Monkith kept his cage in the garden and released his pet *bolbol* every day. It was as if the little bird truly adored him. It nibbled at Monkith's head. When Monkith strolled to school, the bird sat on his shoulder. Perched on a nearby tree, it waited for Monkith during recess. Once Monkith set out for home, the bird fluttered onto his shoulder. The other children approached him, ready to exhibit the wanton cruelty towards animals that overcame otherwise gentle children. But the wise nightingale did not wait for their taunts and fists. It soared high into the sky, and then rejoined its protector once he had signaled safety.

Monkith never forgot the day that his beloved bird succumbed to its mortal enemy. While he was at a friend's house, a spotted black and white stray cat, that had always greedily eyed the bird, finally saw its chance. The cat wrested the cage from a low branch in the garden. It pulled the bird so forcefully between the bars that it was instantly mangled to death. When Monkith returned home and beheld the bloody scene, he shrieked in pain. His tears fell copiously on the remains of his dead pet. He buried his loyal friend near the Tigris, so that its spirit would guard the cities he built there. He swore revenge on the stealthy cat.

Cities of Clay

Oh, you luscious red carpet of clay lining the Tigris, moist with melted mountain snow, sparkling with the reflections of the sun, which enact their casual dance of descent on your fecund surface. I clasp a soft, grainy lump of mud in the palms of my hand. I twist you and turn you into a circle, and then a square. I compress you into quixotic solidity. I elongate you beyond recognition of form, and then I transmogrify you into a human figure, a donkey, and a four-winged jinnee, with whom I take off and fly through the balmy breezes of the sky.

By the riverbanks, two pieces of clay kiss frenetically, and a little bird hatches. My fingers sculpt a proud tall tree in Aytah's foreboding image, and I am transformed into a miniature caterpillar climbing your slender bark. Then I fell you, and nothing remains of you but a small stub I may sit on. Through your intricate warp and weft, I spin a lofty castle no one may penetrate, a secret world no one else may trespass, a magnificent city where no soul sickens at the sight of another. A home for my donkey, a grave for my nightingale, a safe kingdom, like a tapestry that I can weave every day anew. Exotic cities brimming over with two-headed animals with long, slender bodies, winged-people, and spirits floating about and protecting them. But I am not able to preserve you. Other children topple your walls. I cry out in sheer agony, but in my fingers you dissolve into new and more scintillating settlements.

In the stillness of the day and under the heat of the spring sun, the water and clay below remains chilly. I dig deeper into the earth, and reach the freezing water below. My hands, blue from the cold, rub against the brittle clay walls I create and I begin to bleed. My blood seeps and dissolves into your muddy, crimson interior until we become one.

You are my first love, my clay, and no one approves of our fusion. How many times I was beaten for my love of you, and warned not to touch you again. Banished from your kingdom, I find a small stone in my garden and feel it. But I discard it. A stone is not as sensitive and patient as you are to indulge the whimsical desires of my fingers. My clay, you are faithful. A rock may appear firm on the outside, and it deceives me into believing it is strong. But its insides are porous and in my fingers it crumbles. And so I always drift back to you.

I am slave to your larger shape; you are slave to me when you are nothing. I am the creator, the destroyer; you are my creator, my destroyer. How many times I annihilated you, how many times you decimated me... When I am morose, I fling you on the ground. I have twisted your face beyond recognition, but then you abased me, too, the very moment you collapsed me into a sobbing babe.

When I flush out my sore phlegm and my salty tears, and offer my haunted apologies, you befriend me once more. How many times we have argued, but we always come back to each other. I am born of you; you are born of me. I am your god; you are mine.

I shall wander the world over, and shall never find the moisture I discovered in you – you are the shadow, the light, outside and inside, my surroundings and my very center.

Umm Bassam

Not far from the Azawis lived a tall, gaunt, middle-aged woman named Umm Bassam. Her husband's name was Michael. His mother had prayed in a Christian shrine for her firstborn to be a son and when the midwife plucked him out of the birth-canal and into the world, she sprinkled upon him a Christian name. Michael grew up to be shy and quite slight in stature, considerable shorter than the woman he later married. Indeed he was terrified of his wife, who would beat him on almost any occasion she fancied – if he forgot to buy tomatoes at the market, if he bought two kilos instead of one, if the tomatoes were not red enough... She would harangue him until he would flee the house to escape her wrath. However, before too long, she would prowl after the distressed and bewildered man like a quick swinging pendulum, and holler in a voice that pierced the air like a red-hot iron plug, "Look at you, you mama's boy! Come back if you're man enough! Where are your balls? Hah! I forgot, you don't have any!" Then she would spit into the dust and erupt into crackling laughter. Then when she caught him – as she inevitably did after he returned from his refuge in the village's coffee shops – she would drag him back into the house kicking and screaming. One time she battered him so badly that a rib in his side split. No one in Griyat respected this livid man with the deep-set, twitching eyes whose nervous voice sounded like the croaking of a frog.

Depending on whom Monkith asked, Umm Bassam was either crazy or evil – either way, she was a woman of undisputedly bad repute. Everyone knew that she carried on openly with another man. Even her husband was aware of her infidelities, for she invited her lover into their conjugal home. Monkith thought that her lover must have been crazy, too, for even thinking of touching her. Thick green arteries shot out of her forehead, and she had dark, bushy eyebrows and a thick, long nose literally accentuated by a bristly mustache. Her brittle yellow fingernails grew deformed because she played nervously with her cuticles. When she walked in the street, her legs shot out of her short black *abaya* like two bamboo poles. She carried her children matter-of-factly on her thick shoulders with their legs dangling on her chest. Her pace was quick and rigid, and she screeched like car tires grinding to a halt on a hot asphalt road as she paraded like a stiff tin soldier through the neighborhood. The high-pitched reverberation of her voice sounded through the still of the night.

Although Umm Bassam and her husband were miserable together, they had somehow produced four handsome sons – Ali, Abad, Mahmoud, and Bassam. All the children in the neighborhood were scared of them because they knew that if they ever picked a fight with any one of them, Umm Bassam would rush to their rescue. One day, when Monkith was about nine years old, Umm Bassam's eleven-year-old son, Ali – the gruffest of the brothers – began to taunt him. Monkith had joined the children after school for a game of "seven stones," a game in which the boys collected stones of different sizes and split into two different groups. Monkith, his friends Osama and Hatem and his cousin Sateh, joined the first group. Their group piled seven stones on top of the other, while the second group, which was composed of Umm Bassam's four sons, tried to knock over the pile with a ball in no more than three attempts. In the meantime, Monkith and the others in the first group were supposed to disperse. Once Umm Bassam's sons had toppled the pile of stones, they picked up the pieces and pelted the boys in the first group. The rule was that those who managed to reach "high ground" – any surface that was at least ten centimeters from the ground – were safe. A terrified Sateh decided to quit the game and sprinted home without a moment's hesitation. Osama and Hatem searched frantically for a rock to stand on or a tree to hang on for protection, knowing that if they fell, they were liable to be attacked by stones. Ali pushed both of them off their rocks and began thrashing them. As Monkith dangled in "safety" from a tree, with the other children rallying around him and hooting in appreciation of his dexterous rush up the trunk, he noticed Naji ambling at a distance. Without as much as a second thought, he released his grasp and fell to the ground with a loud thump. The stones that laced his arms and legs left their sting, but Monkith knew that this level of pain was much less severe than any punishment, which his father would have meted out had he caught him playing "seven stones."

Ali now had his chance. He forgot the rules of the game, and once he tired of attacking Monkith with stones, he threw him onto the ground and kicked him in the stomach. His brothers encircled him and cheered. Ali had chosen the wrong victim, though, for Monkith escaped his grip, got up, and hit Ali back so hard that crimson drops of blood started dripping from his nose. Ali stood dumbstruck and embarrassed in front of his brothers and the other children, and without a word, a disheveled Monkith raced home before his father arrived.

The following day a livid Umm Bassam stationed herself at the entrance of the school and waited for Monkith to emerge. Her arms flailed and she jumped up and down. The green veins in her forehead burst forth like the branches of an enormous palm tree. She played nervously with her cuticles and began sucking the blood, which flowed from her bony fingers. She scratched her armpits and hollered: "Where are you, you son of a bitch?!! Your sister's a whore – may she rot in hell! Did you see Ali's dirty shoe filled with mud and scum? Well, that shoe has more honor than your sister's ugly face!" Her screeches reached Mrs. Attika's math class, and all the children jumped up in their seats and began trembling.

Mrs. Attika, the new math teacher, was among the most popular instructors at the school. She had thick black hair, which hung past her shoulders like a tar-soaked sacking and made her delicate oval face and wide-set eyes appear even smaller. Yet no one could miss her mouth on which was imprinted a permanent smile and traces of goodwill. After class, Mrs. Attika, who knew that Umm Bassam was violent and possessed by a dirty tongue, offered Monkith to walk him home to protect him. She grabbed her papers, stuffed them in her brown leather purse, and took Monkith's hand. As they passed Umm Bassam, who had stationed herself right at the entrance, she began spitting on them and screaming: "Where are you going you sissy? May your father and all your ancestors burn in a rotten hell! May God shorten your miserable life!" Mrs. Attika pulled Monkith closer to her. She walked decisively with her heavy black shoes, hunching her broad soldiers. At her behest, Monkith quickened his pace.

"I am going to kill you, you bastard! Just wait till I get my hands on your grubby body. I am going to shrivel you up into pieces so small that no one sees you as they stomp on you," Umm Bassam screamed as she pursued them.

"And as for you, you ugly bitch! Mrs. Attika, just wait till I get my hands on your slutty buttocks. I will twist you so out of shape that your husband will throw you out of the house with the filthy evening garbage!

Mrs. Attika tightened her grip on Monkith's hand, who looked up at her and signaled that they were nearly in his neighborhood. When they arrived at the Azawi family garden gate, Mrs. Attika pushed Monkith inside and made sure he locked the gate behind him. When she heard that he had entered his house safely and shut the door, she turned to leave, pretending that she did not feel the salty spits that Umm Bassam fired on her. Even after Mrs. Attika's departure, Umm Bassam stood before the garden door, screaming, "May evil strike you, *Inshallah!*"[21] May the fleas of a thousand camels infest your armpits, you illicitly begotten bastard! You shriveled up piece of donkey dung!"

Monkith watched her from the balcony of his new, independent room, which he shared with no one. His sisters Manal and Ibtihal ran out of their room and gathered around him, eyes wide open. Ibtihal began to cry, and grasped Monkith's arm. Annoyed by Umm Bassam's loud shouts, Monkith climbed down the stairs, stepped into the garden, and grabbed a heavy stick. He opened the gate and ran after her like a wounded bull in a Spanish arena. Umm Bassam, who had not anticipated such fearlessness, suddenly pulled off her shoes and sprinted all of the way home.

---

[21] God willing

Kite Flying

How I wish I were a winged paper plane drifting in the gentle breeze of the sky. It was the early eighties in Damascus and I was in my third year of college. I felt an unspeakable nostalgia for my childhood in Baghdad. I bought a large blue piece of paper, and pasted a tail made of red, purple, yellow, and orange squares onto it. I rubbed the glossy paper against my cheeks. I constructed a small cardboard box for a candle that I would attach to the string of my kite so that it would fly high into the sky. I climbed the rooftop of the University of Damascus dormitory, unraveled the string, and set my kite – with its shimmering candle – free. Within moments there was a rush to the rooftop of several members of the Syrian mukhabarat. Never having seen such a spectacle in the sky before, they thought that perhaps it was a bomb. They laughed when they discovered that it was just a paper plane that belonged to a young man who yearned for the soft breezes of his childhood, a time before flimsy paper planes were replaced by aggressive bombs and warplanes, which ravaged children and adults alike.

Kite flying, the Baghdadi summer sport, was among the greatest sources of pleasure for young Monkith. Like other children, in the beginning he trekked out to the stores to buy a kite. It was not long, however, before he discovered a way to make a kite himself, and soon he was assembling a new brightly colored kite every day, which other children would purchase from him for reasonable sums of money. Every evening, he took out his almost transparent colored sheets of paper, cut up shapes – circles, triangles, and squares. His fingers ran across the slippery surface of the paper. He turned it around, and rubbed the rougher tissue paper surface against his cheeks. His scissors cut a piece of paper, and hesitated between a circle and a square. He scrunched it up, threw it on the ground and began cutting again. He mixed a soft ivory colored powder with some water, and he whirled his fingers around and around until a sticky glue consistency with an unsettling scent formed. He wiped his hands and glued his assortment of pieces together. Blue circles for the windows, a red door, large yellow wings, and he had created an imaginary airplane possessed by a jinnee, which would fly away and discover the secrets of the sky. As he unwound the string, his fingers were rubbed raw, leaving behind a trail of painful blisters. He sat on his knees for hours as he made his kites of all shapes and colors, and tore up his trousers in the process. His parents never quite understood how and why he had so many holes in his clothes.

Throughout the summer, the Baghdadi sky was ablaze with brightly colored bits of paper-trailing long tails. Children took their kite flying seriously, and often engaged in battles with one another. There were moments of peaceful détente. Often, though, it was all-out war. If one kite collided with another's, then an airborne "battle" ensued. These quickly turned into a favorite Baghdadi pastime for boys, since girls in general were not permitted to play on the roof. The boy whose kite broke the strings of another's and remained in tact was the winner. On any given summer day, defeated kites cut off from their owners plummeted haphazardly through the air in downward spirals.

One day, Monkith invented a way to win the kite battles hands down. He searched his home for some old bulbs, but when he found none, he went to his father's friend, Abu Jawwad, who owned a lighting store down the street. Abu Jawwad, an elderly short-sighted man, whose left eye was much larger than his constantly squinting right eye, used his store as a workshop and place to gather with friends. This was his one refuge since his wife, a very jealous woman, threw a tantrum every time he had a social call. Under the pretext that he was slaving away, he stayed through the late hours of the night at his shop drinking *araq* and playing backgammon with his companions. As Monkith reached the shop, he heard the sound of jubilant banter even though the door was locked and the lights were out. He knocked and knocked but no one answered. He heard the sound of shuffling steps and then the laughter grew into a stiff silence, which emerged through the thin cracks of the door. He rang the bell again.

"I'm busy working now, wife!" Abu Jawwad yelled with the voice of a water buffalo injured at the plough. "Please go away. You know I am not a lazy lout! I will come home when I am finished with this order!"

"It's me, Monkith, I have come for some burnt bulbs. Please let me in," he pleaded.

Again there was an obstinate stillness, but then Monkith

heard the sound of approaching footsteps. Abu Jawwad opened the door and led Monkith into a room whose floor was streaked with spilled *araq* and topped with dry flatbreads, earthenware jars, and unwashed plates filled with rotting food. Aggressive flies hovered around the piles of filth. Abu Jawwad's two friends left their hiding place, and continued playing backgammon. Again Monkith asked for some burnt bulbs, and a disconcerted Abu Jawwad searched his trashcans, cabinets, and floors for any discarded bulbs he could find. Without asking what they were for, the tipsy old man handed them to Monkith, who thanked him politely and ran home.

When he reached his room, Monkith locked the door and began crushing the bulbs into tiny pieces, which he then mixed with flour and glue. He lined the first two hundred meters of his thread with his lacerating trapping. The next afternoon when another kite attacked his, he unwound the string a little further to slice his glass string through that of his foe. No one uncloaked his trick, but many peeved mothers would come to him and beg him to be gentle with their sons' kites. "We're at peace," they would declare, but Monkith would answer, "No, we are at war!"

On summer evenings, the sky shimmered with candles in tiny containers, which were fastened onto the kites' strings. Children would fall asleep on the rooftops clutching their strings as the lights fluttered above their heads. Sometimes, the candles burned through the strings. Untethered, the kite would fly away. At nighttime Monkith often beheld differently colored kites flying towards him like miniature meteors descending from the sky.

While his parents and sisters slept on the lower level of the rooftop, Monkith climbed up to the second level and slept there himself. A tall wall enclosed the second level, so he could play with his kite furtively. Before he nodded off to sleep at night, he tied his kite-string to his rooftop bed. He cut a small piece of paper and pierced its middle. He wrote a letter to his kite – "How are you? Are you happy there above in the neighborhood of the stars? I miss you and long to see you again. Tell me how you are feeling. I am waiting for your news."

He lay on his back marveling at the stars. With his eyes, he drew pictures of imaginary animals in the bright clusters – purple elephants with long polka-dotted necks, yellow donkeys with bright blue feet and red horns on their head. When his eyelids finally closed, his kite's bright light still twinkled above him. He fell asleep thinking of his beautiful, magical kite. He fantasized of its journey through the sky, to the mystery of the glittering stars and the creatures he envisioned up above. He dreamed of tomorrow's kite, its magical colors and fantastic shapes – animals, trees, and flowers – that would emerge from his nimble fingers. Suddenly he was startled out of his sleep, and felt fear for his kite's safety. He knew that the kite battles endured even during the darkest hours of the night. At times when he woke up, the other boys on the neighboring rooftops had already cut down his kite. At times it hung low, and was endangered, so he quickly unwound his string and let his kite fly higher into safety, back to the fantastic shapes in the sky.

Eventually, though, the images he drew in the stars of fabulous animals were transformed into Abu Tabar's wounded cadavers. Soon, along with the other children, he stopped marveling at the radiant clusters above and hid his face under the covers when he slept on the roof. By the 1970s, rumors circulated that the Baathists had secret satellites attached to the stars that took pictures of whatever treacherous activity occurred down below. Monkith's neighbor, Osama, had an older brother named Jalil who filled the childrens' ears with stories of the people who caught leprosy and died as they tallied the stars. He instructed them to pull a blanket over their heads when they slumbered on the roof. Ideas of death and punishment cultivated a culture of fear. They seeped in and even altered the kinds of games children played.

Theatrical Muharram

On my cousin Sateh's rooftop, the water boiled in a large cauldron, and I watched as my aunt began to stack up the old pants and shirts from the previous year. She added a black die to the boiling water and she stirred an enormous stick from a palm tree around and around. I became dizzy as the clothes billowed and the water whirled into a red, green and then black, as she added a little more color. When the water transformed into a clear black, she threw in the old, tattered clothes that all the relatives had gathered and given to her from the previous years. I observed silently as the clothes turned into a deep dark black, and then as Sateh's mother hung them on a line to dry, before returning them to the relatives. For it was the Islamic month of Muharram. This was a time of Shii mourning, and everyone needed to dress in black for the occasion.

Every year my father sat me, my sisters, and cousin Sateh around him and recounted for us the famous story: 'It all started when the Prophet Muhammad's grandson and his family were slaughtered in Karbala during the Ashur, the tenth of Muharram in 680 AD.'

'But why did they kill him. Tell us how it started,' I asked, even though I had heard the story several times before. Each year with the new thrill of the event, it captivated me to hear the story told all over again. My father continued:

'Yazid bin Mu'awiya was currently leader in Iraq, but the Iraqis beseeched Hussein to come to Iraq, announcing that they wished for him to serve as their ruler. For you see, he was the son of the fourth Caliph, Ali, whom we Shiis revere as the true Caliph to whom the throne belonged after the death of the Prophet Muhammad. And so the mighty Hussein set off for Kufa to make his claim. But when he arrived at Karbala on the banks of the Euphrates, the wretched Umayyads, led by Yazid bin Mu'awiya, made war against him. Hussein had fewer than one hundred people to fight against an army of about five thousand. The enemy surrounded him and cut off all his water supplies. As it was very hot Hussein and his small brave group became thirsty, and so it was easy for the five-thousand man army to attack. When Yazid and his band slew Hussein, he hoisted Hussein's head on a rod to exhibit his power and authority. He carried this rod to Syria and then Egypt to let all dissenters behold their fate.'

All of us trembled and huddled closer together, and my father paused for a moment. He asked my cousin Sateh, who regularly attended mosque with his father and who was perhaps the most religious of my cousins, to tell the story of Yazid bin Mu'awiya's bitter fate. My father signaled for me to listen carefully as Sateh sat up in his seat, drew in a deep breath, and spoke with pride:

'According to Shii legend, one day, when Yazid bin Mu'awiya galloped through the desert hunting a gazelle, he lost his way. As Yazid became more tired, slowing his pace, a huge serpent slithered towards him. It ate him, swallowed him, and disgorged him over and over again. This devouring became Yazid's fate, until the day of Resurrection as punishment for what he had done.'

My father then reminded us how in the Sumerian tradition, the gods flagellated themselves as punishment for having killed Tamuz. He told us how Shiis appropriated the Sumerian tradition of self-inflicted strikes on the chest and head to punish themselves for not having helped Hussein. And so during the passion performances of Muharram, Shiis struck themselves as a ritualized form of symbolic atonement for their failure to save Hussein's life at Karbala. The Ashur, the tenth of Muharram was a particularly important day, since it is the day Hussein's whole family was killed, except for a few men and children.

For us children this holy season was a strange one. We were mourning Hussein's loss, and yet at the same time the atmosphere in Iraq took on a carnival-like air. Shiis lit candles across all of their sacred cities: Kazamiyyah, Karbala, Najaf, Kufah, and Samarah. Young and old watched theatrical plays of the much-adored soldier, Hussein, represented by the color green, fighting the Umayyad soldiers.

Since A'dhamiyyah was made up of a majority of Sunni Muslims, my friends and I joined the throngs of people making their way to the Shii region of Kazamiyyah on the other bank. We followed the multicolored procession of actors playing trumpets, drums, and cymbals. Most spectators wore black to express their grief for Hussein. Many wept and screamed 'Hussein, ya Hussein' as they watched the actors go by. Even the holy shrine of Musa ibn Ja'afar donned a black garment.

I was both fascinated and terrified by the intense atmosphere. Some of the screaming women and wailing men went so far as to inflict real pain on themselves by striking their heads and chests and, in some cases, drawing blood. Generally, the mourning spectators followed the theatrical procession to the holy shrine of Musa ibn Ja'afar. Here the actors, who were dressed in various hues, mounted a production of passion plays. The fighting between the putative Hussein and his enemies resembled a real war, with the two sides riding horses and drawing their swords on one another. Ironically, I stumbled upon my love for theater during this time of mourning.

The days leading to the Ashur were precious to me as a child and teenager. My father was a stern disciplinarian. Thanks to the mourning period, however, I was allowed to stay out late and see my friends easily. I was not the only one to benefit from the freedom of movement that came with the processions. By Western standards, Griyat was a highly conservative society in the 1960s where interactions between men and women were carried out in secret. Women often wore black abayas, and male-female relationships developed subtly. Generally, the first form of interaction began with darting glances, a coy smile, perhaps some whistling, and exchange of bashful and blushing glimpses. A boy might stand on a stand on a particular street corner and wait for a girl who passed daily, willing her eyes to meet his. Sometimes he might hang a note on a nearby wall as she walked by. If the attraction flourished, the boy might even climb up to his beloved's roof and secretly meet with her.

But in the period leading up to the tenth of Muharram, a newfound liberty descended upon Griyat. Villagers distributed cigarettes, cookies, and tea for free on the streets, and many took up smoking. Impatiently, lovers waited for this ten-day period when they got away with practicing all the things that were ordinarily forbidden. Men and women who were in clandestine relationships were suddenly able to see each other. Even girls were allowed to stay out late under the pretext that they were participating in religious events. When the colorful procession of greens, blacks, and purples passed in the street, there was much confusion and chaos. The men passed in the middle of the procession while the ululating women stood on the sides. They screamed in the throes of their religious devotion. As a child I observed how some men took advantage of the commotion to stand next to the women clad in black abayas to become sexually aroused. They touched themselves on their most sensitive spots, made loud sighs, and aroused the person next to them.

By the mid-1970s, however, as the Baath party gained strength, it sought to erase the collective memory of Iraqis, and one of the ways was to curtail the Shii practice of Muharram. By the early 1980s, the tradition was forbidden altogether. For the Baath sought to create new traditions for themselves – filled with fear, blood, and the mukhabarat.

Tanun and How He Ate to Death

There was once a lunatic in Griyat nicknamed Tanun. He was well known throughout Griyat and even beyond. Yet his true name and origins were a mystery to the inhabitants. He was a huge man, bald with bulging blue eyes and pinched lips, who hauled trash for a living. On his face hung a pair of lopsided brown wide-rimmed glasses, whose lenses were covered in a layer of dust and filth. A small black curl fell at the center of his forehead. He could usually be found sitting on the steps in the front of the local bread oven. There he sat for hours grunting, as his reddened, swollen hands rubbed up and down his bare feet. He peeled the dead skin from between his toes, and lifted his hands in exhilaration to his nose. Sometimes he shut his heavy eyelids and dozed off. Legend had it that when Tanun lost his mind, a hospital exchanged his brain for that of a dog.

He roamed the streets ranting and raving incoherently; the only phrases that could be discerned were his curses against the Baath. Now, this corpulent man took a lover named Entesar, a prostitute, and it so happened that she reported the politics of the men she slept with to the mukhabarat. Rumor had it that the undaunted Tanun heard she was Baathi and each time he had an orgasm and withdrew, he screamed out, 'To hell with your Arab Unity, Freedom, and Community'- popular slogans of the Baath.

And this was not all. Rumor had it that he devoured anything he found edible, that is, anything he picked with his own shovels of flesh. For so delirious was he and antagonistic against the Baath that if anyone offered him food from their hands, he became suspicious and mistook them for the mukhabarat, and screamed, 'Damn you and your supposedly nationalistic government!'

Tanun could be found lingering at the wildest festivities where he ate anything within reach. And so one summer afternoon, he hobbled to a funeral banquet, and gorged himself on rice and meat cooked in a thick homemade tomato paste. He ate and ate, and when not even a few grains of rice were left, he rubbed his chubby hands on his stomach. He stood at the center of the room in his vast frame and glanced around him. Then he stumbled back to his home to nap. It appeared he never woke up.

Days passed and no one had seen him on the steps of the local bread oven. The owner grew suspicious and sent for a doctor to check in on Tanun. The doctor arrived several days later and examined the corpse lying in the middle of the floor in the very same outfit he had worn at the funeral banquet. He squeezed Tanun's cheeks and dug his finger into his mouth to empty it of rice and meat.

He concluded with sorrow that perhaps Tanun had stuffed himself this time with more than even his stretched out stomach could handle. Some were satisfied with this explanation, though they secretly lamented the loss of this colorful local character. There were other more skeptical men who would struggle to learn the story behind his demise...

The next day, Sheikh Khazal al-Sudani, the leader of the mosque, announced the death of a man named Khalil Ahmad, a descendent of the famous al-Shendi family. No one remembered this man living among them, but throngs of villagers attended the funeral procession of this unknown rural notable. During the wake, stories circulated among the villagers that the obscure Ibrahim Ahmad al-Shendi was in fact Tanun.

A Sheikh, a Suicide, and a Loss of Faith

It was two in the morning, and a quiet, steady breathing settled over the house. Monkith grew hotter and hotter. Shiny beads of salty sweat rolled down his forehead like crystals. They mingled with the steady stream of heavy tears, which slid from his eyes. He kicked off his blanket and changed his position. Another day had finally passed, and he longed to taste the sweetness of sleep, the sweetness of escape before he was forced to wake up in just a couple hours to pray. But sleep refused to come to him. It only tempted him. He felt himself falling lower and lower into the darkness, disappearing into the void, when Manal's hoarse coughs wending in from the next room stirred him. It had been several weeks since the horrific images of past events had torn him apart, and stayed up with him during the oppressiveness of the night.

His eyes were wide open. He stared into the familiar darkness with its sinister shadows. Each specter wrapped itself around him and told a story he yearned to forget. As he searched for pleasant shades to lull him and lead him down the tunnel of oblivion, he spotted a pair of hardened eyes in the corner. He imagined Sheikh Khazal al-Sudani drifting toward him and pulling off his sheets. Al-Sudani was a young twenty-seven-year-old man, with a yellow face, a clean beard the pleasant color of cinnamon bark, and a strikingly white turban. He had moved from Basra to the village of Griyat to serve as the spiritual leader of the Zahrah mosque. While filled with treachery, he possessed a magnetic persona that attracted others to him. His voice was filled with an authority that no one dared question.

Monkith grabbed the sheets from the Sheikh's finely groomed, delicate hands now stained with blood. As he sought to banish the Sheikh from his mind, his father's voice seeped in through the darkness and rose in defense of the Sheikh, a former student of Iran's Ayatollah Khomeini and a frequent visitor to the Azawi household. The whispered conversations and secrets his father and the Sheikh shared floated toward him and suffocated him. His shoulders ached in pain. He tossed away the sheets and turned over on his stomach. As he changed his position, he felt his father firmly grasping his shoulders and ordering him to respect the Sheikh. Forcing him yet again to accompany him to the mosque to become better acquainted with him.

"I won't go! I won't go!" He yelled out into the empty space. "You can't make me!" His father's hand swooped over his face and Monkith began to cry. He jerked the blanket, which had gathered beneath his toes and pulled it up over his bruised face. The Sheikh and his father had faded away. Their voices disappeared into the darkness. He beckoned happy visions. The stars outside seemed to clutch his bedroom window and it was as if he could reach out his hand and catch them one by one. He fancied himself twirling around and around on a large canvas of paint the size of his Grandma Fatema's garden. He was barefoot and naked. His toes sank into the green paint and he skid across the canvas into a pond of dark blue. He lay in the thickness of the paint and reached into a corner and plucked a red flower. Its fresh smell soothed him and he breathed it in until his eyes became heavy... "Get up! It's time to go to the mosque. The Sheikh is waiting for you!" his father yelled. "No!" Monkith screamed out. When he opened his eyes, the soft canvas no longer cushioned him. It was his familiar bed. Silence. And shadows.

He closed his eyes and sought to flee to the lushness and peaceful calm of the painted field, to the red flowers and blue ponds, but the devastating images of the past weeks whipped him. He shut his eyes, but it was useless. His thoughts continued to wander off to the evening a few weeks ago when he had turned ten years old. His father grabbed him and took him to the mosque for the evening prayer. A man named Omar sat down to pray next to Monkith and the other boys. Omar was a poor, pale-looking man – his face the sickly color of foaming milk – and to make matters worse, he was a Sunni in a Shii mosque. It meant nothing to Sheikh Khazal al-Sudani, who was preparing to lead the prayer, that Omar considered converting to Shiism. The Sheikh stood at the front of the mosque facing the direction of Mecca, with his back turned towards the men praying behind him. Before commencing his prayer, he turned his head and from the corner of his eyes he scanned the silent, bowed heads. He eyed Omar whose eye-sockets were wrinkled and whose head hung low. The Sheikh grimaced. He called for Nouri, the servant of the mosque and in front of everyone ordered him to throw Omar out.

Nouri's face, which was florid and covered in a carpet of greasy red pimples, did not strike Monkith as particularly unattractive. But the servant did something that forever branded him hideously ugly in Monkith's eyes. Upon the Sheikh's request, he approached Omar, and in a loud, scratching voice he ordered him to leave the mosque immediately. Someone like Omar, who had few worldly possessions, clung desperately to the little dignity he had. When it was trampled upon before the eyes of others, he could not bear the loss. He coughed and threw himself on the ground to regain his breath. Tears blinded his eyes. He quickly gathered his things and fled the mosque as the others began to murmur in prayer.

Monkith struggled to forget the horrible images engraved in the shadows of the wall. The Sheikh's fingernails varnished in blood-red. He closed his eyes and beckoned the colorful canvas full of flowery fields, but there was no escape from the fountain of dark blood. Monkith remembered his father's angry signals as his son pursued the humiliated man out of the mosque. He arrived outside just in time to see Omar fling himself in front of a car. The outcast, who lay in a pool of fresh blood, drew his final breath in pain. His last stammering words ensured that his death was intentional and not the fault of the driver. Bitter tears fell from Monkith's eyes as he stumbled to the ground and inhaled the smell of fresh blood. The men began rushing out of the mosque and shouts filled the air. But the Sheikh turned around and stood as still as an iron pole. He raised his arms to call for the men to return. Everyone grew silent and froze in their places. They continued praying as Naji slipped out, seized Monkith's wrist, and pulled him back into the mosque.

The redness of the blood and Omar's shattered face drifted toward him and clung to his sheets. His eyes had grown used to the darkness. All the horrifying images were clear before him. As much as Monkith sought to toss them aside they adhered defiantly. It was four in the morning, the time to worship God. The stars had vanished. Dawn was breaking. He heard the shuffling of his father and mother's feet as they prepared for prayer. Soon his father would pass by his room to make sure he was respecting the Prophet's law. Monkith crawled on the ground and implored God to pity him. As tears rolled down his eyes, he cursed the Prophet Muhammad over and over again. He cursed Mecca, the site of his father's pilgrimage. He envisioned the Kabba, the black large stone at the center of Mecca that the Muslim pilgrims circled around until they became dizzy. In his mind he transformed it into a large colorless stone around which small black dots smaller than ants rotated. The stone at the center crushed them one by one until none were left, and then a new group of black dots appeared and met the same fate.

He crept back onto his bed, which was drenched in sweat. In just a few hours it would be time to get up and dress for school. At daylight his mother would come in, kiss his drenched forehead, and tell him he had gotten enough sleep. He would open his bloodshot eyes and try to smile. He was growing used to lack of sleep, to the images of the Sheikh's cleanly shaven face, and the skinny Omar lying alone and abandoned in a pool of thick crimson blood.

After a month of sleepless nights, he began to smoke in secret. When this new habit failed to calm his nerves, he began searching frantically in his parent's medicine cabinets for artificial aids to help him to escape the night's shadows and drift into peaceful slumber. From the day of Omar's tragic suicide onward, he was deprived of tasting real sleep. When his parents discovered that their stock of pills was disappearing, he confided his predicament to Jalil, Osama's older brother, who began to steal an unnoticed bottle of beer from his parents and bring it to Monkith in the evenings. One afternoon Iqbal, already a precocious reader, sat in the living room trying to decipher Ibtihal's book. For a moment she looked up and noticed Monkith's puffy, bleary eyes as he passed her in the living room – he was lost in the mazes of his nightmares and did not even hear or see him when she called for him. Frightened, she told her mother about her older brother's red-shot eyes. Nuriya immediately asked Monkith if he had been drinking alcohol. He shook his head and struggled to convince his tears not to fall.

But Monkith's father loved the Sheikh. He even stood by his friend's side during the tragic episode, which provoked a scandal in Griyat. Regardless of his father's tireless attempts to defend the Sheikh, in Monkith's eyes, the man was a criminal. He had heard the Sheikh tell Nouri to expel Omar. How could he command such a horrible action in the name of God? Monkith wondered. From this moment on, he stopped praying in the way his father taught him and felt alienated from exclusivism in Islam. Indeed, he was staunchly opposed to any form of religious exclusivism.

Shortly after, in front of others at the mosque, Naji asked his son to kiss the hand of the Sheikh. Monkith gazed unblinkingly into his father's angry eyes and refused. He stoically bore his father's slap on his face, for he knew he had wounded his father's pride. That evening he told his father: "I am a human being before I am a Muslim, before I am a Christian, or a Jew. I believe in God, but not in your God. My God is sweet, beautiful, kind, and tolerant. Not like your God and that of others, who kill, burn, and destroy."

The Poisoning of Wahida

There once lived in Griyat a woman of astounding beauty named Mehdiyeh. She was blessed with thick blond hair and a round white face. On delightful summer nights, she pranced on her rooftop preparing the blankets and mosquito nets for herself, her husband Yassin, and their sons. She wore a thin, transparent nightgown, which exposed her thick thighs, breasts, and round torso. Although the light of the moon shown down on her, she also turned on the weak lights on the roof. The lamp's glimmer outlined her silhouette even more. She was pleased when she noticed from the corner of her eye that the boys were staring at her from across the neighboring rooftops. She walked on the roof swaying her hips to and fro, wishing to incite them, and perhaps relieve her own boredom. She sat on her silk white blanket and cracked open a juicy rosy watermelon. Her teeth sank into it, the juice dribbled down her lips onto her chin and down her neck. Moments later, her husband returned from the café, and her seven handsome sons joined them, and they each went under the mosquito net.

It so happened that her husband Yassin was a taxi driver, a weak-looking creature deemed stupid by the villagers in Griyat. He had a large forehead and thick eyebrows. His hair was a faded black, the color of old, worn-out clothes dyed during the month of Muharram, and used over and over again until they were dusty and grayish.

Mehdiyeh remembered her hopes and joys the day he and his brothers had come to her village to ask for her hand. If truth be told, she felt no love or attraction toward him, but she hoped to escape the control her father exerted over her. A pathetic husband, she reasoned, was easier for her to maneuver with than a domineering father.

She remembered the day she first arrived in Griyat and how the men and women observed her from their windows. Everyone had heard how the meek-looking man had wed a beautiful girl from outside the village. An outsider was a novelty, and a beautiful girl such as Mehdiyeh provided the villagers something to talk about for years to come.

As the days and then years flew by, Mehdiyeh discovered that there was nothing she could do to fall in love with her husband. The only thing that soothed her was the glances she received from the men and boys when she strided through the streets swinging her hips. This became her game, and she went hunting for admirers who became so easily entangled in her silk net.

The villagers mocked her husband Yassin for although he went on to become the proud father of seven beautiful children, none of them resembled him.

Indeed it was rumored that different men fathered Mehdiyeh's children. The gossip became even hotter when several villagers in Griyat learned that Mehdiyeh's husband was sterile. For he once had the ill luck of picking up a woman facing the scandal of a pregnancy without marriage. Eager to find a scapegoat, she recorded the taxi's number. She set off immediately to the police station, where she accused her driver of raping her. The police stormed the 'criminal's' house and hauled him into the station. When the doctors examined him, however, they discovered his unfortunate medical condition.

But there was one man who envied Yassin, and sought Mehdiyeh's younger sister, Salome's hand in marriage. And soon her sister, another outsider, came to live in Griyat. On some summer nights, Salome spent the night with Mehdiyeh and observed her rooftop prancing. Salome also tried to seduce the observers by wearing a thin nightgown and tiptoeing about the roof, but she was not able to incite the same attention in her frail frame. Alas, she drowned in the Tigris without any man other than her husband eying her. She left behind her husband, young son, and daughter Wahida.

Wahida, with her large protruding forehead and thick unibrow, was not particularly beautiful. A rather dull expression played about her dark brown pinched lips. Her unruly, frizzled black hair hung like wild spinach around her neck. Now motherless, the plain girl looked upon her aunt Mehdiyeh as her second mother and confided to her everything. Mehdiyeh, for her part, enjoyed having the company of 'her adopted daughter,' as her sons were independent and rather secretive.

'Dear Aunt, I have something I think you should know. I am besotted with a man who lives not far from our small home. I pass by his home every day, and I can feel him observing me from his kitchen window,' said Wahida, breathing a sigh of relief that she had finally revealed her secret to her aunt.

Mehdiyeh stopped looking at herself in the mirror and her voice grew serious as she whispered to her niece, 'Tell me what his name is child, so that I may inquire about him, to make sure his intentions are respectable.'

Wahida grew ever more confident now that she knew her aunt would help her. She continued, 'I heard from a neighbor that his name is Fuad, but I do not know much else about him. I can tell you where he lives, and you can go on and probe.'

'Very well then, tell me the exact location of the apartment and I shall let you know.' That evening Mehdiyeh invited Mulla Aboud to her home. He was a mysterious old man whose origins were unknown. People believed that a jinnee had possessed this strange man's soul. According to local legend, when he turned one hundred years old, his blond hair resurrected, he began to teethe, and he grew vigorous like an adolescent. Only his stubborn sight never returned. He shuffled quickly through the streets with his head leading the rest of his body, singing strange tunes and chattering to himself. He slept by the Tigris or on the streets, and knew everything about everyone, as he somehow happened to linger everywhere at once. Sometimes several people swore they saw him in three places at exactly the same time of the day.

Without much ceremony, Mehdiyeh began, 'My dear Mulla Aboud, I am desperate for some help. I need you to acquaint me with the background of a young man named Fuad who resides here in Griyat.' After she informed him of the address, he lowered his head in silence. She slipped some money into his coat pocket and watched him closely. For a moment it seemed he had fallen asleep, but then he began to hum and frantically twirl his prayer beads between his fingers.

'My dear Mehdiyeh,' he finally said, 'that young man is a very wretched sort. He arrived years ago from some village in the south with his father and his younger brother. It is said that his father had murdered his wife and her lover when he found them making love in his bed, and he never made the required recompense either by delivering a sum of money to the victim's family or by offering up a life from his own family. And so he escaped his village and came to settle in Griyat. He built an isolated house with a palm tree roof and wooden walls. When the derelict shelter became overcrowded, the family abandoned it, and erected a new one. Like squatters, they relocated repeatedly. But that was many years ago.'

Mulla Aboud stopped speaking for a moment and fiddled nervously with his prayer beads. Mehdiyeh became faint. She burned seeds of wild rue and sprinkled the powder over her niece's picture, trying to fend off the evil spirits. She closed the kitchen door so that her husband and sons would not interrupt the session.

After a few moments, he resumed his story: 'No one in the family even owned an identity card. They were among the poorest of Griyat's working class. Indeed, their one donkey was the family's sole source of livelihood. With it, they ran errands for people and moved goods, such as vegetables and construction materials.'

'Okay, but what about Fuad, please tell me,' pleaded Mehdiyeh, who already was tortured about her niece's prospective suitor. 'It seems some evil eye has touched the young girl. May God protect her.'

'I am getting there, my child, but please be patient,' the Mulla responded. 'I must search my mind for the scattered information I have.'

The Mulla lifted his eyes to the ceiling as if searching for something and then spoke again: 'The younger son, Ali, loved the cinema. He learned English, Hindi, and the Egyptian dialect by watching motion pictures at the cinema in

A'dhamiyyah. He especially loved Hollywood cowboy movies from America. The shooting thrilled him. He adored nothing more than to watch a showdown. Once, the cinema made the mistake of showing a romantic movie filled with love and tenderness. An agitated Ali confronted the projectionist and complained that the film contained no gunshots or brawls. He later traveled to Najaf, and no one knows anything else about him.'

Mehdiyeh began to worry, bracing herself to hear about the older son's fate.

'Now, let's return to Fuad,' said Mulla Aboud. 'As an adult, after his father died, he joined the Baath. Before he knew it, he earned a decent salary working with the mukhabarat who promised a gun, a car, and power to anyone who joined. He began to point his fingers as if shooting a pistol and frighten the local inhabitants into doing as they were told. If he wrote a complaint against someone, he or she would be sent directly to jail. Well, the wretched Fuad from the very lowest echelons of society, never dreamed of wielding such intoxicating power before.'

Mehdiyeh moved to say something, but Mulla Aboud signaled with his prayer beads that she must remain silent as he gathered together his recollections. He continued: 'In his new position, he earned enough money to buy a small house. Not far from his home lives your niece in whom he soon took an interest. But you must put an end to it. His intentions are not honorable, and his background speaks for itself. You must speak to her as soon as possible, before it is too late.'

At this he rose from his seat and darted out the door. Mehdiyeh burned some more rue for her niece, took a shower, rubbed a moisturizing cream on her body, and fell asleep. No sooner had the sun risen the following morning than Mehdiyeh called to warn her niece, but it was indeed too late. For the very same evening that Mulla Aboud spoke those frightening thoughts, the cunning Fuad discovered that Wahida was an easy target for quick pleasure. With one fantastic phrase as she passed by, he was able to convince her to come to his bed the very same evening. After midnight, she stole past the rooms of her father and brother to meet her awaiting lover, treading very carefully so that the floors would not squeak. Fuad took her into his room without uttering a word. Her lips trembled and her body quivered as he took off her abaya and embraced her. In the early morning twilight of their first encounter, she was no longer a virgin, and pregnant at that.

It was to Aunt Mehdiyeh that the young woman confided her secret as soon as she figured it out: she was expecting a child and the wretched man had abandoned her. The older woman was mortified by the shame that awaited the family. She buried her face in her hands and prayed desperately until a solution came to her. And so she invited Wahida to join her husband and sons for chicken in a thick pomegranate sauce, rice, and yogurt one cold winter evening.

The shrieking wind beat hard against the kitchen windows. Hoping to induce an abortion, Mehdiyeh lowered her eyes and quietly slipped poison into a bowl of garlic sauce, which she then mixed with some maroon pomegranate sauce. She appeared at the dinner table glowing:

'Well, my dear Wahida, I have made you your own special portion of chicken with garlic sauce. My husbands and son never touch garlic and don't allow me to savor it either. But I always make a special dish for our guests, so they don't have to suffer like me.'

'Oh, my dear, please get that garlic away from me,' her husband moaned meekly.

'Thank you, Auntie, you didn't have to go through any trouble. Really I would eat anything. I am just happy to be with you, my uncle, and cousins,' she said, smiling as she drew her plate with the fatal garlic sauce closer to her.

Mehdiyeh watched as Wahida slowly chewed and swallowed the chicken and drank her yogurt drink. After dinner, as Mehdiyeh's husband and sons grumbled wearily about the strong scent of garlic, which had impregnated all the corners of the house, Wahida complained of fatigue and her aunt prepared her sheets in the guest bedroom. The night was as black as charcoal and the shrill cry of insects penetrated the air as Mehdiyeh slipped into bed, and eagerly awaited the results of her plan.

The next morning Mehdiyeh, her husband, and sons sat around the kitchen table for breakfast and awaited Wahida, who did not appear. Finally, Mehdiyeh knocked on her door and entered. From the kitchen table, the family heard Mehdiyeh's shrill scream, and she fainted. Her plan was all too successful, for not only did the unborn child die, but so too did its mother.

Her husband splashed water on her, and Mehdiyeh rose. They carried Wahida to the hospital and the police doctor examined the lifeless corpse. The doctor glanced at Mehdiyeh, who looked remarkably beautiful and glowing that day, despite the sudden shock. She stared at the doctor as she spoke faintly:

'What is wrong, what caused her death?'

'Hm, are you aware that the girl is two months pregnant?' the doctor asked. His eyes scanned hers as he waited for a reply.

'Of course not, how can that be?' she said struggling to maintain her composure.

'Well, then,' said the doctor, 'it seems that the only explanation for her untimely death is that she has committed suicide.' He began to jot down a few words, but then Mehdiyeh placed her hand on his.

'Please help us keep this secret. Our family cannot handle the public scandal.' She began to weep as she brushed against him.

The doctor solemnly recorded a few observations with illegible writing on a piece of paper, with Mehdiyeh breathing closely next to him, and nudging her soft elbows against his arms. The police officer who later looked over the medical papers, simply recorded this information onto his public records. Then he put his head down, took his glasses off, and closed the book and said, 'God wished it so.' The matter never went any further. Oh, how many dossiers have been closed in this way in Griyat…

Two-year-old Monkith on
Habooba's rooftop

Above: Monkith (at center),
his cousin Sateh (to the left),
and neighborhood
children

Left: Nine-year-old Monkith

145

Monkith (fourth boy to the left)
in elementary school portrait

Portrait Monkith took of sister
Manal before her wedding

Monkith (left) and cousin Zaid
in Habania, north of Baghdad.
Zaid was later executed by the
Baath

Young Monkith (far right) and
cousins. All were later executed
by the Baath except Monkith and
his cousin, Hussein (to his right)

Monkith and his uncle Mohsen
swimming in the Tigris

Monkith (third from the left)
and classmates at the Central
Secondary School in Midan

Monkith at the Central Secondary
High School

Above: Monkith and friend by
the Tigris

Above: Monkith (far right) with
Saadi (far left) and friends in
Griyat

Below: Monkith meditating by
the Tigris

Teenage Monkith with his
paintings

Above: Monkith (fourth from the left), Saadi (fifth from the left), and friends at the Central Secondary School in Midan

Right: Monkith and Saadi.

Monkith's maternal grand-
parents, Fatema and Jawwad
al-Salman

Above: Monkith drafting an
interior design project at the
University of Damascus

Right: Polyester sculpture by
Monkith entitled: "The Camps"
(1986)

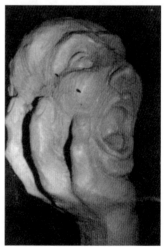

Portrait from a large panel by
Monkith entitled: "Eastern
Details," which he exhibited in
1987 at the Damascus National
Museum. The detail here is of the
face of Umm Fadi, the proprietor
of the ground floor apartment on
Shah Bandar Square.

Hond & Hamer Exhibition
organized by Monkith with the
cooperation of Queen Nur at the
National Museum of Modern
Art, Amman, Jordan (1995)

Monkith in Damascus with
Iraqi exiled poets Saadi Yussef
and Abdel Wahab al-Bayati
(1996)

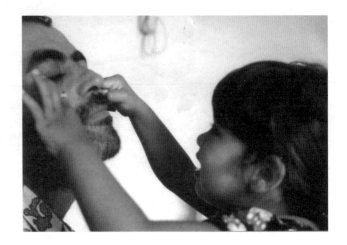

Monkith with daughter Maya
in 1995

Monkith back in Baghdad after
long exile – in the picture:
Monkith with his parents, and
sisters Amal (on the left) and
Iqbal (right)

Miran al-Saadi's Sculpture

A miraculous shade covered the walls I propped myself against, until a luscious light appeared and lifted the veil. It left behind the devastating glare of the summer. I sprinted home to avoid the heat, and the punishment I was sure to receive for my long absence from the house that morning.

When I was about ten years old, Miran al-Saadi, a famous Iraqi sculptor, was commissioned to create a large metal statue of the black poet Antara in A'dhamiyyah. Every morning I strolled forty minutes from my home to reach the spot where the sculptor and his assistants worked. I sat against the wall covered by shade for five entire days witnessing the birth of the statue.

I tried to approach the sculptor and his workers, but each time I did, they yelled, 'Get away, you dirty dog, we are working, and it is dangerous here. You could have an accident and we'll be held responsible.'

But this did not deter me, and each day I attempted to touch the monument. Each time someone shoved me away, and I would lie near the wall about thirty meters away from the work site. When the sun set and the yellow glare appeared to touch my head, I tried to hop on a bus home, but the bus driver would shove me off since I did not have money with me. As I did not own a bicycle, I had to walk.

Upon arriving home, my mother placed her one-year-old son Muhammad in Manal's arms. Then she slapped me and screeched, 'Where were you? Why are you late again? Wait till your father finds out!' But the punishment did not inhibit me from returning the next day to follow the development of this spectacular form. I was especially fascinated by the sculpture since I knew the story behind the subject.

On vacations, my father bought each of us short stories. For every book we read, he offered us one hundred felas. A child could buy lots of candy with that sum. As a result, I used to read prodigiously. I knew that Antara bin Zabiba was a black poet from the Jahiliyyah period, the age of ignorance before Islam. His father was the head of a tribe, but his mother was a slave, so Antara never took his father's name. When Antara grew up, he became a great fighter and his father wished for Antara to fight alongside him. But Antara said: 'Slaves are not allowed to kill.' His father responded: 'That is so. But you can kill, because you are not a slave but a free man.' Antara replied: 'So you acknowledge that I am your son?' And his father said: 'Yes.'

I think the story touched me because of the love and pride that Antara's father finally showed his son. I watched the sculpture's construction in awe, eager to witness the marvel that each new day proffered.

Secret Art

Art inhabited my essence. There was never a before and after. For as long as I could remember I searched the bathroom trashcan for my father's tossed away razors, and with them, I transformed common objects such as soap and chalk into whimsical figures. I frittered away my time dabbling in paint. As I turned the pages of my favorite art book, I was intrigued by El Greco's elongated figures, his thick contours and shadows, the lush greens, yellows, reds, and blues that danced across his canvas. When my own hands touched the paintbrush and dipped it in water and colors, it was a secret world I created, and in it I laid claim to all my joys and fears.

Art was with me as I ambled by the riverbanks of the Tigris. It accompanied me to school, and in class it hindered me from focusing on my lessons. I scribbled and sketched in my notebooks images that spun in my mind like a whirlwind. Many teachers complained to my parents that I was inattentive in class, but in the end some turned a blind eye in my direction and allowed me to sketch.

But art class, which should have been my truest joy, was the source of my greatest frustrations. My art teacher, Mr. Shukr, was a short, hairy man who shuffled about like a penguin. He cultivated many rules and technicalities in class, which crushed me under their weight. When he asked us to draw the palm of their hand, unlike the others who traced their hand and its five fingers, which they lay directly on the table, I twisted my hand into the strangest and most awkward positions. I searched for all the contours and shades in my design, and the end result was always part fantasy, part reality. This warranted a scolding and a slap on the back from Mr. Shukr who had instructed us to copy and imitate that which lay before us.

Despite my blunders in art class, starting at age eight, I began to win awards for my creativity. This I kept a secret from my family. For in Griyat, it was considered a 'tragedy' for a boy to be interested in becoming an artist. Parents boasted of their sons studying medicine and engineering – the hard sciences. A boy's artistic inclinations and ambitions were a source of embarrassment that should never reach the eyes and ears of gossiping friends. Whenever Hajj Abbas or other gossiping neighbors told my stern father that they had seen me drawing, he fumed at my betrayal of him. In order to continue sculpting and painting, I hid in the garden behind a bushel of trees.

One day, my father discovered that I was not in my room studying and he felt a tremor of rage. He began screaming out my name from the top of his lungs. From my balcony, he spied a little figure stirring behind the garden trees.

He flew down the stairs and secretly approached me from behind like a wolf encircling a sheep. I was lost in my own world. I was painting a woman on a dark brown horse – with rich contours and thick outlines –swimming in lush shadows on the ground below. Images floated toward me, I grabbed them, and rushed to capture them on paper. I had not heard my father's angry shouts. My father tiptoed closer to me, and then stood in front of me, glaring. In terror, I lifted my brush from the paper and stared back in silence, as tears welled up in my eyes. I sat frozen in uncertainty. I did not dare wipe the sweat gathering around my brows. My father crinkled his eyes and his look became ever more menacing.

He snatched the brushes from my young fingers and broke them with a snap that sounded like cracking bones. He dumped the bluish purple water on the ground. He grabbed the sketches and drawings, and ripped them into small shreds. He twisted my arm by the wrist: 'Now lead me to your other paintings and sculptures. How many times have I told you that you must not disrespect me by making these idols?'

I was frightened and led my father to my special cache under my bed. He pulled out a treasure trove of clay and soap sculptures, paintings, sketches, and drawings. With fury, he tossed the sculptures on the floor and stomped them into small pieces. He tore the paper artwork into fine shreds and threw the pieces out my bedroom window, to join the other fragments that were scattering in the whirling wind that had just begun. In desperation, before he left my room, he screamed, 'You are a failure, my son! My God, how I wish you were as bright as your cousin Sateh! His mother always talks about how he focuses on his studies and does not play around like you! Why do you insist on bringing shame to my good name?!'

In utter terror, I stood on my balcony for hours under the nervously dancing clouds and watched as my mutilated artwork flew about the garden, like wild birds, only to be drenched later by the evening rain. The rain began falling on the rooftops, on the balcony, lashing my soul. As I stood on my balcony, I watched as the colors of the torn papers melted into the stream of water below. I became depressed and sick for days. How could my passion, which was so much a part of the fabric of my being, be considered by my father to be a betrayal? How could all this rage be poured onto my true love? I wondered.

About a year after this heartbreaking incident, when I was about ten years old, I discovered the style of twentieth-century Swiss Surrealist Sculptor Alberto Giacometti[22] when I accompanied my uncle Mohsen to the university. My uncle Mohsen was in his last year at the Academy of Arts in Baghdad, and Giacometti's famous tall, thin figures influenced Iraqi students of art at the time. That entire year, I visited the academy with my uncle, to admire the works of these students. Giacometti's sculptures enticed me, although I did not yet understand why and how he created such elongated beings. Probing an artist's creative spirit was still a mystery to me.

Nevertheless, I was enticed by Giacometti's style. I dreamed of joining the Academy of Arts. It did not take long for my uncle Mohsen to become jealous of the wealth of ideas that tumbled so easily out of his nephew. He did all he could to dissuade me from studying the arts, but he was no more successful in breaking my resolve than my father had been. The disapproval of friends and relatives, and especially the merciless approbation of my father, could not sway me. Eventually, I would apply to the Fine Arts Department at the University of Baghdad, but that was many years away.

---

[22] Giacometti lived from 1901 to 1966.

Uncle Majid's Well

They were there – several of Habooba's sons – Hamid, Majid, Kafeeh, and Naji, their wives, as well as their children. The sounds of the stones they threw made a splash, but still no one could determine how far the well's water lay below.

"My God, I think there are about nine meters," said Majid as he listened to the spatter of the stone as it hit the well's bottom. He tossed his cigarette butt on the ground, and lit another despite his wife's grimace. As she stood with a large bowl filled with fresh fruit in front of the kitchen window, she continued to scowl at her chain-smoking husband from the corner of her eye.

"No way, it can't be more than seven meters," said Naji dryly as he paced back and forth like a cooped up lion. "I have already told you that for several days. It is not as deep as it seems."

"What are you talking about Naji, the well is at least ten meters, but most probably it is more," said Hamid as he peered down the well. He was sweating profusely, and he took off his shirt.

Thick black hair brushed up his neck and husky shoulders, sweeping down his backside. The hair growing out of his ears waved with the wind. He cracked a walnut as he scrutinized the water below.

The men argued among themselves, tossed more stones, and theorized on the possible depth. As the other children ran and played in the vast garden, the eleven-year-old Monkith stood still. The sounds of the stones, the suspense, and the heated discussions that followed enthralled him.

"In any case, we have to figure out the depth. I have no idea how much water we have, and I need to know it before the peak of summer arrives," said Majid. He and his wife had recently bought a new place in central Baghdad, a beautiful house with an elusive well, and for several days his relatives and friends gathered there to help him figure out the mysterious depth.

"Why don't you send me down to the bottom. This will be a sure way to measure the depth," said Monkith eager for adventure.

"Well, perhaps that is a solution, but the only problem is that the well is quite thin. I am not sure if it is safe for you. What do you think Naji?" Hamid asked patting his brother's back.

"No way," he said as he hit Monkith on the head. "Absolutely not. It is not safe to do such a thing."

It seemed like the same discussions took place every day. Monkith would lie in bed at night dreaming about the well and its depth, and in class he sketched the well in his notebooks until the teacher became angry with him and tore the pages in half. And then one day he found a solution.

Everyone clustered around the well again, listening to the resonance of the stones. Monkith hovered around them. He had brought a clothespin and attached one positive and one negative wire to each side. He placed an aspirin in the middle of the clothespin, which forced the prongs apart on one end of the long wire and at the other end a light bulb. Everyone watched as the child silently lowered the long wire down the well. They were surprised to see how much of the wire holding the aspirin was still descending and still there was no indication that it had touched the water. All eyes continued to peer down the well as the wire fell further. Monkith imagined what it would have been like to travel to the depths of the well. He fancied himself descending further down the narrow well, not being able to breath and hearing his parents' screams above.

When the clothespin finally touched the water, the aspirin dissolved and the prongs came together, completing the circuit. An electric current flowed, and the bulb connected to the wire at the top of the well lit up. Majid measured the wire and learned that the well was fifteen meters.

"My God, I never imagined it was fifteen meters, so I guess that means we need to buy equipment for the well that can descend fifteen meters. Monkith, how did you ever come up with such an ingenious idea? Naji, how proud you must be of your son," exclaimed Majid.

Monkith's mother, in her eight month of pregnancy, stood beaming with pride at her son. His sisters and cousins gathered around him and clapped.

"His idea was no big deal – it was not that difficult to think of," answered Naji as he glared at his wife and the rest of the children. And then he stormed off, and said that thank goodness the silly matter had been resolved.

The Hypnotist

Upon arriving in Mosul, the little party found its way to a chubby dark-skinned magician with a white beard. He was dressed in a faded yellow *galabia* and he draped a brown cape over his shoulders. They entered a small room filled with smoke and strange scents and sat down in bewildered astonishment. The old man summoned his son who entered wearing a striped *galabia*. He was a short, thin boy with hollow cheekbones and an amazingly long neck. His face wore a dumb, perplexed look and his eyelids were red. He carried himself heavily, and his hands dangled low and limp. It seemed as if he were about to fall down. The old man with wrinkled eyes stood up, and in a trance, the boy sank into his father's seat. The old man began flapping his hands up and down. At first the boy gaped at his father's dark green eyes as if mesmerized, but then he stared at the agitated hands. He fixed his eyes on them as if he were dreaming, and then he lowered his head in silence.

◆

Monkith's uncle Annisse became engaged. Ordinarily, this was one of life's happy occasions, but his family staunchly opposed the union. Annisse had fallen in love with Soad, a Kurdish woman, and a Sunni Muslim at that. To make matters worse, his family considered her beneath his station. Annisse was a professor and an engineer. Soad was comparatively uneducated.

Annisse's sisters immediately made it known that they found the match entirely unsuitable. But no one protested more furiously than Monkith's mother Nuriya. She pleaded that Annisse was like a son to her. She had worked hard to help raise him, and she would never give up her "son" so easily. In short, it was absurd to suppose that she would have no say in his choice of spouse.

The words were not mere rhetoric, for his older sisters, Nuriya most of all, had spoiled Annisse. He was the first son born after eight girls, and he was now the only son still living at home now that his younger brother, Mohsen, had left for Dubai that very year. The sisters could not be blamed for wanting the best for him. Still, it must be said that the family was very proud. Two of the sisters – Layla and Annissa – who were both exquisite, were in their thirties and still not married. The prospective grooms were always found too short, too tall, too bald, or too hairy. And every time they did manage to become engaged, the family protested and the engagement was broken.

Soad's family, on the other hand, was neither proud nor religious. They were simple people without a pedigree. As Kurds, they were influenced more by Iranian than Iraqi culture. They even celebrated Nuwruz, the Persian New Year, when men and women wore special dresses made of glittering blue, red, and yellow colors, designed in the Iranian tradition. They poured out into the gardens and parks in their colorful celebration. They swayed in beautiful dances under tents. Many Iraqis looked on in fascination. Some even joined them in their bright festivities.

But despite his sisters' objections, Annisse was determined to marry Soad. After the couple had been seeing each other for two years, they announced their engagement. Perhaps Annisse's family had hoped that their mutual passion would lose steam. It did not, and the betrothal caused much pain and sadness. Only a few members on the groom's side attended the engagement celebration at Soad's home. Those who did were very tense. Everyone that is, except for Annisse's parents, Fatema and Jawwad, and his nephew Monkith. Fatema took the engagement in stride because she was very spiritual, and never had a problem, ever, with anything. Monkith's grandfather, Jawwad, was quite relaxed at the party because enticing women surrounded him; he busied himself flirting with the bride's mother. A pretty cousin of the bride named Firuz captivated the eleven-year-old Monkith. Although Monkith spoke only to the girl's brothers, he noticed her smile. She also cared for him, but in silence.

Annisse's sisters, however, refused to accept defeat. After the engagement, one hot summer day, the family called upon Monkith – who at eleven-years-old was the eldest male in the family after his uncle Annisse – to accompany his unmarried aunts, Layla and Annissa, to the famous hypnotist of Mosul. It was a desperate attempt, but the sisters hoped that the magician might be able to rid Annisse of his love for Soad. Along the way to Mosul, Monkith and his aunts took their meals in restaurants whenever the bus stopped. The trip seemed interminable to Monkith, who expressed relief as much as curiosity when they finally arrived at their destination. Yet again, his family forced him to shoulder a responsibility that seemed so cumbersome at his tender age.

◆

The fat, bearded magician continued to flap his hands up and down passionately. As he grew excited, a thick, bulging blue vein that darted across his dark forehead, burned like lightening. The session involved not only the magician but also his own son who sat in the room. First the magician hypnotized his son, and then allowed the spirits to speak through him. To prove his credibility, the old man first asked Annissa for her identity card. In a display of mental telepathy, the old man read silently from the card. The hypnotized boy trembled and shook. He cited aloud all that was written on the identity card in the exact order it appeared:

The Iraqi Republic
The Ministry of Education
The Teacher's Identity Card
Annissa bint Jawwad al-Salman

With this first test successful, the magician proceeded to focus on the reason for his guests' visit. He signaled for his son to speak of the problem.

In a trance, the boy told the two women, "Your brother, Annisse, wishes to marry a Kurdish girl, and the whole family is saddened."

The boy lowered his eyes again, and the little party stared at him in astonishment. The old man tread toward his cabinet and reached for a blue bottle marked with a large X, and he poured its contents into a small glass tube: "Well my dears, take this tube with you, and upon your return home, immediately splash the magic vinegar in front of your brother's door. I assure you that this shall help your brother renounce his love for that Kurdish girl."

After he slipped the tube into Layla's hand and she tucked it gently into her purse, the clairvoyant turned his attention to Monkith, who sat wistfully in a corner watching the magical event in bewildered astonishment.

The magician turned to his own son again. "Tell me, son, what do you know of the young lad perching in the corner? What is the mark underneath his eyes? he asked in a serious tone.

The boy uttered in a trance, "There is a small black mole under his hazel eyes." Monkith and his aunts stared in silence as the magician prodded his son for more details. The listless boy continued: "He is eleven years old. This odd boy does not really fit in the family. He shall live most of his adult life outside Iraq. He shall leave and never return to live there again. He shall receive higher degrees and make a name for himself. He shall travel to London three times, and following the third trip, he shall die. He'll be buried far outside Iraq in eternal exile."

This was a strange experience for Monkith, but no less unnerving than the fate that awaited his uncle. Upon their arrival home, Layla tiptoed outside her brother's door and sprinkled the magic liquid exactly as the magician had instructed her.

Several weeks later, Annisse sundered his relationship with Soad, but his life was beset by problems. His heart, once filled with love, became a well of bitterness. The family may have looked down their noses at Soad, but he would search for a way to even the score...

Sabiha

I feel loneliness and desperation.
I have thought to draw a train on the sand
and travel with it to the unknown.
There I will build a very simple cabin, a shelter
to an upset lover... Such is my destiny.

◆

Monkith held his breath, opened the door, and walked into Mrs. Beydoun's class. He politely apologized to his teacher for his tardiness, and when she nodded her head in assent, he slipped into his seat. He glanced at Sabiha, the prettiest girl in the class, who giggled and looked down. His classmate Sherif, seated at a neighboring table, noticed the glances that Monkith and Sabiha shared. As Mrs. Beydoun gathered her thoughts and resumed her history lesson, a plotting Sherif passed a note to Monkith and asked him to divulge to him the real reason he was late. Monkith chuckled and handed his friend a ripped up piece of scrap paper filled with the lyrics of Abdel Halim Hafez's song, "Don't Give Me Feelings of Guilt" written half in a faded blue felt-tip pen and half in a black ballpoint on a piece of paper torn from a notebook.

"As I was dressing this morning I listened to the radio, and found myself embroiled with writing down these lyrics," Monkith whispered to Sherif, who examined the torn piece of paper. Sherif, who noticed that Sabiha was still admiring Monkith, dutifully raised his hand and informed Mrs. Beydoun of the reason for Monkith's tardiness. She once again interrupted her lesson and the line in her frowning forehead became as thick as a piece of chalk. Although she was a frail woman, she walked with heavy steps, which sounded like the shuffling of a cow. She darted across the room, struck Monkith on the shoulder, and threatened to inform his parents. Later that day, when Monkith caught Sabiha's eyes, she smiled in secret complicity with him.

At the age of eleven, Monkith fell in love with his classmate Sabiha. She had almond-shaped brown eyes and dark black hair –

a girl so lovely that she enamored many other boys in Monkith's class and often was the cause of serious rivalries. When she smiled, her mouth opened like a butterfly spreading out its wings and wrapping them around Monkith's small body. He was not careless with his feelings, for he knew that any wrong movement on his part could result in punishment from the teachers. At first, he did not tell Sabiha to her face that he loved her. Instead, he wrote her an anonymous love letter and slipped it into her red backpack when all the children were outside at recess. When she discovered it at home while doing her home-work, she stared at the walls and dreamed about the identity of her admirer.

After the secret letter, Monkith was careful not to be caught admiring her. He was frightened that she would divine his secret and inform the teachers. But one day, during recess, when all the other children played outside, Sabiha approached her classmate.

"Monkith, you barely notice me anymore. Have I done some-thing wrong? Please tell me," she whispered softly. Her eyes were grave, her voice shaking.

Monkith's cheeks began to burn and his heart race. In an utter trance, he murmured that he loved her as she gazed at him in bewildered silence. He leaned over to kiss her. As his lips touched hers, Mrs. Baydoun entered the room in search of her papers and witnessed the scandalous event: "May a fever strike you! You have brought shame to all of us!" she yelled as she spanked him again and again.

After the incident, he and Sabiha became inseparable friends. But through the years, not once did either of them ever mention the secret letter or his profession of love. He escorted her home every day after school and often they visited each other at their families' homes. On weekends, they developed a favorite pastime of ringing on their neighbors' bells, and then running away when someone finally answered. Once when neighbor Hajj Abbas grew irritated by their taunts, he ran after them in his tat-tered *galabia* swinging a shiny black belt. His two broken front teeth – as sharp as buffalo horns – protruded forward as he screamed. They fled his grasp and arrived panting near the Tigris where they hid for several hours.

They lay by the rocks giggling and looking up into the sunshine. Their bond of friendship grew ever deeper and they promised that they would never hide anything from each other.

"Monkith, I have a secret I want to share with you. I am not really my mother's daughter – I am the daughter of the maid," Sabiha whispered.

"What do you mean?" Monkith asked gently.

Sabiha explained, with her eyes turned down: "My cousins used to tease me about it, but I never believed them. Then a few weeks ago I eavesdropped on my aunts. Apparently my mother was barren and really wished for a child. After visiting countless doctors, she tried pilgrimages to the holy shrines and brought back blessed water. When that did not work, she visited a famous herbalist-doctor in Najaf named Fadhila, who filled my mother's purse with small bags filled with wild rue, coriander, indigo, and numerous animal body parts. But still her womb remained barren. Just as she despaired, a miracle occurred. Her maid was engaged to be married to one man, but pregnant by another. So my mother helped her maid deliver the baby in secrecy and then she raised me as her own. No one wants me to know I am not her biological daughter – it is apparently a big family secret." Her eyes were drowned in tears, and they lay together cushioned by trust and intimacy.

"Well, your real mother must have been a stunning gem," Monkith said as he inched closer to her.

Monkith was with Sabiha when he lost his close friend Osama to a tragedy. It was the year they were thirteen years old. Monkith had learned that Osama had scored the highest grade on their yearly exam. The scores were posted outside the classroom, and the students tripped over each other and pushed and shoved in order to behold the results by their name. Monkith had done less than average, and had failed English, and thus was required to retake English during the summer session. But he was exhilarated when he discovered that Osama had attained top honors. Osama was absent from school that day, and so Monkith set out running to Osama's home to share the good news. He sprinted so fast that he tripped several times. When Sabiha learned that Monkith had gone to Osama's home, she set off to join him.

Monkith arrived panting at the familiar gate – the door was open. He entered the garden and saw Osama's mother standing at the entrance of the house, her eyes overflowing with tears. She choked on her words as she stretched out her arms and pulled Monkith's head close to her heart. Monkith held her tightly, feeling that there was something terribly wrong. He noticed many unfamiliar mournful faces gathered inside the living room and whispering away. After a few moments, Osama's brother Jalil approached them, his eyes were hazed, and in a barely audible voice, he whispered, "Dear Monkith, Osama is not here, and he shall never be here again. He and our brother-in-law, Amer, went for a swim this morning in the Tigris and drowned. We found their footprints in the sand and their clothes washed over by the water."

"No, no!" Monkith screamed. He ran out of the house and to the Tigris, so fast that he could barely breathe. Sabiha, who had just reached Osama's home, sprinted after him. Monkith threw himself on the ground at the feet of the river and began to claw his nails into the dirt and dig. He vomited uncontrollably as Sabiha pat his back.

"Osama has drowned! How could God take such a kind human being? It makes no sense," Monkith whimpered as he caught his breath and spit into a napkin to clear his throat.

"Perhaps God missed Osama. He needs his beloved creature with him in heaven," a shocked Sabiha reasoned, as she wiped her tears and brushed her hair away from her face.

"I think I'll never accept that he has drowned. I'll always long to see him again. I'll wait for him to come through the door for a visit, smiling and saying hello," Monkith announced. Every day for months on end they returned together to that spot at the Tigris to grieve for their lost friend.

When Sabiha entered her teenage years, she became even more enchanting. Her family, who owned a factory, arranged for her engagement to her paternal cousin Adnan in order to preserve the family wealth and secrets. Never mind that she did not love her chubby cousin whose red skin was as rough as a tortoise shell.

One day after school, Monkith's close friend Nabil approached him.

"I need to confide in you about something. I have been in love with Sabiha since I first saw her with you many years before. Is there anything between you and her or do I stand a chance?" Nabil pleaded.

"Sabiha is like a sister to me. There is nothing between us, but you know, she is engaged to be married to her cousin," Monkith responded sadly, for he knew Sabiha did not love Adnan, who always dragged himself awkwardly with his head bowed down behind her.

"Please introduce us," he beseeched Monkith. "I am not really worried about her loveless engagement. I am more anxious about whether she canever permit herself to accept me for who I am. She is affluent, and I have nothing to offer her at this point."

"Sabiha is kind. I doubt she thinks about wealth and status – perhaps she will also fall in love with you, and you can save her from entering a disastrous union with her cousin. I'll arrange for you to meet each other tomorrow at the bus stop, and then you can walk her home," he said quickly as he set off to make the necessary arrangements. That evening he called Sabiha and the flattered girl agreed to meet with Nabil after school.

Nabil skipped class that day to prepare for their first meeting. He changed his clothes several times until he was happy with his ensemble. Sabiha, who had also made herself up, met him at the bus stop and in silence the two nervous teenagers walked home. From that day onward, Nabil called Sabiha from Monkith's home, and soon an attraction blossomed between them despite the fact that she was still engaged to her cousin. She often called Monkith to talk to him about her feelings for Nabil and he listened to her as if he were a close brother.

Not everyone was as complacent about these goings-on as Monkith. Nabil's brother, Yussef, was a powerful member of the *mukhabarat*. As it happened, he was set against the idea of a relationship between Sabiha and his brother. Yussef knew that Sabiha was soon to be married. He protested his younger brother's love for a "plucked rose". To make matters worse, she was a Sunni Muslim and he was Shii. Yussef convinced Nabil to break up with Sabiha, and when he did, she became unbearably fragile.

Monkith grew angry with Nabil for hurting her, and was determined never to speak to him again.

Ultimately, Sabiha proceeded with the marriage to her cousin. Once, when her husband furiously protested her friendship with Monkith, she screeched between her tears that if she had been given the choice between the two of them, she would have chosen Monkith.

One day, her husband searched for Monkith and asked him, "Do you love her?"

"Yes, I love her as my sister. That is it. How about you, do you love her?"

"Love, I do not know what that is. But the fact is that she and I share a common family wealth, which we must safeguard," Adnan insisted.

The tumultuous marriage left both the young bride and groom miserable. After the wedding, Sabiha's mother consulted with Monkith about whether she had done the right thing to marry her daughter off to her cousin. Monkith was forthright in voicing his disapproval.

Sabiha later divorced her cousin, and she immediately tumbled from wealth into poverty. For after her father died of cancer, her paternal uncle, who was also her father-in-law, stole the family factory and Sabiha's father's fortune. When she left her husband's bed and board, she returned home to her now impoverished mother and siblings. They subsisted on her mother's teaching paycheck. Sabiha followed in her mother's footsteps and became a teacher. At the time, anyone teaching or involved with the education system was required to become a member of the Baath party. Sabiha had no choice but to take the fatal step and join the party – a move that severed the friendship between her and Monkith since he was already adamantly against the Baath.

She visited Monkith almost every day, sometimes just stopping by saying she just needed to see his face and then leave. But she began to notice a change in Monkith's eyes. He no longer beheld her with the love he did before.

"What have I done? You no longer care for me," Sabiha asked him desperately one day.

"I am a stranger among all of you," Monkith said without

looking directly into her eyes – eyes that sat in a heap of premature wrinkles. Her body had grown frail, her face haggard. "I have learned that Nabil has recently joined the *mukhabarat* in the hope of escaping his lower middle-class existence, and now you are a member of the Baath party. Don't you know that the Baath will pollute your blood?"

"But I have no choice. I need to support my family," she pleaded.

"But I would rather die than defile my blood," he said tersely as he walked away.

Little by little the communication between her and Monkith faded and he heard her news from afar. She later married and divorced again. But the intensity of the love she felt for Nabil would never be recaptured. Meanwhile the headstrong Monkith felt he was losing all his close friends to the *mukhabarat*. He felt like a languishing and profoundly solitary shadow in their midst.

Hamoudi and His Four Virgin Wives

There was once a man named Muhammad, nicknamed Hamoudi, who owned a local vegetable store. There was no mistaking him. He was tall and he had astonishingly long legs. He compensated for his baldness with a long beard and mustache. An elongated, hooked nose accented his angular face. As if his looks did not set him apart already, the villagers marked him with stories of impotence and abnormal sexual behavior. He had married four women, and all four women were still virgins when they divorced him.

Hamoudi took his first bride – a young girl who was brimming with excitement for the passion of her wedding night. On the eve of the ceremony, as was custom, the married women of the family gathered around the innocent girl and explained to her how to share herself with her husband for the first time, how her fingers were to crawl gently on his skin in search of his most sensitive spots. The girl giggled in embarrassment as each woman conjured up the lovemaking spirits and caressed the curves of her own body as a demonstration of passion to the young bride.

But the next evening in the bridal suite, as she approached her husband with her twinkling eyes and flushed face, he felt a surge of disgust. He pleaded like a sheep hoping to escape its slaughter: 'Do you remember the drum they beat at our wedding celebration? It is still ringing in my ear, so please let me rest and fall asleep.'

She lifted the covers over her tired husband, and lay down next to him, unable to taste slumber. Bright and early the next morning, her sisters, aunts, and mother appeared at the door of the bridal suite, carrying an exquisite silver tray filled with cream, milk, bread, and chicken. Hamoudi was still asleep, so the bride let them in.

'You must be starving this morning, my darling. Here is enough food to last you through the night, so that neither of you will even have to leave your bed,' her mother said, winking at her. The other women chuckled and nudged her.

As was custom, the women had come to recuperate the white handkerchief drenched in blood, which flowed from her previously untouched sex. But the young girl explained how her husband was exhausted and in need of rest the night before. The women would have to return the next day for the magical handkerchief, which would be waved in delight before the neighbors and friends. That day the mother of the bride burned wild rue and frantically swayed around the house, sprinkling the magical powders over pictures of her daughter to ward off the evil spirits.

The bride waited patiently for the second night, but as her eyes passed over him and her hot breath brushed against his gloomy face, Hamoudi answered her sharply, 'Do you remember the trumpet they played on our wedding night? It still resounds in my ear. So I beg you to let me sleep.'

'What shall mama and the other women say this time,' she asked herself out loud as she pulled the covers over her face to hide her tears from her husband. She tried to approach him and let her skin touch his, but Hamoudi turned his back to her and grumbled, 'Wife, I need space around me in bed. Please do not come so close.'

The next morning at the crack of dawn, the women appeared again with a beautiful tray filled with delicacies, eager for news. Hamoudi was still asleep, and the bride was drowned in tears as she recounted the story of the night before.

'My darling, perhaps he is shy,' whispered her mother. 'You must take more initiative. Upon the advice of our neighbor, Umm Mehdi, I bought you a transparent silk nightgown, which you will wear to seduce him tonight. Your young breasts and beautiful thighs will shine like the stars and he will not be able to resist. Gently take it off before you turn out the lights.'

'Mama!' the young girl shrieked in embarrassment.

'You shall do as you're told, my darling, and tomorrow I shall behold your happiness. Tomorrow I shall wave my daughter's honor for all to see.' Without another word, she kissed her daughter, and ran home to burn some more wild rue.

On the third night when the young girl approached Hamoudi, her cheeks were blushed and eager. She slipped off her lavender robe and stood before her husband in her transparent silk nightgown. Grasping his covers over him like a timid virgin, the frightened man stared at the girl as she danced around him, let down her hair, and her nightgown fell under her legs and lay beneath her like a glimmering silver pond in which she was wading. She turned off the lights, and brushed her soft skin against his. Silence choked the room, until she heard him whisper impatiently, 'Do you remember the cymbals? They still resonate in my ear and are giving me a headache. I crave sleep.'

The next morning, the retinue of women once again left unsatisfied, beseeching her patience. For surely there was some explanation, the young bride's beauty must have provoked an evil eye filled with jealousy. This happened on the fourth, fifth, and sixth night, until, of course, the bride lost patience and asked her family to grant her a divorce.

And so Hamoudi married his second, third, and fourth wife. Each met the same fate. A joke circulated in Griyat that the shopkeeper had managed to marry and divorce four girls who bore the distinction of having remained virgins throughout their marriage to him.

Despite his rather odd reputation, Hamoudi became one of the most popular personalities in Griyat, and there was always a long line outside his vegetable stand. His stand was among the least expensive, and he was most generous with his clients. He always slipped at least an extra half-kilo of fruits or produce into his clients' baskets. When he weighed tomatoes, he glanced at the scale, ignored the true weight, and announced the purchase was only one kilo. Then he dipped his hands into the piles of tomatoes and added more to the bag. His customers watched in amazement, sure that he would remove a few bright red clusters to reconcile the value of the purchase with the weight shown on the balance. But he never did.

Precisely because of Hamoudi's legendary sexuality – or lack thereof – the shopkeeper's vegetable stand became a social hub. Married women regarded it as a safe haven. They knew that Hamoudi would not flirt with them or harass them. Even their husbands did not question the long hours they spent at his stand. On hot summer days, some of the women took things a step further by wearing provocative clothing. Despite Hamoudi's annoyance, some entered the stand wearing low-cut thin shirts that barely covered their breasts and no panties. Sitting on the ground, they spread their legs as they chose vegetables. Sometimes they stretched their legs wider, as if testing to see how far they attracted Hamoudi's attention. But he was incorruptible.

Naturally, a stand filled with bare flesh, brazen behavior, and local women became a magnet for the boys. Unable to freely associate with women because they were no longer children, boys were drawn to the stand like bees hovering around honey. They used any excuse to loaf there and peak at the layers of forbidden flesh before them. It never ceased to amuse villagers in Griyat that the shopkeeper's stand – the man whose own intimate relations with women were deficient – was a beehive of latent sexual activity.

Once a group of older boys gathered together in a cluster around Hamoudi's vegetable stand. Mulla Aboud rolled off the sidewalk and stumbled with his prayer beads to the stand, which was teaming with boys watching women count their vegetables. He chuckled as he heard the heavy breathing of the boys. He, a newly rejuvenated old man, understood that the adolescents masturbated upon returning home from Hamoudi's stand. With a bright smile, he whispered to the boys that he had a secret he wished to share with them. They huddled around him as he hummed mystically, jingled his prayer beads, and then in a soft voice informed them that those who 'abused themselves' would grow thick black hairs on the palms of their hands. Before he finished his story, he heard the boys gasping as they desperately rubbed and searched their palms for traces of stubble. Mulla Aboud burst into laughter and flopped himself on the ground. He kicked his feet up and down in jest, like a mischievous adolescent. For it was now clear to him as well as the others standing there that all the boys there had engaged in the forbidden act.

The Bicycle

"I'll take this one, how much is it, sir?" Monkith asked Abu Rabih, an obese young man with a greasy red tinted face, who had not taken him seriously from the moment he had entered his square meter shop, which was filled with all sorts of second-hand bicycles, as well as broken household gadgets, and an odd assortment of tattered odds and ends all packed on top of each other on the dirty rubbish-heaped ground.

"I am busy now, kid, give me five more minutes," Abu Rabih said in a carefully muted voice. He was busy negotiating with a client who had spied a broken television at his neighbor's stand, which cost eight dirhams.

"I'll sell that very television to you for seven dirhams, come back in just a moment and you shall see." He shook hands with his client, who went on to rummage through the pile of used radios on the ground nearby.

Meanwhile, Abu Rabih approached his neighbor's stand to bargain for the broken television his client wished for. "I'll take that television for four dirhams," he said as he tried to lift it.

"My goodness, this television cost me seven dirhams, and I am only selling it for eight dirhams. I'll lose if I sell it for any less," the merchant said firmly.

"Give it to me for six dirhams, and we can strike a deal," responded Abu Rabih as he tapped his fingers on the television. In the excitement of the deal, his sweaty face had become the color of tomato paste sizzling in the sultry summer sun.

His neighbor's wrinkled blue eyes danced with avarice. He stood silent for a moment and then lifted the television from the ground and handed it to his neighbor. "Congratulations," he said as he pat Abu Rabih's back.

"May God bestow his blessings upon you. I'll bring you six dirhams in just one moment." He shuffled back to his own stand, and summoned his client who was foraging through the radios nearby.

"Give me seven dirhams, and the television is yours," he said beaming with delight.

The client handed seven dirhams to Abu Rabih who immediately placed one in his pocket and granted the remaining six dirhams to the owner of the next stand. He called for some boys in dusty *galabias* to help his customer transport the television home.

Meanwhile Monkith continued to stare at the rusty blue bicycle, with the broken bell and old peddles, waiting patiently for Abu Rabih to finish his business dealings. After school, he had taken the bus to the Junk Market, in the Old City of Baghdad, a bustling, crowded and dirty market filled with rubbish and second-hand objects; everything from old beds, chairs, and tables to shoes, coats and towels. Sometimes a man, who had just stolen a chicken or two, hollered about the pair of live chickens he sought to sell. People came from afar to test their luck, hoping to turn up some desperately needed spare part, either stacked on the ground, heaped over the trash, or flying through the air. An odd assortment of music and noise flowed through the dirt filled market as sellers played their own cassettes from broken radios, disregarding the neighboring tunes.

But Abu Rabih's stand filled with bicycles was all that interested Monkith. Each day Abu Rabih's stand was located on another square meter of the ground of the junk market, and Monkith's eyes had to scan the whole street for him. When he located his square meter, he watched as other children went with their parents and picked out the bicycle of their dreams, and on many an occasion, he begged his father to buy him one.

"Good Heavens, no way, son. Bicycles are forbidden in my house. Severe bicycle accidents have befallen both your uncle Kafeeh and I. Uncle Kafeeh still limps from his accident, and I continue to have nightmares of the time my breaks stopped working and I bumped into the tree and fell on the ground so hard that my left arm broke. I'll buy you children anything but a bicycle."

But the evening before, Monkith had determined that most probably the main reason his father would not buy him a bicycle was because it was expensive. He figured that because his younger brother Muhammad still needed attention and because his new brother Ahmad was still an infant, his parents could not spare the money. So he counted up his allowance and determined that with his four dinars he could certainly buy a second-hand bicycle from the Junk Market the next day. And so after school, with four dinars jingling in his pocket, he rode the bus to the Junk Market, his eyes seeking out Abu Rabih. Abu Rabih was busy with an older client, but Monkith stood firm, dreaming of riding his bicycle, his feet peddling away so fast that he flew through the air, high above the houses of his family and neighbors. He fantasized of how he would paint it a bright blue. He would wash it everyday, and when he saved up his allowance, he would pamper it with new peddles, gears, and tires.

Having just closed a business transaction, Abu Rabih examined the dazed boy, with his freshly washed hair and sparkling white *galabia*. He determined that this boy must have some money and could in fact be taken seriously. "Which bicycle did you say you want to buy, kid?" Abu Rabih asked, shaking Monkith out of his dreams, "I am done with my client and can help you now."

Monkith turned to him and smiled. He pointed at the rusty blue bicycle in front of him: "This one, how much is it?"

"Four dinars and two hundred and fifty felas," Abu Rabih responded tersely as his eyes scanned the market to see if there were any approaching customers.

"I have four dinars, is that okay?" Monkith asked, looking Abu Rabih straight in the eyes.

"No way, this bicycle is in good shape. I would lose if I sold it to you for any less." Realizing that Monkith did not have the required sum, Abu Rabih turned away.

"Wait, I can save up my allowance. Do you think the bicycle will still be here in a couple months?" Monkith entreated Abu Rabih who looked at him again.

"Yes, probably," Abu Rabih said with impatience, as another client had entered his stand and he wished to tend to him. He shuffled Monkith away, promising him nonchalantly that he would keep the bicycle for him.

Meanwhile, Monkith dreamed of owning the bicycle. Every week he counted his allowance, and smiled with each new cent that he added. Often he lingered around the Junk Market, and hovered over the blue bicycle, before Abu Rabih shoed him off with his cane. No other bicycle mattered to him; his dreams were centered on the rusty blue bicycle. After two months, he had saved up another two hundred and fifty felas. That evening he counted his allowance and then returned it to the sock, which he would take with him to school the next day. That night he could not fall asleep as he envisioned the adventures he would embark upon with his bicycle. He fantasized how on the festivities when his parents gave him money, he would save the money to repair his bicycle, which would become well groomed and taken care of.

When he returned to the market the next day, his eyes passed over the whole ground, trying to locate Abu Rabih's stand. When he finally spotted the old man, he fumbled around in the hope of finding his blue bicycle, but it was gone. Monkith felt a sudden stab of disappointment and ran toward the young man.

"Hey, Abu Rabih – What happened to the bicycle? You promised you would save it for me," Monkith reminded him.

"By chance, someone came two days ago and bought it. But look, here is another one," he said out of the side of his mouth as he pointed to a large red bicycle. "This one is five dinars."

"I don't have five dinars," Monkith said sadly and then turned slowly away. Like many an object of desire, it eluded its beholder. He returned home that day covered in disappointed tears.

A few days later, as he held his younger sister Amal and passed Hamoudi's vegetable shop, his eyes spotted a green delivery tricycle in the heap of the brightly colored clusters of peaches, apricots, and apples.

"Hamoudi, could I deliver your vegetables? You don't even have to pay me," Monkith beamed as he placed Amal on the ground beside him.

"Sure, why don't you start now? Could you dispatch this heap of watermelons to Hajj Naji's home down the street?" Hamoudi said as if his prayers had just been answered.

"Yes," Monkith cried in excitement, and Amal began clapping her hands. For a moment Monkith forgot that Hajj Naji was his own father, and that he would surely beat him if he spotted him and Amal riding the beaming green tricycle.

Hamoudi filled the basket in front of the bicycle with a load of large watermelons. Monkith perched on the bicycle with Amal clutching him from behind. The watermelons piled up in the basket and blocked his view, but Monkith began to peddle away as a joyous Amal sang an incoherent tune she had heard her grandmother Fatema chant a few days earlier.

It chanced that Naji was running some errands that day and was just then walking home. From afar, Naji discovered his son joyfully peddling the tricycle as hard as he could, with his hands floating freely in the air and Amal holding onto to him from behind. Monkith sped up the street and the tinkle of his bicycle-bell and Amal's singing could be heard from afar. Naji followed stealthily after his son. As Monkith approached the house, one of the watermelons flew to the ground and cracked open. This was enough for Naji. He flew into a rage.

Naji grabbed Amal and placed her on the ground. He dragged his son by the ear, and screamed: "God curse your father and the father of the one who gave you this bicycle! Don't you know that it is not safe for little girls to ride bicycles?! And what do you think you are doing by involving your little sister in your errant behavior?"

"But I promise, Amal and I never fell. I made sure she grasped me very tightly. It is only a tricycle, so it is not dangerous!" Monkith insisted as Amal began to cry. His mother, holding her infant Ahmad, and his sisters Manal and Ibtihal, who were playing hopscotch on the veranda, came running into the street to see the cause of all the commotion.

"Don't talk back to me and contradict me in front of others," Naji told Monkith as he slapped him again on his cheeks, which became as bright as beets. After that, Monkith received a severe beating and a lecture on who served whom. It was not members of their family who should deliver, his father pronounced. Rather, he was part of a family to whom fruits and vegetables were sent. It was a scandal for the eldest son to be working as a delivery boy. Monkith should know and respect his proper station in society. These class distinctions forever eluded Monkith, though, whose tears never seemed to dry from his father's beatings. A sense of longing for a bicycle filled him for many years after that incident.

And so I had a complex when it came to bicycles. Later in life when I went to Holland with its flat terrain and friendly bike paths, I thought it was high time I fulfilled my childhood dream. I bought five bicycles the first year I arrived there.

Sexual Awakening

It all began one hot summer day when the nine-year-old Monkith sat in his room fiddling with his beloved kites. He placed a large piece of yellow paper next to his knees, and cut out rectangular shapes of other colors from his books so that he could add them to the kite's tale. With a dark blue pen, he began to draw the face of a nightingale onto the large yellow paper. His mother had gone to Fatema's home with the rest of the children. The house was empty, except for the maid, Zaynab, who was the fourteen-year-old daughter of their neighbor, Umm Hassan. She was stunning, with honey-colored eyes, long lashes, large red lips, and thick curly black hair. On this day, she crept up the stairs and slipped into Monkith's room on the second floor. She nestled next to him, and asked if she could play with him. Drowned in his imaginary world of colors and shapes, he said nothing.

As she joined him in coloring the face of a nightingale onto his kite, she began to shake and perspire. She removed the colored pens from his reluctant fingers and rubbed his hand against her leg. Then she stroked his hair, laughing flirtatiously and breathing deeply. Her body trembled, and her forehead glistened with sweat. He immediately sensed that there was something especially odd in the way she caressed him.

Each day, the game with its strange sensations continued. As soon as Zaynab knew she was alone in the house, she climbed the stairs to Monkith's room. She sat down next to him and stroked his hair, kissing him and clasping his knees. As he became more comfortable with this new element of their game, she grew bolder. She took off both their clothes. She placed his hand on her breast, and then positioned his leg close to her body, bending his knee so that it pressed gently against her sex. Then she brushed herself more quickly against him. Confused, Monkith felt her breathing as she fondled him. She moaned as her body tensed, and then she fell quiet. Her breathing returned to its relaxed rhythm once again. He sensed her relief – it permeated the room. This became their secret ritual. Zaynab warned him each time never to tell his mother about their trysts.

◆

The village of Griyat during the seventies in the midst of Monkith's adolescence was much like a cauldron of simmering desires. Children were not encouraged to ask adults about their changing bodies, and their passions were held in check by taboos and strict parental guidelines. Parents warned that even a glance of the eye to the opposite sex, not to mention a kiss, could result in pregnancy, blindness, and madness. Girls were taught to protect their virginity at all cost – they were barred from vigorous physical activity, riding bicycles, jumping from heights, or squatting on sharp surfaces, in order to ensure that their hymen remained safe. They were told to avoid mixing their clothes with male members of the family on the wash line lest they become pregnant. Boys were warned of the dire consequences of masturbation – such as paralysis or even the widely known superstition of dark black hair sprouting out from the palms of their hands. And so it was not unusual to see a thirty-year-old man or woman with little knowledge of his or her own body. Those who sought to gain sexual experience were often compelled to take extreme measures. One teenage boy, Jamal, came to Griyat with his family from the south. His family was poor and they sold chickpeas to the locals. But the youth had an extra source of income – he engaged in prostitution with other boys in town. With access to girls so difficult, this was a way for at least some boys to gain exposure to the forbidden.

Underneath all the layers of secrecy, however, there were some girls and boys who explored their sexuality with each other. With kisses, hugs and caresses, they unmasked the pleasures of the flesh while avoiding full penetration. Because purity was a necessity for marriage, most girls ensured that they remain virgins throughout their experimentation. Once these children learned how to navigate safely in forbidden territory, however, they gained an introduction to their sentimental education.

◆

When the maid Zaynab first introduced Monkith to the mysteries of sex, he did not understand the whirl of confused emotions that filled his soul. As he neared his teenage years, his friend Osama's older brother Jalil, opened Monkith's eyes to his sexuality.

"Did you know," Jalil asked Monkith, "that when a boy becomes a man, he can make a girl pregnant?"

"How do you know when you have become a man? Are there particular signs?" Monkith asked gravely.

Jalil counseled Monkith, "Well, naturally, you can mastur- bate: if white sperm emanates, it means you are a man."

But Monkith was hesitant. He had often heard of the dire con- sequences of "abusing oneself." So then, how could he find out if he were a man? He decided that the beautiful Zaynab could help him. He had not seen her for over a year, but he sought her out in the local vegetable market the next day. He recognized her imme- diately, though she was taller and more beautiful.

"Hello, Zaynab. I am the Hajj's son. Do you recognize me? It has been a while since you've been to our house. Aren't you working for us anymore?" he asked energetically.

She could hardly recognize him, but when she did she tilted her head back and blushed in embarrassment. She answered shyly. "Yes, but I come in the mornings when you are at school, because I have another job in the afternoon. And my mother is sick so I need to tend to her and my sisters more. I am not in school anymore."

Monkith inched closer to her and whispered softly as if divulging a great secret, "Well, I understand what you were doing several years before when you used to touch me and hold me."

Zaynab's face became flushed. "I am not sure what you are talking about. Anyway, I need to run now, as I told you my mother is ill and I need to help her prepare dinner," she said with agitation as she turned to run off.

"Wait. Please don't be scared," he replied. "I have matured. Could you come over some time when no one is home, and teach me some more? I want to understand if I have become a man," he said in the most serious and confident tone he could muster.

She hesitated but then replied, "Well, maybe just once. When will the house be empty?"

"Tomorrow afternoon, my parents and sisters will be at my Grandma Fatema's house. Why don't you come at around four o'clock," he said softly as he examined her closely. She nodded her head in agreement and they nervously said good-bye.

When Zaynab arrived the next day, he opened the front gate and they both quietly entered the house and crept up the stairs into his room. They both slowly undressed and lay on the ground giggling timidly. She kissed his hair, ears, and cradled her neck on his shoulder. Then her hands crawled over his feet and onto his legs, further upward. She continued caressing him steadily as he lay on the ground barely breathing. As her hand pressed against penis, she rubbed it rhythmically. He felt his head and legs tighten up. He panicked that paralysis would creep through his body. He was certain he would die. Then the white sperm shot onto Zaynab's hand and splashed across her body. She gently kissed his eyes and tried to calm him, as her fingers fiddled with the fluid.

"Calm down silly. This is normal. You have officially reached manhood," she said as she stroked his hair.

They both lay on the ground for a few more moments. Half-dazed, Monkith could barely move. Zaynab rose, dressed, and kissed him on the forehead before leaving.

If he had misgivings, it did not take long for them to vanish. Shortly after this incident, he sought Zaynab out and asked her to touch him again. And slowly as he began to understand the sensation it caused, he learned to caress her as well. He was curious about uncovering her body and the secrets of his own.

In the midst of the sweaty summer heat, he continued his discoveries. He climbed to the top of his roof to spy on Zaynab and her sisters. The four pretty girls walked around their private garden in their underwear. When Zaynab's sisters saw him, they told their mother and she banished him from the roof. But he found a way to observe them. He made a little box and put it on the roof as if it were a birdhouse. Then he placed a mirror strategically inside so that it reflected the images dancing in Umm Hassan's garden back to him.

Zaynab and Monkith continued their secret trysts. She began to sneak into his room uninvited. On the days she was not working at the house, she stole into his room by climbing the grapevine trellis directly under his balcony. At other times, she slithered from the roof where their homes were directly connected. Once her sister tattled on her, and Umm Hassan stormed over to the Azawi household in search of her eldest daughter. When they heard the frantic voices of the approaching mothers, Monkith hid the naked Zaynab in his closet and raced to his bed. He drew the covers over his head, and pretended to be fast asleep. And not even Umm Hassan's urgent calls for her daughter could awaken the "sleeping" young man.

"Creatures of God"

It was a secret Dawood Adeeshu shared only with Monkith. Dawood, one of Monkith's best friends, was also his study partner, and they had developed a special bond over the years.

It began one Monday after the festivity of Zacharias,[23] when they were in his grandparents' garden, studying, with the sparkling Tigris before them. Monkith told him, "You know, although you are Christian and I am from a Muslim family, we share many of the same traditions. Last night we, too, commemorated John the Baptist's conception."

"What do you mean, how did you celebrate?" Dawood asked, lifting his eyebrows in confusion.

"Well, you know, we fasted for the day and then in the evening, we ate *zardeh*,[24] and my mom prepared beautiful trays filled with candles, bowls of sweets, and grape leaves. See, even though we are a Muslim family, somehow we still observe Christian festivities, along with you. Why? How does your family celebrate the festivity of Zacharias, Dawood?" Monkith asked, lifting his eyebrows in curiosity.

Dawood looked down and his face turned red like a wounded cherry. "Monkith," he said, "There is something I should tell you but it is a secret, you must tell no one at all, not even your sweet grandma, Fatema."

"Go ahead, Dawood, you know you can tell me anything, anything at all. You are my close friend, my brother," Monkith assured him.

Dawood then confided the truth to his friend, "You know, although I pretend to be Christian my family is really Jewish. If our classmates discovered the truth, they will surely harass me and most likely beat me up."

Dawood knew his secret was safe with Monkith, for he had heard Monkith say that the Jews were part of Iraq's cultural

---

[23] The festivity of Zacharias takes place on the first Sunday of the Muslim month of Sha'aban.

[24] This is a special dish made with rice, saffron, and sugar.

mosaic. When he blurted out his secret, Monkith smiled, "We are all brothers, Dawood, we eat from the same bread and share in each other's sorrows. In fact, I think you are definitely more Iraqi than I am."

For Monkith recalled the days, not long before, when Jews had been accepted. He remembered when, as a young child living with Habooba, there was a Jewish family next door to them. The mother, Georgette, frequently visited Habooba. Her son, Adil, became a close friend of his. This Jewish family associated harmoniously with their neighbors. Despite an inherent cultural prejudice – one that became more flagrant as the Israeli-Palestinian issue came to dominate Arab politics – the neighborhood took care of the family, protecting them as best as possible. The landscape began to change for Iraqi Jews with the ascendancy of the Baath party. Monkith's neighbors began receiving threats from the government informing them that they would be deported to Israel. Soon this Jewish family, along with many others, disappeared. And Monkith pined away for his lost friend.

But times had changed since Monkith had played in the garden innocently with Adil. Fear and distrust were now planted in the hearts of Iraqis. When Dawood's parents learned that their son had revealed their secret to someone outside their community, they were terrified. In addition to threatening to send the Jews back to Israel, the Baath party had forbidden them to follow their religious traditions. Furthermore, the *mukhabarat* were constantly on the lookout for Jews who defied the Baath party decrees. In fact, in its effort to erase the Iraqi cultural and historical memory, the Baath party opposed many types of religious practices. And so, the 1970s were a difficult time for the Jews in Iraq, as they were a particularly disliked minority in a society under siege.

Despite the danger Monkith put himself in by associating with Jews, secret or not, he and Dawood remained steadfast friends. Monkith's grandparents, Fatema and Jawwad, who welcomed all of their grandson's friends, often invited Dawood to the house when the teenagers prepared for their exams.

Once, as Dawood departed, Fatema said to him: "May God, Muhammad, and Ali be with you." Monkith was embarrassed by his grandmother's words. She always seemed to assume that all his friends were Shii Muslim. Monkith adored Fatema and longed to tell her that Dawood was Jewish, but he was sworn to secrecy. The flustered Monkith merely said: "Grandma, Dawood is Christian, not Muslim."

His heart swelled with gratitude when Fatema responded, "But my son, we are all creatures of God."

A Fake Death

It was the year that the month of Ramadan – the Muslim month of prayer and fasting – fell during the impossibly hot summer month of August. Monkith, robbed of energy by the fasting and intense heat, often crept languidly up to his room and fell on his bed in the afternoons. He closed his eyes and struggled to summon sleep, which stubbornly refused him. Beads of perspiration gathered under the wisps on his forehead, and clung to his brows. They rolled down his cheeks and became entangled in his long sideburns. At that time, the Beatles were in fashion, and Monkith, a lively thirteen year old – wore his hair with sideburns and a few wisps in his face. How proud he was of his fashionable hairstyle and the Charleston pants he wore!

"Your son is wearing long sideburns. He looks very sloppy and undignified," Hajj Abbas told Naji one day when they passed in the market. "You should make him cut his hair – people are starting to talk about the scandal his hairdo is causing," the Hajj insisted, knowing he wielded influence over Naji.

Later that day, when Naji returned home, he told Monkith, "Son, you need to cut those sideburns, people are starting to talk. Hajj Abbas told me so today. You have to remain dignified, son. You are, after all, the son of Hajj Naji!"

"Oh, it is okay, let him wear his hair as he wishes," Nuriya responded. "Hajj Abbas is a miserly and depressed man with nothing better to do than fill people's minds with lies. His tightness is becoming renown. Yesterday, he divided some leftover portions of meat for Umm Hassan and sold them to her for double the true price. Apparently he is stingy even with himself and his own family. I heard that at home he only gives his new wife discarded bones and old meat to cook with!"

"Don't contradict me in front of the children!" Naji screamed as he threw a glass dish on the floor. Nuriya lowered her head in silence as her husband flew off into a tantrum. She nudged a wide-eyed Manal and together they bent down and picked up the scattered pieces of glass from the floor. Naji left the house, slamming the door behind him.

The next day, an exhausted Monkith unable to sleep grabbed a pill from his father's medicine cabinets. He entered his room, closing the door behind him. As he swallowed the slippery pill, he lay his tired head on a pillow, beckoning deep sleep. He forgot the bitter heat. Sweat clustered at his forehead and dripped down his neck as he descended into a tunnel of darkness. Delightful sleep. As he napped, Naji approached him quietly. He observed his son closely, brushing his hands against the soft wisps on his forehead. He placed a pair of large scissors close to his forehead and like a lawnmower cut the dangling wisps down to the root. He rubbed the scissors along his sideburns, and the small particles of loose hair decked the sheets, drenched in perspiration. Upon waking, a still exhausted Monkith rinsed his face, but did not yet notice his humiliating haircut. When he sat at table for the *fatoor*,[25] he could not understand why his father laughed and served him food in uncommon good cheer.

"Father can you pass me the pickles," Monkith asked quietly as he held his youngest brother Ahmad in his arms and fed him from his spoon.

"Of course, son, what else would you like?" Naji replied, his eyes sparkling with triumph.

Everyone else gaped down in silence, frightened to utter a word. With her large hazel eyes, Iqbal motioned to Monkith to check his hair, but he ignored her signals. She was accustomed to bringing a book with her to the dinner table and she would read as she ate. Hoping to capture Monkith's attention, she let her book fall on the floor. But still Monkith paid no attention as he struggled to feed Ahmad who as usual was not particularly cooperative when it came to eating. Only after the meal, as Monkith washed up, did he notice his hair. He ran his fingers across his forehead in disbelief, and tossed more and more water on his face to drown away the tears. He was so self-conscious about his shorn locks that he decided that he would not join his friends for days after. He heard his neighbor Hatem calling for him from

---

[25] The Breaking of the Fast

the street outside their garden gate, but Monkith shut the window so he could not hear.

Every day he glanced in the mirror to see if his hair had grown any longer. He touched the soft fuzz in the place of his former bangs, which seemed to stubbornly stay short. When he realized how long it would take to grow back, he decided to have it professionally cut. But he was embarrassed to go to the barber who would certainly ask what happened. So he took a pair of small black scissors and began cutting his hair aimlessly. With each shorn lock, tears filled his eyes, reddened by sadness. By the time he was through, uneven strands of hair sprouted from his defeated scalp, and he had no choice but to ask the barber Mr. Haddad to help him fix it.

He looked up at Mr. Haddad in tears and said, "Please, can you fix my hair? I messed up trying to cut it."

"Sure, let me shave the whole thing off for you," the older man replied patting Monkith gently on his back. Monkith nodded his head in agreement and Mr. Haddad set the razor loose on his head. Several minutes later, when he observed his shiny scalp, Monkith could hold his head up again, and he confidently ran out to meet his friends.

Monkith continued to bear his father's humiliations with only his fragile pride as a defense. But one day, when his father hit him very hard in another unprovoked incident, he decided to take his revenge. At first, he was not sure how he could recover his dignity following such an unwarranted affront. His father was much stronger than he. He fell deep into thought by the Tigris and then conceived a plan.

◆

About four o'clock one late summer afternoon, he grabbed a pair of jeans and a T-shirt, and flung them from his balcony into the street that lay beyond the wall surrounding his house. He descended the wooden stairs, passing the living room, where the whole family sat and talked as usual. He wore his everyday clothes, jeans with a red and white striped shirt. Calmly, he walked out the front door of the house.

Once he retrieved his jeans and T-shirt from the street, he ran to the Tigris River. He knew how fearful parents were of their children drowning in its treacherous waters. He chose the most dangerous spot in the area to execute his plan. He stripped off his shirt and pants, and donned the clothes he had thrown from his bedroom window. He placed the discarded outfit in plain view by the dangerous eddies of the Tigris. He set off to execute his plan of revenge against his father.

Around seven that evening the family gathered for their meal, but Monkith was nowhere to be found. "My God, I have told you over and over again that this boy has a problem with discipline. He is probably out playing with his friends, even though he knows it is dinner time," Naji said to his wife as he sat down at the table.

"But this is unlike him," retorted Nuriya. "If he is going to miss a meal he always calls. He has never remained absent like this. Monkith knows Ahmad won't eat one bite unless he feeds him." As her husband and children sat down for their meal, she called Fatema, as well as several of Monkith's close friends to see if they had seen him. No one had. A few hours later, the family realized that something was terribly wrong. Monkith was missing.

The whole family searched frantically for him and even asked friends and neighbors to join the pursuit. Finally, Umm Hassan reported that she had seen some abandoned clothes on the banks of the Tigris at a particularly perilous spot. The whole family ran to the river, and when they recognized the heap of clothes, his sisters and brothers began to weep. Nuriya fainted and Naji screamed out into the dark air. Fatema quietly mourned her grandson and held her grandson's shirt close to her, while Jawwad stood still in disbelief.

Meanwhile, Monkith was at his uncle Aziz's house, playing with his cousin, Samer. Uncle Aziz, a moody man with a flaring temper, was not particularly close to the Azawi family. Clinically depressed, he was usually in bed by eight in the evening, despite his wife's complaints. It had been years since he had spoken to his younger brother Naji, and so Monkith's parents had never thought of calling his home to inquire about their missing son's whereabouts.

"Well, my son, how odd that you should visit today at this time of the day. Aren't you expected to be at home now?" Uncle Aziz asked suspiciously as he stretched out his arms and yawned. He had heard that his brother did not allow his children to stay out late on a school night.

"No, I already ate before coming. No one will mind," Monkith insisted.

After nine, though, when his cousins went to sleep, Uncle Aziz became irritable. He threw his head down and gnashed his teeth. It was then that Monkith revealed his plan of revenge to his uncle and aunt. Aziz immediately called Naji to let him know that his son was safe. In just a moment, Naji's tone moved from mournful to furious, and he swore he would beat his son when he returned. Only the intervention of his grandfather, Jawwad, spared him. But the seeds of rage were planted for Monkith. One day, Monkith knew, he would leave the patriarchal family structure that was so inexplicably intent on crushing him. He always knew that he would not return.

Mr. Rooster

Not long after I turned fourteen years old, my grandmother Fatema told me that I was now a man and that I could sacrifice a chicken. I felt so grand and important in front of all my sisters and brothers. I prepared to perform the sacrifice in the Muslim tradition. Just as I had observed my family elders, I placed the chicken's wings under my left leg and its claws under my right leg. Then I pushed its tongue aside so that I could slit its throat. But as my sharp knife approached the tender feathers, I grew nervous. In the end, I cut my own finger so badly that I fainted. Alas, I was not able to prove my manhood in front of the children.

◆

Monkith's youngest brother, Ahmad, was the wildest son in the family. He took great pleasure in provoking his siblings, especially his brother Muhammad. Ahmad had the annoying habit of loudly crunching his food as he ate. In response, Muhammad yelled for his mother to spank the uncivilized child. Yet, the moment she appeared, Ahmad put on his best table manners. In desperation, Muhammad left the table for a few moments, and when he came back, he always found his supper gone. It was not that Ahmad did not have enough to eat; he usually threw pieces of his own meat onto the floor when no one was paying attention, or he hid pieces under the cushion on his chairs. It was just that he thoroughly relished eating his older brother's food. But Ahmad's worst assaults were launched against Muhammad's schoolwork. Muhammad had always been considered an excellent student until the day the mischievous Ahmad opened his notebooks and erased all his answers.

Ahmad's relationship with Monkith was different, though. When his older brother arrived home from school, the little boy dashed out of the house and through the garden to meet him and jump into his arms. As Monkith did his homework, Ahmad nestled by his side. And when it was time for dinner, it was only at his older brother's insistence that he agreed to touch his plate. He threw temper tantrums when it was time for bed, and in the end he could only sleep when he laid his head on

Monkith's chest and heard the beating of his heart.

One day when he was almost three years old, Ahmad acquired a stinking rooster. He had accompanied his mother to the house of Umm Amin – the young wife of Hajj Abbas – where there was a shelter filled with chickens. As his mother and Umm Amin drank tea and chattered, Ahmad secretly grabbed some pieces of sugar and Amin led him to the chicken shelter. As he touched a rooster's feathers, he jumped up and down in delight. When Amin grew bored, Ahmad stayed alone with the roosters. He crushed the sugar cubes in his mouth. Sugar mush fell down his chin and onto his clothes and stuck to his hands. He searched for pieces, which he held out to the hungry mouths of the roosters. When his mother prepared to leave and called for him, Ahmad refused to leave the roosters and began to holler desperately. Nuriya and Umm Amin entered the shelter. Ahmad tugged at his mother and rubbed the sugar mush into the folds of her skirt. An irritated Umm Amin yielded, handing the child a rooster with a skin disease that even her miserly husband was just about to get rid of.

Monkith took Ahmad's new pet seriously. He washed it, and taught Ahmad how to feed it. The delighted little boy began to lavish it with love and affection. Gorging itself on its new diet of food and affection, the rooster gained weight, plumped its feathers, and strolled with its head raised in pride. It was a beautiful red, with purple and blue feathers. It began to grow and grow, until it became the most enormous rooster they had ever laid eyes on. The children even began to wonder if it was a real rooster, or if some dangerous *jinnee* possessed it.

With a newfound confidence, the rooster began to jostle and scratch everyone in the family with its sharp claws. It spared no one except Ahmad, who only had to whisper to make the rooster cease an attack. At the sight of Ahmad it would open its beak wide and shake its plumage with delight. But his sister Ibtihal named the ill-tempered creature "Mr. Rooster," and no one, not even their father, dared to offend it – for it fancied itself the man of the house. Even the garden was not spared its authority. Mr. Rooster dug up the soil and ate the flowers with its sharp ebony beak, and often escaped to plunder neighboring gardens. The neighbors were terrified of the strange creature that pecked away at everyone and warned the Azawi family that they better not set their rooster loose again. But Mr. Rooster always managed to find new gardens to pillage.

Naji and Nuriya concluded that it was time to end Mr. Rooster's destructive habits. They gathered with their neighbor Abu Hassan to find a way of ridding themselves of the new household menace. Abu Hassan put forward a solution: Naji and Nuriya should offer to purchase the rooster from Ahmad for three dinars.

The unknowing Ahmad readily agreed to sell his rooster, and Naji quickly whisked the rooster away, taking it to the butcher, Hajj Abbas. Hajj Abbas performed an Islamic style sacrificial slaughter, pushing the rooster's tongue to one side, shutting the beak over the tongue, and quickly slitting the throat in its most vulnerable spot. Naji brought the dead rooster home, and Nuriya prepared a dish of cooked rooster with soup and vegetables. Soon the news leaked out among the children, and by that evening, everyone in the family, except Ahmad, seemed to know exactly what they would be eating.

As usual Ahmad sat next to Monkith so that his older brother could feed him. Monkith would say, "There is still room in this part of your tummy for another piece of food," and Ahmad would yield and allow his older brother to gently put another morsel in his mouth. But this evening, Ahmad did not wish to eat anything – not even from his older brother's hand. No one knew how he figured it out, but he suddenly dropped his head. When Monkith lifted the child's chin, he saw that his dark eyes were filled with tears. The child's grief was contagious. Monkith refused to take another bite. Silence choked the room. Mother, father, sisters, and brothers put down their knives and forks. The divided rooster lay on their plates, dead but victorious.

Suicide

It all began during his first year of high school at the famous Central Secondary School, just a fifteen-minute bus ride from Griyat. Basima, the most beautiful woman in Griyat, had long captivated the fourteen-year-old Monkith. With her hazel eyes, dark lashes, long black hair, and golden-brown skin, Basima was brimming with desire she herself did not understand. Often, when she left her home, she did not wear her black *abaya*, leaving the silhouette of her figure open for all to see. When the dazzling Basima walked in the street, all the men turned to catch a glance.

Monkith gave Basima a compliment whenever their paths crossed. One day, at a distance, he spotted her walking towards the bus stop. He ran home and changed into clean clothes so quickly that he hardly had time to make sure anything matched – green pants, yellow shoes, a striped white and blue shirt. He quickly returned to the bus stop where she was still waiting.

He approached her, and introduced himself in a barely audible voice. Right away, he noticed an expression of sadness dangling over her lovely eyes. They stood alone together at the bus stop, and after a few more minutes of small talk, he boldly asked for her telephone number. He promised to call late that evening when both of their families were sound asleep.

Basima's sad eyes followed the young man as his outline faded out of sight. Her heart began to race, and her emotions wavered between excitement and fear. Rather than running her errands, she returned home in an impassioned fury. Several years earlier she had been married – and she was now trapped in a loveless union. Her cold and unattractive husband, forever gone on business trips, was busy having his own love affairs. Even when he was at home, he was indifferent to her pleasure.

As moments of intimacy between them slowly decreased, Basima never complained. In time, she repressed her body's desires, and her very sense of self. Basima did not understand it, but a depression descended upon her and left her young body with an old woman's soul. The only reminders she received of her femininity were the men's whistles and approving stares as she walked the streets. But rather than lifting her spirits, they only plunged her deeper into despair.

To make matters worse, she did not work. Basima's lonely days were filled with routine visits to relatives and neighbors. She did not even have the potential for children to comfort her. Over the course of stomach surgery a few years earlier, the doctor had accidentally cut one of her ovaries. He told her then that she would never be able to have children. She now faced the stigma attached to a woman who could not bear her own son, and often she was referred to as Umm Khaieb, "mother of the absent one." She could hear the whispers "what a shame, what a shame," sometimes spoken just loud enough to pierce her ears.

But on this day, she later told Monkith, "I ran home, heart racing. I entered my bathroom, and looked at myself for the first time in many years. I noticed the freshness of my youth, the innocence of my expression. My moist mouth glistened. Although I was a married woman of several years, I realized how little intimate experience I actually had. Your face, filled with self-assurance, your faraway look, was firmly carved in my memory. I could think of nothing else, and when the phone rang late that evening, my heart beat in excitement."

After several phone calls back and forth, Monkith and Basima decided that he would secretly visit her at her home. Here, she lived with her husband, brother-in-law, his wife and their children. Monkith would come at two in the morning when her brother-in-law and his family were asleep. Her husband, as usual, was traveling. On the appointed night, after confirming that all of the members of his own family were asleep, Monkith stepped onto the balcony outside his bedroom window. He climbed carefully over the grapevine trellis, and then shimmied down the outside of the garden door, landing in the street.

He walked for several minutes, and then caught his breath as he arrived in front of Basima's house. With great care, he opened the already unlocked front door. Basima stood by the door, anticipating his arrival. As she saw it open, she grasped the teenager's hand and led him to her room near the entrance of the house.

He entered a space that reminded him of a dull hotel room with no spark of life. No photos lined the tables, no paintings hung from the bare walls. Gold trim lined the dark beige bed, cabinets, and table but everything looked untouched and ghostly. With the exception of the small figure breathing next to him, the room held no trace of life.

Basima was so ecstatic that Monkith had come that in the next few hours, the two impatient teenagers lost no time. She looked up at him and pressed her moist mouth against his neck. They undressed each other and within moments, their bodies were intertwined. For the first time in his life, Monkith was struck by the warmth and tenderness of the inside layers of a woman's soft flesh. Without uttering a word, the two teenagers lay close to each other in a dreamlike state, gently caressing each other.

Sadly enough, it did not take long for the enchantment of the late-night relationship to take its toll on Monkith. He visited her at two o'clock every morning, but when he returned home and woke up at six a.m. in his own bed, he was exhausted, having caught only a few minutes of sleep here and there. He began to neglect his homework and fall asleep in class. He had an impossible time concentrating on his lessons. Often due to lack of sleep, he felt impatient and irritated.

It was inevitable that things would come to a head, and they did, one winter day. It was seven in the morning. Monkith arrived at sports practice exhausted and particularly irritable that morning.

Everyone knew that the sports coach with his unevenly dyed black hair and eyebrows as thick as a bush adored peering at the teenage boys' naked legs. He would order them to take their tracksuits off, leaving only their thin shorts to cover their legs. On that day, the fatigued Monkith dug in his heels and refused to take off his tracksuit. All of the other boys had already shed them. They stood around him, shivering in their thin shorts and T-shirts. It was a cold day and the blood had flowed towards their exposed flesh, turning it red. The hair on the bare parts of their bodies stood straight up. The teacher ordered Monkith one last time to take his tracksuit off, but he refused. In a fury, the coach struck Monkith and, much to his great surprise, Monkith hit him back. The strikes developed into a full-blown fight, as the freezing boys cheered for their classmate.

In the end, the sports coach hauled Monkith to the headmaster's office. The headmaster, Sami al-Jaffari, a staunch member of the Baath party, was a short, bald man, with flimsy stubble that covered his face. Before his employment in the education system, he was a high-ranking military officer. But when his brother-in-law, Harden al-Tikriti, the defense minister, was killed by the government, the Baath party expelled Mr. Jaffari from his sensitive military post and forced him into the civil service. Now headmaster, he dealt with the students as if he was a stern officer in an army and they were the soldiers under him. If he caught students coming to school late, wearing necklaces, or smoking cigarettes, he either expelled them, beat them, or forced them to sit outside under the glaring sun while he sat in the shade and admired the sweat beads, which rolled down their forehead.

Mr. Jaffari now locked the door to his office so that Monkith could not escape. He told Monkith to stretch his hand out, palm up, so that he could hit it with an iron rod. Monkith closed his eyes and held out his hands, but jerked them away just in time. The rod hit the older man's leg, and then the tube of iron dropped to the floor. Mr. Jaffari then screamed and expelled Monkith from the entire education system in Iraq forever.

Devastated, Monkith left campus and headed straight to the Oil Ministry where his cousin Ali Hadi Jabber worked as an expert. He knew he had nowhere else he could turn, and that if anyone could help him it was this cousin who had many contacts in the government. Another employee with a body as broad as a bean and large spectacles on his dark green eyes led Monkith into Ali's office. Ali lifted his eyes from his papers and rose to greet his younger cousin.

"Why hello, Monkith, how nice to see you! How are your parents, brothers, and sisters? Please assure me that they are all happy and healthy," Ali said as he patted Monkith on the back.

"Everyone is fine. They all send their regards," Monkith said quietly, and then he looked down to avert his cousin's searching stare.

Ali, who had already figured something was wrong, rubbed his tired eyes and said, "Tell me what is wrong, Monkith. God willing I can be of help." And then he signaled to his secretary to bring Monkith a bottle of pepsi.

Monkith told his cousin about the day's events and his subsequent expulsion from the education system in Iraq. Immediately Ali called the Education Ministry, and after a friendly chat and some careful negotiations, it was agreed that Monkith would be expelled for only one year. Ali promised he would keep the whole matter confidential. For Monkith was determined to keep his expulsion a secret from his father. During this time, he was already having difficulty with him. It had reached the point where the two were not on regular speaking terms.

To make matters worse, a week earlier Monkith's older cousin Kazem spied the teenager leaving secretly for a rendezvous with Basima. He pursued him as he set off stealthily in the middle of the night. Perhaps he was jealous that Monkith was involved with the most beautiful woman in the village. Perhaps he was worried about the prospect of family shame. In any case, Kazem went straight to Monkith's mother the following morning and informed her of the affair. The honorable woman broke into tears and screamed in despair. She pounded violently on her head and beat at her heart. But she did not tell her husband, for she feared the magnitude of his wrath towards Monkith.

Now Monkith had been banished from his first year of high school and his relationship with Basima had been cut short forever. His only contact with her now was a phone call from time to time, and even that slowly faded. To hide his expulsion from school, Monkith woke up every morning at 7:00 a.m. in the morning and left the house every morning at the usual time and pretended that he was heading to class. At first he would walk to the Corniche, near the Tigris, and sit by the river, lost in thought. The streets were virtually deserted at that time of day. After a few weeks of aimless wandering, just as Monkith grew bored, he discovered by serendipity a public library. The library became his daily destination. Sitting at a desk, he plowed his way through Darwin, Marx, Sartre, Hesse, Hegel, Tolstoy, and much other classic works of European literature in translation. He memorized the verses of such Arabic poets as Abu Nuwas and al-Mutanabi and wrote summaries of the books he read. After about a month, the kind looking librarian, impressed by his literary voracity, approached him:

"You're too young to be a researcher. What are you doing here?"

Monkith divulged the truth to her, and they soon became friends. She prepared him tea, and placed it by his side as he perused his new treasures. In turn, he shared the sandwiches his mother made for his lunch. They ate together, and discussed what he learned. She shared with him secret papers filled with the poems of the condemned and exiled poet Muzaffar al-Nuwwab, which her brother had hand written. Al-Nuwwab's forbidden verses imbued Monkith's soul with hope and courage. From an unfocused student with an intense distaste for academia, he turned into an avid self-taught pupil who devoured books and gave himself freely to learning. Without the stress of formal schooling, a sense of calm infused his ever-restless spirit.

By the start of the next school year, however, Naji learned that Monkith had to repeat a grade. He did not know that he had been expelled. Monkith only told his parents that he had failed his English exam. Everyone knew that the school system in Iraq was extremely harsh. If a student failed three or more subjects, he or she had to repeat the entire school year again. But if they failed only one or two subjects, they were given the summer to repeat them. It was only if they passed the failed subject by the end of the summer session, that they could continue to the next grade with all their classmates. However, if they failed the subject again in summer school, they were forced to repeat the entire school year. The whole family knew Monkith was weak in English. He always received fifty per cent out of one hundred, so they had no reason to doubt his story.

This was the last straw as far as Monkith's father was concerned, though. That day, he unleashed his rage towards his son. "You're nothing but a reject! I will hang you from the large fan in the living room and let your neck turn round and round," he threatened his son. Then he cast him from the house, screaming, "Get out of my house. I never want to see your ugly face under my roof for as long as I live."

To make an already desperate situation worse, Monkith's mother told him that he would have to become a soldier. This exacerbated his gloom, for he knew that in Iraq failures were always told that they would be forced to join the army.

On that day, he did not need to hear these threats to feel terrible about himself. During the days leading up to it, he was already overwhelmed by his own sense of failure. His friends had passed on to the next grade while he stood still. His spirits plunged. He was now smoking up to a pack of cigarettes per day. Unable to sleep in the days leading up to the new school year, he lay in his bed throughout the long nights, worried about his safety and his future. He either took sleeping pills or asked Jalil to bring him a bottle of beer. When he did fall asleep, his nights were filled with vivid nightmares that he recorded in his journals. On the eve of his expulsion from home, he had written:

Last night I had a strange dream. I drifted into a dusty garden. Everything was dusty, dirty and trying to attack me. I tried to defend myself. When I left that garden, I reached an alleyway filled with dogs. They, too, began to besiege me. Even though I was frightened, I ambled slowly. I knew that if you run, dogs would begin to run also. I slowly ascended the street. I tried to remember the telephone number of our house. As the dogs surrounded me, I began to sweat. I remembered a bunch of telephone numbers I had memorized, except my own. The dogs barked loudly around me and posed to aggress me. I woke up screaming out my telephone number...

But on the day he was cast out, he was at the peak of his depression. His family's refrigerator was always filled with aspirin to soothe his father's frequent headaches. Monkith took a handful of pills and lay down in the guestroom. His stomach began to ache. He closed his eyes and began to lose consciousness as sleep came tumbling down upon him. Little by little, the severe pain in his abdomen began to disappear, and he felt as if he were floating through a beautiful tunnel.

I was flying through a tunnel that was filled with beautiful hues of purple and green. For the first time in a long while, I felt a sensation of sheer happiness as I flew ever higher. I was floating higher when suddenly I felt a shock. I imagined my mother's face in front of me, screaming out my name, and I opened my eyes.

◆

He opened his eyes to the harsh light of consciousness, and was startled by violent convulsions in his stomach. He started to moan. The eyes of his mother and father peered down on him in his hospital bed.

Hours earlier, Monkith's parents had opened the refrigerator and realized that the aspirin was gone. Some pills were scattered on the kitchen floor. Manal screamed, "Monkith has committed suicide!" and the children filled the house with panicked shouts. Naji and Nuriya took their son to the hospital. A doctor pumped his stomach and examined him. He concluded that their son had indeed attempted suicide.

The news spread like wildfire through Griyat and became a common subject of gossip. Monkith was so mortified that he refused to leave the house for several weeks, hoping to avoid the inevitable sidelong glances. He entered an even deeper depression, not bothering to shower or comb his hair. He could do no more than stare at his bedroom wall and imagine neighbors lurking in the corners of his room, laughing and pointing at him.

Shortly after this incident, his grandparents, Fatema and Jawwad, invited Monkith to live with them permanently. Despite their kindness, Monkith would feel forever transient after this experience. He felt he no longer had a home. Already he had lived his childhood between his grandparents' and parents' houses, never fully establishing his own roots. Now he was compelled only to visit his mother and siblings on days his father was not home, or they would come and see him under his grandparent's roof. But he never considered moving back. Nor did he speak to his father again for several years, not until he decided to leave Iraq for good.

◆

Later when I was preparing to leave Iraq, I called Basima, whom I hadn't seen for years after my mother discovered our secret. I told her I needed to see her because I was leaving for good. She brought me a bag containing a kilo of gold – traveling money – and begged me to take it. But I refused. I had hardly any money of my own, but I felt I could never take money from a woman.

Dr. Razak

For as long as Monkith could remember, beholding images reflected on the Tigris was akin to being close to God. In the morning, he observed the rebirth of the sun on the surface of the Tigris. In the late afternoon, he descried the sun drowning in the water, and in the evening, the moon dancing on the rippling river waters. He grew accustomed to performing his "Tigris worship" in the same spot by the ruffled waters. He found a small stone and with it he began to sculpt a seat out of a large rock on the riverbanks. He continued smoothening the surface of the rock until he transformed it into a comfortable chair. He placed another rock in front of it for him to stretch out his legs for comfort. Implicitly, villagers in Griyat knew this was his rock, and if someone sat on it when he arrived, he or she rose and returned the stone to its sculptor.

Sitting on his hewn perch, Monkith gazed at the palm trees in Kazamiyyah, about four hundred meters' distance away. The juxtaposition of the trees' brown bases and their dark green leaves reminded him of a line of women in dark *abayas* advancing towards him. When the sun set, its light covered the green palm tops with a mantle of red, purple, and dark blue.

As he nestled on his rock, he thought about his hometown. Over the years, he had grown ever more critical of Griyat. He was convinced that his neighbors could not see anything beyond their narrow borders. They seemed to have little curiosity. Although many of the inhabitants were comparatively educated, they did not know anything beyond their own private lives. They appeared to have no interest in other countries or people.

Religion and tradition virtually ruled most people's lives. But to Monkith, the line between religious zeal and hypocrisy ran perilously thin. Although the inhabitants of Griyat prided themselves on the strength of their religious devotion, he felt their prayers were formulaic. Their prayer, it seemed, had little to do with God, and were more a display for the benefit of their interfering neighbors. Most lived an agrarian life tilling the land. Anything new shocked them, disrupted their conventions, and caused confusion. When Neil Armstrong stepped on the moon in 1969, some villagers stopped praying because they felt that humankind – at that point – had reached God.

Monkith knew that even if he graduated from university, he would not be able to speak about culture and philosophy in the village without sparking controversy. If he spoke a foreign language, for example, he would be considered arrogant. If he espoused any knowledge other than what he was taught in school, he would be considered insane. Monkith believed Griyat was a village that created many geniuses who became outcasts in the eyes of society. This drove many of them crazy. Monkith thought to himself, God himself would go crazy if he chanced to visit Griyat.

Dr. Razak was one genius considered to be crazy by the villagers of Griyat. As a child, he was a prodigy and no one knew from whence his genius stemmed. He was from a poor, uneducated family. His father sculpted chairs, tables, and beds out of palm trees, and his mother – thin and pale as a lump of chalk – was a mere shadow behind her husband. In high school, Razak ranked highest among students, and was admitted to medical school at the University of Baghdad. At medical school, for the first time, he saw men and women conversing naturally with each other. He observed girls in short skirts and with bright red lipstick. He began to doubt the religious beliefs he had been taught.

According to local folklore, Dr. Razak's eyes fell upon a beautiful woman at the university, and he stared at her continuously. No relationship ever developed between the two, as she was wealthy and he was poor. But he adored her from afar. Soon his unrequited love became an obsession. He developed schizophrenia and epilepsy. He dreamed and spoke about the object of his love incessantly. Villagers threatened to tell his religious father about his behavior. He was brilliant, but after he completed his studies he went crazy and was unable to practice medicine. As he babbled incoherently and hallucinated, this figure on the margins of society became a general object of ridicule in Griyat.

Things went from bad to worse for Dr. Razak. He began to dress like a woman to remind himself of what he had lost. He wondered where he had failed as a man, and donned women's clothes to take revenge on himself. He forgot the meaning of femininity and masculinity; he could no longer feel the heat or the cold. He grabbed whatever clothes he could find, so he would be practically naked in the bitter cold of winter, or wrapped in a thick woolen sweater in the heat of the summer. He stopped praying, fasting, and gradually even believing in God. He learned to speak English perfectly. That in itself did not constitute insanity, although people thought it was an indication that he was on the verge of madness.

Having never had contact with women, Dr. Razak had no idea how to conduct himself around them. If a woman accidentally showed some skin or was simply polite to him, he interpreted her interest as sexual. His *galabia* grew damp with sweat, and shivers ran down his spine. Unable to make love to the momentary object of his desire, he attempted sex with a palm tree or even the dirt on the ground. Often he was hospitalized. Doctors pricked him with needles and forced him to succumb to electrical prods as a way of bringing him back to reality. Dr. Razak was only in his mid-twenties but he had already developed a slight hump on his back.

Many children and teenagers made fun of Dr. Razak and threatened to throw stones at him if he did not make love to a tree or dirt. "Dr. Razak," they would yell. "We order you to have sex with a tree at this very moment."

Dr. Razak complied in front of the children. He began to breathe deeply and kiss the tree, he rubbed his tongue up and down the branches and his moist saliva touched the branches as he wrapped himself around the body of the tree. Then he threw himself on the ground and began licking wildly. He swathed himself in the dirt, his mouth filled with the soil. Still the children threw stones at him and beat him with sticks.

Even as an unknowing adolescent, Monkith knew that this man was a poor creature. Dr. Razak often sought Monkith out to tell him stories about his lost love. Dr. Razak called his little friend "Allah."[26] For when the children saw the doctor talking with Monkith, they put down their stones. Monkith always asked his mother – and then his grandmother when he lived with her – to give him two sandwiches so he could share one with Dr. Razak. He would often join Monkith near his carved seat on the Tigris.

Dr. Razak's mind hovered between reason and insanity. What made his ramblings so disturbing was that they were part truth. At times he might regain his faculties enough to help Monkith with math, physics, and English. But then he might lose his mind a moment later when he spoke of the girl he loved. At times, he started to drool and shake and became unaware of Monkith's presence. Monkith learned to place a branch in Dr. Razak's foaming mouth so that he would not swallow his tongue. He sprinkled water from the Tigris on Dr. Razak to calm him down.

The doctor's mad ramblings always drifted into the past. "But it is time for you to think of the future and move on," Monkith told him as he stared at the ruffling waters of the Tigris.

The doctor became upset, but to please the adolescent he said, "Yes, I shall forget her. Yes, I shall forget her..." But he never failed to broach the subject again.

During one rare, lucid moment of conversation, Dr. Razak asked the fifteen-year-old Monkith, "What are you planning to do in the future?"

And he responded, "I aspire to leave Griyat and chart my own course. My dreams are too large for the confines of this village. You can't imagine the alienation that engulfs me."

Dr. Razak, who could not understand Monkith's desire to leave his family and country, recommended that he abandon Baghdad and take up residence in Mosul. Monkith never responded. He knew that the doctor – like most others in the village – would never be able to comprehend his need to see the larger world.

Monkith then gazed at the sun. He began to sketch, wondering if he would ever become an artist. He drifted off into his own dreams and told himself: "Everyone rejects art here – only medicine or engineering are open to me in the eyes of my parents and society. But look at this crazy, delirious man before me. He, too, went to medical school and now look at his fate. I don't want to conform and become a medical student like everyone else. I don't want to slowly fall into madness."

---

[26] Arabic for God.

Monkith fantasized about how he would study abroad. He imagined how he would not have enough money to buy shaving cream to cut his beard. It would grow and grow, until it touched the ground. He thought of how after many years he would return to Griyat in a Porsche with an automatic shift. He would drive up to a beautiful girl and say, "Do you remember that young man you used to know, that young man whose eyes and heart were choked with dreams?"

As if cradled by Monkith's daydreams, the doctor whispered: "I feel safe with you, like I used to feel with my parents. But now I repel them. They say I am crazy. But I am not crazy. I am not crazy. I am not crazy."

Monkith felt sympathy for the doctor. He always wondered why such people were deemed mad, for he believed that there was a thin line between insanity and reason. "Perhaps they are the reasonable ones, he thought out loud, "and we are the ones who are unhinged."

Saadi

The country I lost, I find again in Saadi...

When Monkith returned to the Central Secondary School after having been expelled the previous year, he was uneasy about having to repeat the grade while his former classmates moved on to the next level. He entered his classroom, embarrassed, and imbued with a deep sense of failure. Already he felt odd in this school, filled with young men from the wealthiest families in Iraq, while he was from the middle-class. Most of the other students owned cars and expensive clothing, while he did not even have his own bicycle. To make matters worse, his father refused to renovate the house, whose paint was chipping and tiles were cracking. Very rarely did Monkith choose to bring his friends to a home that did not bespeak the comfort of middle-class life, but rather gave off the impression of impoverished living. It was only when he recognized Saadi, a long lost childhood friend, that he once again felt a glimmer of hope.

Monkith's friendship with Saadi had begun in the summer of 1970. That summer, he would have been perfectly happy spending his vacation flying kites, but his father ordered him to enroll in an English class at a summer institute in A'dhamiyyah. Naji believed that his eldest son needed to be better prepared for his foreign language class when he returned to school in the fall. Monkith hated the thought of not being able to play with his friends that summer, but only a few days into the course, he met a fellow dreamer, Saadi. The two passed notes back and forth, teasing fellow students as well as each other. Their friendship blossomed, and soon they were inseparable.

When the course ended, however, the two parted ways. It was not until now, five years later, at the Central Secondary School, that Monkith and Saadi crossed paths again. Monkith immediately noticed his friend walking down the corridor, although it took Saadi a little longer to realize it was Monkith standing in front of him. They picked up exactly where they had left off five years before, and in no time at all, they were once again close friends.

Saadi hailed from a liberal family of ten sons and one daughter. He was the youngest child in the family, and his advantageous birth position in an unusually open-minded family bestowed upon him astonishing liberties. By spending time at Saadi's house, Monkith was exposed to many things outside the narrow world he had known until then. In Saadi's older brother's room, the teenagers indulged in erotic magazines imported from abroad, cartons of cigarettes, and bottles of liquor. Monkith saw his first pornographic films, courtesy of an older brother who projected them from a reel onto the garage wall. What a contrast to his own household, where Monkith had always been forced to employ great cunning just to enjoy a smoke. In his father's home where he used to live, he always had to say that the family had run out of toothpaste or that he needed to buy bread – anything to get him out of the house and bestow upon him a chance to light up. Or, if on a weekend evening he wished to stay out late, Monkith had to rely on his younger sister Iqbal who would sit downstairs in complicity, and when Naji searched for Monkith, she would lift her head from her book and assure her father that she just saw Monkith doing his homework upstairs in his room.

Saadi's father, who was a famous leather trader, was among the most affluent men in Baghdad. The family owned an expensive Rolls Royce that had once belonged to Princess Rabiya of Iraq's deposed royal family. The young men sat in the Rolls, and played with the fascinating electric windows for hours. Saadi's family home, which sat on prime real estate close to the Tigris, was immense. The family also owned a building that was rented by the government to house the Museum of the Army.

Much to Monkith's surprise, Saadi's father hauled his money home in enormous bags, and there he emptied it out. Sometimes he beseeched Saadi, Monkith, and Saadi's older brother, Wahab, to organize the bills according to denominations. Saadi's stealthy brother often tried to steal money, and when he was caught, he simply emptied his pockets and said, "Ooops, it must have stuck to my hands."

At this time, Monkith had become a more focused student. The many hours he had spent in the public library the year before had given him new drive and ambition. Subjects that had always come naturally to him such as science and math became his true strengths. In contrast, Saadi detested the way math and physics was taught at school. He knew that he could depend on Monkith to tutor him before their exams, for even when Monkith cut school, he was never at a loss. Saadi did not hesitate to capitalize on his friend's inherent grasp of these tedious subjects.

Sometimes they skipped a class or two and meandered off to find shade under a large palm tree. Once as Saadi closed his eyes and whistled, Monkith took out a notebook and began to sketch his portrait. Saadi marveled at his friend's talent and it was then that he discovered Monkith's dream to become an artist. As Saadi unshrouded his friend's most glorious aspiration, and displayed the portrait for his fellow classmates, many a lover discovered a way to get a girl. In exchange for a pack of Roffman, a popular brand of British cigarettes, star-struck lovers asked Monkith to sketch a portrait of the girl they loved from a picture they gave him or their own detailed descriptions. Saadi managed his friend's list of demands, which often caused them to skip class to remain on schedule, and the portrait-for-a-Roffman-exchange was the cause of many a heart fluttering as well Saadi's disclosure of his own innate business aptness.

Sometimes, when the weather was particularly hot, Monkith and Saadi cut school to watch movies in the cinema. Inside, it was cool and refreshing. Once they were thrilled to discover Anthony Quinn, star of the epic motion picture The Passage, sitting in the theatre among the applauding public. Quinn had come to Iraq as part of the publicity for the movie's opening, and Monkith and Saadi joined the throng begging him for his autograph. Although neither Monkith nor Saadi could speak much English, they signaled for Quinn to sign their notebooks. He patted their back and began writing his name. Monkith watched him closely, this man who was a symbol to him of the outside world he yearned to learn about. A world he had yet only dreamed about.

They returned to school late that day after jostling for Quinn's autograph, and snuck into the bathroom to smoke a cigarette before class. As they puffed and chuckled together, they failed to hear the sound of approaching footsteps. It was Mr. Farah, the headmaster's assistant who had entered in search of delinquents he could report to Mr. Jaffari. He flung open the door, fuming with anger. At the sight of Mr. Farah, Monkith threw his cigarette on the ground and Saadi flung his in his mouth, only to cough it out a moment later. Neither young man was able to hold back his laughter.

"Get the hell out of here, you sons of bitches!" Mr. Farah yelled as he pulled them by the ear and led them to the front of the building. "Now get the hell out of here – you're both expelled for the day. Tomorrow I expect you to bring your fathers here so Mr. Jaffari can speak to them about your delinquency! Now get the hell out of my face and don't come back until you drag in those responsible for you!"

"Shit," Monkith whispered under his breath. "What the hell am I going to do? I don't live with my father anymore and we are not even on speaking terms!"

"Don't worry – we'll find a solution. But for the moment, I am happy to get out of school for the rest of the afternoon. I am going to see my new girlfriend, Nada!" Saadi gleamed as he waved good-bye to his friend.

With nowhere else to go, Monkith went to a small café next to the school and sought to hatch some kind of plan. As he ordered his coffee, his eyes settled on the waiter – a long and slender, feminine looking man who wore a sparkling clean white turban and walked swaying his hips. The waiter looked at Monkith affectionately – he had noticed Monkith and Saadi several times before when they visited the café, and now he was happy to see Monkith on his own.

"You look so sad today, young man, are you okay? Is there something I can do to help you?" the waiter asked him with a strange, cracked voice, which sounded like pepper corns pounded fine with a mortar.

"No – there is nothing you can do – my life is now ruined. I have been expelled from school and I need to bring my father to the school tomorrow. But of course," Monkith laughed with irony, "my father will probably come to my grandparents' home and kill me tonight when he finds out, so we'll never even make it to the school. I have no idea what to do!"

"I wish I could help," said the waiter whose eyes seemed to lock on his.

"Wait, I have an idea!" Monkith exclaimed. At that the waiter seemed suddenly startled out of his reverie. "You can be my father tomorrow and I'll pay you a quarter of a dinar for your time. What do you say to that?"

Before the shocked waiter could answer, Monkith continued, "My name is Monkith and your name is Naji Saaid al-Azawi – that is the name of my father. Can you remember that?"

"Yes – you are Monkith and I am Naji," the waiter said, smiling at this chance opportunity.

"Okay," said Monkith as he sipped the last drops of his coffee and rose from the table. "Let's meet tomorrow in front of the school and we'll head straight to Mr. Jaffari's office."

The next morning, Monkith met the waiter, who had dressed in a formal gray *galabia*, just for the occasion. Monkith paid him a quarter of a dinar and they entered the headmaster's office. At the sight of Monkith's father, Mr. Jaffari grimaced and rose from his desk.

"What kind of father do you take yourself for? Did you know that we caught your good-for-nothing son smoking a cigarette with his friend in the bathroom yesterday?" Mr. Jaffari yelled.

Without a moment's hesitation, Monkith's "father" screamed, "Monkith – You bastard! What the hell do you think you are doing?! Wait until you get home – you have no idea about the punishment that awaits you!" As Monkith thanked God for his ingenious plan, his "father" stretched out his arm and slapped him so hard on the face that he began to bleed.

"Damn," Monkith whispered to himself. "I did not think the waiter would strike me like this. Is this what I paid my money for?" He pressed his hand against his cheek to ease the pain and scowled at his "father" who looked at him triumphantly.

Mr. Jaffari was beside himself with happiness at the sight of this responsible father, and declared: "Well, you good-for-nothing – I see you have your own special punishment in store for you at home – I guess you can begin school again today – but if I ever catch you smoking again..." Mr. Jaffari thanked Monkith's father, shook his hand, and led him to the door.

That afternoon Monkith found Saadi at his girlfriend's home. He had not yet been accepted back to school. Monkith took him to the café so they could see if the waiter could also help Saadi. The waiter happily agreed to act as Saadi's father. In the suit Saadi took from his father's closet and brought for him, he looked completely different and was able to fool Mr. Jaffari. Indeed their plan was so successful that soon another expelled student called upon him to act as his father – but that day Monkith and Saadi spotted the waiter leaving the school with his turban disheveled over his head, his eyes red from the punch of the headmaster, who had finally discovered his deceit.

At the end of their junior year, Monkith learned he had achieved above a ninety per cent average in his classes, and was therefore exempt from final exams. In the rigid educational system of Iraq there were three semesters and at the end of the year, the student added up his or her grades in each semester and divided by three. Only if the average in a subject was ninety per cent or better did the student not have to take the final exam. Otherwise he or she was forced to study for the rigorous finals. Saadi had not achieved the ninety per cent average, and therefore was not exempt from any of his finals. Even with Monkith's help, he had a hard time preparing for his math and physics exam. All of those sweltering afternoons playing hooky in the cinema or managing his friend's portrait-for-a-Roffman-exchange were lethal to his grasp of the drudging course material.

The inherently brilliant Saadi searched for a solution. At last, one seemed to come to him from the heavens. By chance, one afternoon while the forlorn Saadi was at the Brazilian Café sipping a cup of tea, he spied his Egyptian math teacher, Mr. Chamaa, waiting tables. Because Saadi knew about a law in Iraq that forbade a teacher to denigrate his profession by taking a job that was considered beneath him, he realized that he now had a valuable piece of information, perhaps something he could use to his advantage. With sharpened joy, he ducked down and carefully slipped away from the café. Then Saadi triumphantly called his sidekick. He confided to Monkith the next day:

"You will never believe it, my friend. I have made a discovery worth more than a million dollars."

"Tell me, what it is? You look so excited," Monkith exclaimed.

"Well, yesterday I saw none other than Mr. Chamaa. He was waiting tables at the Brazilian café," he said as he clasped his hands on his stomach to keep from laughing.

"Wait, I thought teachers are not allowed to take second jobs," Monkith said with a wicked smile.

"Yes, you are right my friend, it is against the law," Saadi said rejoining with a smile.

Monkith and Saadi chuckled and put together a plan. The next day, the two sneaky young men set out for the café to "study." They kept their heads buried in their books until the moment their teacher came to ask them what they wished to order. As Mr. Chamaa stood still at the table, Saadi looked up from his book and exclaimed with feigned surprise:

"Wow, Mr. Chamaa. What do you know? Is that really you? What a surprise. I did not know you wait tables! Monkith, can you believe it? We have the pleasure of seeing our dear Mr. Chamaa outside of class also. What a wonderful surprise!" Saadi said as he glanced at Monkith who was pinching himself to keep from laughing.

The old man's yellowish eyes and thick fleshy nose began to twitch uncontrollably. His lips – two thin lines – only became visible when he opened his mouth to mumble an abashed answer, "Yes, it is me. Um, can I get you anything to drink?"

Saadi scrutinized him for a moment and then continued, "But I thought you were not allowed to do this."

Mr. Chamaa was too humbled to speak. His facial expression grew ever more pinched. He understood that moonlighting as a waiter could land him in trouble, and he also realized that Saadi now had powerful leverage over him. For a moment he appeared transfixed, but then he came to and fled from their table. The two teenagers looked at each other and laughed.

Saadi lost no time in capitalizing on his victory. One night, shortly after the surprise encounter in the café, he and Monkith paid their math teacher a visit. They rang the bell. Mr. Chamaa was not home, so the two young men spent the rest of the evening drinking champagne by the garden gate. When Mr. Chamaa returned home later that evening, he was astonished to find Saadi and Monkith tipsy and dancing around his house.

They presented him with a glass of champagne, which he took with hesitation. Then Saadi sweetly demanded the questions to the exam so that Monkith could help him prepare. Their frightened teacher began to shake, and then readily agreed to provide them with the information they requested. What else could he do?

In the last couple months of high school, Saadi and I saw very little of each other, for the mid to late 70s was a time when everyone became scared of everyone else for political reasons. I joined the leftist student groups, while Saadi did not. Anxiety and suspicion reigned. The mukhabarat became ever more relentless and spies were now planted everywhere. Sadly, our relationship virtually ended, though we were both against the Baath party. Indeed Saadi had an expression that 'the blood of anyone who joined the Baath party turned dirty.' There was a student in school, Mazen, who had joined the Iraqi mukhabarat and by coincidence, his face was a bright red. We called him Mazen al-Ahmar (The Red), and began to avoid him early on.

But we also began to shun each other. It seemed that the paranoia systematically fermented by the Baath party touched everything, including my relationship with Saadi. It was not until many years later, when we were both in exile, far away from Iraq, that we resumed our friendship. I was happy to learn of his success as a businessman in California. I was proud of this man whose friendship I had chosen as a teenager, and whose friendship I was delighted to rediscover in our adult years.

Manal's Engagement

One day, Monkith's younger sister, Manal, approached her parents and told them that she wished to marry Hussein, an aspiring engineer. He was the son of Grandma Fatema's sister Zahra. Monkith's parents were delighted, for the radiant Manal was obviously happy. A few days later, an entourage consisting of Zahrah, Hussein, and his brothers paid a visit to the Azawi household to ask for Manal's hand in marriage. Monkith's parents received them warmly, but to show their daughter's incredible value, at first they feigned refusal.

"My daughter Manal is a precious pearl. I need to think about this matter more before I can give an answer," Naji said decisively. For several weeks, Hussein's family sent messages and made frequent visits to the Azawi home beseeching a positive answer. Finally, Naji – after carefully pondering the matter, conceded.

"Are there any special conditions you would like to make on the arrangement?" Hussein's eldest brother Ahmar asked Naji one afternoon.

"My only request is that both of Hussein's parents ask for Manal's hand in marriage," said the proud father.

For Hussein's father had not come on the first visits to ask for Manal's hand in marriage to his son. It happened that Hussein's father hoped for his son to marry one of his older brother's six daughters. Only at Hussein's insistence did he finally agree to ask Naji for Manal's hand in marriage to his son, but he never truly supported the union. Still the date of writing the marriage contract was soon to be set.

Hussein was about twelve years older than Manal, but he had not yet completed his engineering degree and he had still not begun to work. The family elders agreed that although the marriage contract would be signed, the marriage would not yet be consummated. As was the custom, the two would continue to live separately until Hussein had finished his education. Indeed, Naji was quite liberal with all his daughters, but he knew that neighbors such as Haji Abbas could come and fill his ears with disapproval if they ever spied his unmarried daughter unchaperoned with her cousin. Signing the contract now meant that

Hussein and Manal were officially man and wife. This ensured that the couple could go out to dinner and the cinema unaccompanied.

Thus, shortly after Hussein's father gave his reluctant blessing, friends and relatives gathered in the Azawi home. A local religious leader sat down with Hussein to review the wedding contract and establish the amount of the bride's dowry.

Meanwhile, Manal sat behind a closed door, surrounded by the female guests. As was custom, to ward off the evil eye, only married women with luck were allowed to join her. Divorced women and women who had lost children had to wait outside. The "lucky" women placed a white veil above the young girl's head and rubbed sugar over it to symbolize the sweetness of marriage. Then the religious leader appeared behind the door and asked the bride if she accepted Hussein as her husband, along with the terms of the dowry. The religious leader repeated his question five times,[27] and only on the fifth time did Manal answer, "Yes, and you represent me."

Now that they were officially married they could be seen together alone in public. Hussein spent the next year finishing his education, and then he began to work. He now felt he was ready to bring his bride home with him and share a life with her. When the day of the wedding celebration finally arrived, it was a happy one for all but the groom's father.

Perhaps that is why, despite his vast wealth, the groom's father refused to dip his hand into his pocket to help the newlyweds. It was custom for the bride and groom's families to divide the wedding expenses and the cost of any furnishings for the young couple's bridal suite in the home of the groom's parents. But Hussein's father contributed nothing. Naji, who was always generous with his daughters – paid not only one hundred percent of the cost of the wedding, but also spared no expense furnishing the newlyweds' bridal suite.

The day of the wedding celebration was one of great excitement in the Azawi household. Only close friends and relatives were included. The beautiful Manal glowed in her simple white gown lined with tiny pearls. How spectacular and glittering she was. Family members wrapped bangles of gold around her wrists, and hung precious gems from her earlobes. She wore a bracelet of beautifully scented jasmine around her wrists. Women in the groom's family as well as her mother and grandmother presented her with all these gifts and more.

Manal was a happy woman. Her bridegroom was the man of her choice and was very much in love with her. He arrived at the end of the party, since he had been busy making arrangements for their honeymoon the next day. When he appeared, he looked at his new partner with deep admiration and respect. Relatives chanted *Mashallah*,[28] *Mashallah* from all of the corners of the house, and there was much clapping and singing as the bride and groom socialized, dazzling everyone with their love. The joyous evening ended with many of the female guests ululating as the bride and groom left the house for their hotel. The next day, Manal and Hussein left for their lavish honeymoon across Morocco, France, and Germany, all at Naji al-Azawi's expense. Included in his generous expenditures were suitcases brimming with not one but two trousseaux, one for the bride and one for the groom, including all new clothes, nightgowns, creams, and shampoos.

Manal's betrothal left a bittersweet taste in eighteen-year-old Monkith's mouth. At the time of the wedding the headstrong young man was living with his grandparents. It confounded Monkith that his father could be so kind and generous

---

[27] Five times is meant to signify an incident referred to as the Kisbah in which the Prophet Muhammad visited his daughter Fatima's home. Her husband Ali and their sons, Hussain and Hassan, were also there. All five slept under one blanket that night. Sometimes, though, the religious leader will ask for the girl's consent and she answers after twelve times, signifying the twelve Imans. And sometimes, he repeats her phrase fourteen times since there are twelve Imams in Islam, and the thirteenth and fourteenth additional times are meant to symbolize the presence of God and Muhammad.

[28] This is a phrase that beseeches God's eternal blessing and protection from harm.

towards his brothers and sisters, so tolerant and liberal-minded with anyone else of close acquaintance. He wondered, Could this be the same man who was so severe with him and stomped on his artwork?

It has been said that no son truly understands his father. Strange rivalries spring up between strong-willed patriarchs determined to mold their sons in their own images, and their progeny who must struggle to establish their own identities. Perhaps Monkith, free spirited and independent, never stood a chance of gaining his father's approval. Perhaps his sister Manal, who was not her father-in-law's first choice, experienced her own disappointment. Maybe, Monkith concluded, Griyat would be a better place if fathers were not so intent on imposing their will on their children. Since Monkith would never be able to change the traditional family structure – and it would never change him – one of them would have to give up its hold on the other.

Prison. Torture.

*"I long for the prison dove. I long for you, and you
long for me. If you wish to long, just long..."*

Muzaffar al-Nuwwab

I strolled through central Baghdad circulating political pamphlets secretly.
With long, unruly hair, which reached my shoulders, dark black sunglasses, and
blue Charleston pants I appeared as if I was on the way to a social gathering. No
one could guess that underneath the carefree smile hovering on my face there
was a political dissident. On the streets, I provoked no suspicion. I appeared as
if I were just some teenager with ordinary concerns. And this is why the Da'wa
Party,[29] an Islamic party, used me. They chose me to work with them although
I was leftist, for in those days all of us dissenters shared a common trait: we were
all against the Baath.

It was 1978, the year I graduated from high school. The Iranian revolution
was well underway. Many of us Iraqi youth – whether Shii, Sunni, or
Communist, supported the revolution, which we viewed as a nationalist revolt
of the masses, another Bolshevik revolution. We identified with the Iranians
and supported the fall of the Shah and his imperialist allies. We also wished for
an end to the oppression Iraqis suffered at the hands of the Baath. Many students thronged the streets. Demonstrations were strongest in the Shii regions of
Najaf, al-Amara, Karbala, al-Samawa, al-Nasariya, and Kazamiyyah following an age-old tradition of rebellion in Shiism dating as far back to
Hussein's revolt against the injustice of the Umayyads and his massacre at
Karbala. Sunnis, Christians, and Communists participated in the Shii led
revolts against despotism.

Every day the unrest continued. When I was not distributing pamphlets, I
joined the throngs starting in A'dhamiyyah. We crossed over the bridge to reach
Kazamiyyah where we gathered around the holy shrine, screeching slogans
against injustice and imperialism. The Baathi police fired tear gas and bullets,
and the crowd scattered. One day, though, as shots streaked through the clear
blue sky, someone clutched me from behind. Before I had a chance to notice who
it was, my captor tore the shirt that my uncle Mohsen had sent me from the

---

[29] Party of Prayer, Supplication.

Emirates and wrapped it around my eyes. The next thing I knew, he hurled me into a car with a group of my friends and others I did not know.

I spent forty-five days in prison. It was summer, and for forty-five days we saw no sunlight whatsoever. The prison guards stole our clothes and ordered us to settle our hands behind our back by our buttocks. From that position, they hung us with a hot cable. It scorched my hands. I was scared I would fall. My shoulders felt as if they were going to pop out of their sockets. Every day they tied my hands with a lever and lifted me up, so that I dangled in the air horizontally.

The prison smelled like a car garage, but in reality, I had no idea where I was. The guards blindfolded us throughout, and threw us bread as if we were dogs. I recognized those around me only by their sounds. We slept piled on top of each other on the sticky stench, which spread across the ground like a thick blanket. In the middle of the night, the guards entered and randomly whipped us with cables. They shot their guns to frighten us. I was asleep, but I woke up to their screams as they threatened to kill us. Every moment, I thought I was hit and began to shriek. But they did not shoot at me. I thought I was going to die, but then I realized I was still alive – I felt as if my life was in the hands of the devil.

And then there was the daily problem of confessions. They hung us one by one and growled, 'Okay, you son of a bitch! If you want to walk out of here alive, you'd better start to think of the names of the people responsible for organizing these protests.' Every day, more and more prisoners informed them of instigators against the Baath.

Every day, they held me up by a lever and ripped my skin with cables, 'You dirty dog, tell us what you know.'

'My God, I don't know anything,' I pleaded in a voice I no longer recognized as my own.

'What did you say, you son of a bitch?' someone asked me as he continued to strike my blood-streaked back with the hope of compelling me to cough out more information.

'I said I do not know anything. I was just visiting a friend that day. I was caught in the crossfire by chance. I swear I do not know anything,' I ranted in barely discernable words.

But they slashed me with their cables and flung me on the ground and every day the routine persisted. It seemed that more than half of those present had begun revealing names of the men responsible for the demonstrations in exchange for their own freedom. Every day a few more names were whispered and the leaders duly executed by the Baath.

Then one day, by some miracle, they dressed the remaining stubborn half-crazed bodies in dirty galabias. They dumped us into a truck packed on top of each other and tossed us out like stray dogs in the center of Baghdad. We all managed to return to our homes that day – broken, half-dead corpses. Some of us later escaped Iraq, some were executed, and some eventually went on to become members of the mukhabarat.

A Desert Escape

Perhaps this country promises me one less year of sorrow.

Such deep optimism. Perhaps this is what it augurs, so that I may hold on to one more year. I am exhausted and cursed. For how long shall I inhabit this exile and where shall it lead me?

I carry Monkith on my shoulders. His weight is as heavy as a wounded wild animal.

He tires me not only because of his extraordinary weight, but because of his heavy sorrow... restlessness... loneliness...

Tell me...Oh, my dear guiding star, my judge, please tell me...

Where shall I discard Monkith? Do I cast him in a deep pit, in the wounded gutter of an alley lined with trash, or in a dark and lonely hell?

I shall lift him from my shoulders. I shall be kind to him just this once.

I shall dump him in an empty station, and deceive him into imagining that someone shall come and pick him up as he leans on emptiness and stares at nothingness.

For I am lost... lost... like him.

I am alone and respected by no one... I have no lover... family... or homeland... only alienation and grief...

◆

At ten o'clock one cold December morning in 1978, I sat desperately at a small café in al-Rutbah, at the Iraqi border. My cup of tea – untouched in front of me – cold. I was entangled in a dark gray web of thought, wondering where my future lay, or if I even had the right to one.

I longed to join the Fine Arts Department at the University of Baghdad that year. But when I learned that I had not been admitted, I was as crushed as the sculptures broken under my father's feet. After my initial shock, I made an appointment with Faegh Hassan, one of Iraq's most important realist painters who also chaired the Department of Painting at the university. The sympathetic Hassan told me that I had received a highly competitive score on the department's entrance exam. But Abed Najem, a prominent member of the Baath party and head of the Iraqi Student Union, rejected my application on the grounds that I was not a Baath party member. To enter that department – in fact, to enter any university from the late 1970s onward – required party membership. The Baath party watched their membership closely, for as soon as computer technology arrived, they immediately put it to use monitoring the population.

'When I saw your work,' Chairman Hassan said, 'I told the department committee that if they did not accept you, they would lose an extraordinary artist.' He paused, looked down, and then continued, 'But my words to the committee were in vain. Without Baath party membership, there was no way you would be admitted.'

The rejection, in whatever terms it was couched, carried ominous implications. If I could not enter university, I would be forced to become a soldier. At first, I was relieved to see that my name had appeared on the list of those accepted at the University of Sulamaniya, in the northern region of Iraq populated by the Kurds. But alas, I was allowed to attend the university for only one day. By the time I finished filling my entrance papers, I was cast away since I had not attended classes in September, October, or November. Never mind that I was absent from class during those months since my name had not yet loomed on the list of those accepted. The Baath party devised this strategy for the very purpose of keeping all non-party members out of the Iraqi university system.

I was despondent and turned back to Baghdad with thick, knotted nerves. I knew I would soon be drafted. In any event, the Baath party would note on my enlistment that I had demonstrated against the regime, which meant they would lose no time in killing me. As a last resort, I begged my father for money to leave Iraq. But my father – who had recommended to me that I become a taxi driver when I returned from Sulamaniya – refused to grant me travel money. 'God curse you, son – you and your demands. In the end, you will be the death of me,' he hollered as he pushed me aside and stormed away.

To make matters worse, in order to gain permission to travel, an individual had to procure an official document, which ensured that the person intended to return to Iraq. The document required the sworn testimony of someone else. That way, if the individual did not reappear, the person who had vouched for him would be forced to pay a huge sum of money. My father refused to support me, and also dissuaded others from helping me.

'Please, Sinan. I will never ask you for anything else. I can feel that I need to leave Iraq as soon as possible,' I implored my older friend one day as we sat by the Tigris.

Sinan stared unflinchingly at me and then looked down as he mumbled the words, 'I can't… Please understand… Do you understand?'

'Has my father spoken to you, Sinan, tell me. Has he come here?' I cried as I shook my friend.

Tears swam in Sinan's blue eyes, and then he ran off without saying good-bye. I never saw him again. It was then that I understood the extent of my father's power over others.

Just when I despaired, though, my brother-in-law, Hussein, and his friend, Rashid, stepped forward. In this case, I needed two signatures, since both Hussein and Rashid were newly graduated engineers and still did not make enough money to serve as witnesses on their own. With his usual sense of irony and humor Rashid nudged me, chuckling, 'Enjoy your new life far away from Iraq. Please know that I am vouching for you only if you promise not to return to this God-forsaken land.' I hugged him with gratitude – this man who barely knew me, but still took the risk to stand by me.

And so on a cold December day, in 1978, I left home at six a.m. and took a taxi to al-Rutbah, a checkpoint in Iraq. My friend, Hatem, had also planned on leaving Iraq that day. But on our way to al-Rutbah, Hatem jumped out of the car, fearful of attempting an escape from Iraq. Years later, I would learn that he was executed shortly thereafter by a Baathi informer. But that morning, an impending sense of doom compelled me to flee Iraq at any cost. Never had I felt more like a foreigner in my own country. In my heart I had a strange sensation that I could not wait one more day.

From al-Rutbah, I planned to cross over the al-Tanaff desert and arrive at the Syrian border in a taxi I had reserved. But shortly after I reached the Iraqi border, I discovered, much to my alarm, that my name decked the list of those forbidden to leave the country.

Now, in the face of apparent defeat, I sat in stunned silence at a little café near the checkpoint, wondering what to do next. I was surrounded by a suitcase, small backpack, and unfulfilled dreams. A young Bedouin, who appeared in his mid-twenties, must have seen the desperate look shrouding my face and approached me.

He asked gently: 'So, you want to leave Iraq, don't you?'

I was frightened. I thought the desert nomad, with his bushy black beard and mustache, dark black eyes and heavy eyebrows, was in the mukhabarat, and so I abruptly answered: 'No.'

The Bedouin went away and left me alone, but he soon returned and persist-ed: 'Why don't you trust me?'

'Who trusts who in Iraq?' I replied tersely

The relentless man pressed further, 'But I think I can help you. I will deliver you to safety. I promise.'

'How?' I asked sadly – his insistence finally won me over as I realized I had no choice but to have faith in him.

'I can help you escape from the vigilant eyes of the police at al-Rutbah, but then you have to tread the lonely and vast desert of al-Tanaff to arrive at the Syrian border Abu Shammat,' he said with a curious sense of authority.

I was nervous and twitched in my seat.

The stranger continued without any inflection in his voice: 'You must follow a large star. Beware of wolves and Iraqi border guards that monitor the al-Tanaff desert in their rugged Jeeps.'

He handed me a flashlight and continued instructing me, 'Wolves are scared of light, so shine this in their face if they approach. If you see the light of the Iraq border guards, lie on your stomach. Once you have reached the Syrian frontier, just inform the border guards that you have fled Iraq. They will surely protect you, since at this time Syrian border guards do all they can to aid fleeing Iraqis.'

In gratitude, I tried to offer the young man my large suitcase. 'Please take this, it is too heavy for me to carry,' I pleaded. 'I do not know how else to thank you.'

Instead, the stranger politely refused, 'No, I'll return it to your family.' He took out a piece of paper to write down the address of my parents.

Again, I pressed, 'Please, my family will not need this. I really would like to give it to you.' I pushed the suitcase toward my new friend and patted his shoulder.

The Bedouin issued a fresh refusal, but then he relented. I reached over and pulled out two books by the Egyptian writer Mustafa Mahmud and some tattered clothes. I donned three thick sweaters and a leather jacket. Then I handed the suitcase to the Bedouin who accepted shyly. Now all I carried was a small backpack stuffed with two books, a towel, a Quran, some sketches, my high school diploma, a family album, a box of dates, a bag of homemade sandwiches, and one hundred and ninety dinars my mother had slipped into my pockets when my father was not paying attention.

'Wait in the café until about three in the afternoon. The best time to set out across the al-Tanaff desert, and escape the attention of the alert border guards at al-Rutbah, is at sunset. By then, it will be dark enough for you to see the large shining star you must follow. You are lucky that the weather is clear today. You should be able to make out the brilliant star with no problem,' the Bedouin said before he disappeared behind the thick desert shadows.

As instructed, I waited until late in the afternoon. Then I started what seemed like an endless march through the desert. The unknown stood before me. But the desperation to leave my country bestowed upon me strength to survive the interminable hours of walking before the sun rose again.

All that existed was a young man, a trackless desert, a guiding star, and the deathly cold. Although I wore heavy padding, I froze. Yet, my cumbersome backpack and rapid pace made my skin burn. I lost all trace of time. My teeth chattered and my ears were so cold that they ached. I began to blow my warm breath into my hands so that I could clasp them against my ears. My feet turned numb as if pricked by icy needles, but I did not know how to unthaw them. Then in my fear, I quickened my pace and began to sweat. Exhausted, I threw myself onto the ground to cool the sweat on my shoulders. But the sand felt like shards of ice. I wavered between feelings of unbearable cold and scorching heat. Once again, fear was my constant and loyal companion.

My throat became dry as the summer drought from the salt I tasted on my lips. My teeth sank into a sandwich, but my tongue was enshrouded in sand. I could only eat half of it and tossed the other half to the backpack. Then I remembered that I had another sandwich, so I flung the sandy one on the ground. But after walking a short distance, I grew nervous as I remembered the spy stories of Sherlock Holmes. I retraced my steps to the discarded sandwich and buried it so that no one could track me. Then I pulled out my towel and covered my head in order to warm my frozen ears.

As I stepped, it seemed as if my backpack turned to lead. In order to lighten my load, I stopped to entomb the Quran my grandfather had offered me on the night before my escape. For an instant, I allowed myself to drift back to the moment I had taken leave of my grandparents. They had thrown a glass of water behind me as I passed under the Quran, whispering: 'This water is so that your enemy's heart grows cold, so that your enemies cannot hurt you. May you step under the Quran for your safety.' My grandfather – who believed laughing and crying were beneath him – was now paralyzed by his tears. I felt him trembling as he grabbed me and held me close. I embraced grandmother Fatema and as she laid her head on my shoulders, I inhaled the lovely scent of her scarf for the last time – her sweet perfume, which had enveloped me in my childhood, but somehow was not able to protect me.

I resumed my pace and began pondering my life. I thought about my mother, my father, Griyat, my country that had lost its hold over me because it took away much more than it gave. The country I longed for would shelter me, not throw me out. I buried the dates, and then sat on the ground for a moment to rest. But an instant later, I jumped up, realizing that if the desert guards caught me, I would be executed, or worse, sent back to prison. As I resumed my agonizing trek, my mind drifted off to recent nightmares.

I quickened my speed into a run, imagining all the ways I could face an untimely death. I knew that if a hungry and vicious wolf approached, I could do nothing to protect myself. My hands were frozen in my pockets. The wolf would be sure to tear me at my neck and devour me. There were one thousand other ways I knew I could die. I began to sprint quickly, as if trying to escape these terrifying thoughts. Sometimes I told jokes to myself so I could escape my fear. At other moments, I recited an elegy commemorating my death in the hostile winter desert.

'He's dead! He's dead! Who will bury him?' I raved deliriously. I visualized the wolves tearing my remains so that no bones could be interred. I sensed the sweat on my shoulders, although my hands were frozen. It felt as if my toes were falling off. As my legs sank in the sand below me, I wondered how my guiding star – who I imagined as a beautiful woman – could save me if the sand covered my whole body. I searched for areas where glistening dew had blanketed the sand, enabling me to run without descending deep into it.

As I dashed, I begged my bright star to lead me to a safe place. The star became my friend – my beautiful lover. I promised to pamper her with affection. It seemed sometimes as if she were laughing at me, poking fun at my fear, for she always smiled and danced above. I convinced myself that she was happy to help me escape, and I ran faster and with more confidence. I knew that if I were lost in the desert she would augment her light to save me, to encourage me to start my life anew. But sometimes her light flickered and grew dimmer as if she were about to vanish.

'Oh my darling, please don't leave me. You are all that matters to me in my exile,' I would scream out into the emptiness, wondering if she even existed, whether she was just an illusion. But then I grew silent again; anxious that someone would hear my shouts and carry me off to be executed.

Fearful that she would fall asleep and forget me, blackening the sky in a thick veil of darkness, I recited silent poems. I told her more jokes. I asked her whether I would live or die. Her light twinkled, and in my mind, I could hear myself declaring my love to her under my breath so no one could hear:

You ask me why I love you, but how could you answer why you love jasmine or the air you breathe?

How could you explain why you drink water and cannot live without it, why when you are drowning in the sea you struggle to live?

How could you explain the feeling of excitement when you are starving and then smell the scent of fresh bread, or feel excitement when you are in a desert with no drop of rain and suddenly there is a shower?

You are my safe haven and shelter after my first country banished me, erasing all traces of me and shattering my existence. You are my freedom, you are the future I live for, oh, my beautiful guiding star. You are all my contradictions.

You are my candle in the lonely darkness, you are the drop of water in my dry desert, you are the tree that gives me shadow from the burning sun, but you are the sun in my dark life, you are my happiness and sorrow, my hope and despair. You are my success and my failure, you are my bright night, you are my day.

But when I saw you carrying all my life in your lovely hands, you kept my heart close to your breast.

And so from the evil of humanity, I leave my life and land to find some place and call it my home. I yearn for your eternity, your pure heart, which has become my shelter. You are my heart that has come alive again after such a long death.

◆

After several hours, exhaustion forced me to slow my pace. I entombed the family picture album, but one less object in my backpack brought no relief. As I pushed forward the sand, tears crushed my eyes.

My father and I had not spoken to each other for years; until the day I told him I was departing. That day my family surrounded me. My younger brother Ahmad pressed his head against my legs and wrapped his arms around my body. He would not let me go. He threatened that he would never sleep again, since he could not be lulled by my heartbeat. Manal was pregnant and stood crying – she felt she was losing a brother who had also been a friend. My sisters, Amal, Iqbal, and Ibtihal, stood around me sobbing, not understanding the events occurring around them. Even my father wept alongside my mother. But now, none of that seemed to matter anymore.

I adored the poetry of al-Mutanabi, but when I crossed the desert in the bitter cold, I even cursed him. His verses rang in my tired head and pierced my ears:

'If you long to follow an adventure, which leads to the highest honor, don't accept less than the stars...'

'I wish to reach a point unattainable by time itself.'

Al-Mutanabi had shaped my dreams. But now, as I rubbed my hands mightily to withstand the sharp needles of the wind, I resented al-Mutanabi, for teaching me about ambition, in a village where I felt there was no way to realize my dreams.

The Bedouin had informed me that when I finally crossed over a large pit, I had reached the Syrian border. By the time I arrived at the Abu Shammat checkpoint at five a.m., I had few material items left in my possession – only some sketches and my high school diploma. I was ready to discard my backpack *as well, but then I realized that I would need it. I would never stop traveling. From that moment on, a suitcase would be my only country.*

Tears fell from my eyes as I remembered my country and family – my younger brothers and sisters. I longed to embrace them again, but then I remembered the exhaustion, prison, and images of death. I spit across the border, and then unzipped my fly and urinated into Iraq. I yelled and screamed with delight. I danced and jumped in the air – peering over the border at the vastness of the desert that I had crossed on my own. But then I remembered that someone special had led me to safety. I glanced up to my guiding star to thank her, but she had already vanished. The purple color, which spread through the sky before the moment of sunrise, dabbled the earth's canvas with colors of magnificent radiance.

Inside the Syrian checkpoint, I was frightened once again. There was a large metal object in the center of the room that had an extensive metal network climbing the walls. It looked like a huge spy network. When the border guards asked my name, I answered with a question, pointing with alarm at the metal pipes: 'What is that?'

They all laughed and told me that it was the sobiya, a heat pipe, run on diesel oil. It was used to warm them in the winter, and not an object to be feared. Then one of the men asked me in surprise:

'Why, what do you use in Iraq to heat yourselves during the wintertime?' I explained that our heaters were smaller and run on gas and a kerosene liquid, not diesel. The heating units were small, independent pieces of heating apparatus, not connected by a huge network of large pipes that clung to the wall around them.

Then I calmed down, and told them my name: Monkith Saaid. I donned my paternal grandfather's first name as my own last name, dropping Naji al-Azawi forever. It was not only a move to assert my independence from my father but more important, I wished to protect my family, who could easily bear the brunt of the Baath party's wrath for my political activities. I knew that moving forward, I would be traced by the Iraqi mukhabarat. Any misstep on my part could result in the death of my entire family. I knew that perhaps even the very next day, my father would be questioned about the whereabouts of his missing son.

Even after I had finished giving the Syrian border guards my personal information, I had to linger several hours until a driver could take me from the border to the nearest village. There, I could catch a taxi to Damascus. With many hours in front of us, I entertained the curious border police with stories of my childhood in Griyat and why I had conceived of the plan to finally leave. Later that afternoon, a large rusted bus carrying suitcases on its roof and filled with villagers pulled up to the checkpoint and I stepped in. The driver crossed over into a nearby village and from there I found a cab heading into Damascus. Along our way, the beautifully lit Ghasseoon Mountains surrounding Syria's ancient capital were the first wonder that struck me. To me, they resembled a beautiful bride with glittering multicolored gems adorning her bosom. This was an image – a dream – I would always find myself drifting back to.

A New Identity

"Oh my God, for the age spent in exile moving
from one hotel to the next.
Oh my God, I shall taste no comfort in hotels.
Please let me find rest, please.
For all my life, I am wounded."

Muzaffar al-Nuwwab

Thus began a new chapter in the life of Monkith Saaid. He was scared and uncertain of his new identity, as well as his future. As he marveled at the images carved into the Ghasseoon mountains, the taxi driver with the stubby yellow mustache glanced at him through the front window.

"Well, where exactly do you want to go? Do you have a hotel address?" he asked Monkith.

"Can you take me to the cheapest hotel around? I will need inexpensive lodgings as I start to look for a job," Monkith replied in a tired trance.

"I can see from your accent that you are an Iraqi. My name is Abu Anjed. Please consider me your older brother here in Syria, and let me help you in whatever way I can. In fact I do know of a reasonable hotel. We'll get there in about ten minutes."

When they arrived, Abu Anjed parked his cab and escorted Monkith to the hotel. Abu Anjed quickly whispered a few words to the tall and lanky Egyptian hotel manager, who subsequently slipped some money into his pockets. As he darted out, Abu Anjed smiled at Monkith and wished him luck. For his part, the drained Monkith was shocked; the hotel was like a thick brew bubbling with prostitutes and Syrian *mukhabarat*. For the Syrian secret police enjoyed a strongly established network throughout the country. If he had not been so enfeebled, he would have chuckled at the irony of escaping the Iraqi *mukhabarat* only to find himself forced to savor the Syrian *mukhabarat*'s eager questions.

As he left his passport with the manager, the *mukhabarat* surrounded him. "Who are you, kid, and what are you doing in this hotel?" one of them asked grouchily as he picked through the field of lint on his own dull gray sweater.

"I am just a tourist. I checked into this hotel just for the evening," he said tersely, trying to disguise the fear that nibbled away at him.

No one replied or asked him another question, but they vanished behind the thick shadows and odors that impregnated the decaying walls. Carefully, he trudged through the corridor and found his room. He entered the small room with the peeling yellow paint and locked the door behind him. He concealed himself in a corner of his room, and several times he hovered by the door to make sure he had shut it properly. When he was convinced that it was bolted, he gained the courage to shed his clothes and take a shower. Barefoot, he tiptoed over the damp, black-stained bathroom floor. He placed his shivering, naked body under the loose showerhead, which emitted a few thin drops of cold water. Then he wrapped the reeking towel around his body and fell onto the bed, pulling the flimsy sheets tight over his face to escape the images of death and decay that the fierce humidity had encrusted on the discolored walls.

Frightened that the *mukhabarat* would send him back to Iraq, early the next morning he checked out of the hotel, and for a few months he changed hotels frequently enough so as to make it difficult for anyone to trace him. Then one day he met a Syrian man named Ali who was traveling to Turkey. He asked Ali to contact his parents and let them know he had arrived safely; he understood that he might endanger his family if he telephoned them directly at this point. A month later Ali called Monkith from Turkey. He told him that when he called Naji to let him know that his son had arrived safely in Damascus, the nervous Naji immediately replied that he must have the wrong number and hung up the phone.

To his horror, Monkith discovered through some Iraqis who arrived in Syria a few months later that his name was listed second on a Baath party execution list. The list had circulated in Baghdad the day after he fled. Everyone on the list but him was duly executed. He was then placed on a list of names of men who had escaped and whose family was now surveyed. Years later, Monkith learned that his father was summoned once a week by the *mukhabarat* and questioned as to his missing son's whereabouts.

"Listen, Hajj Naji, any correspondence or telephone contact with your son must be reported, or else the entire family will surely suffer," one of the prominent *mukhabarat* officers promised him.

Naji was terrified. "As I have told you before sir, I am a fervent supporter of the regime, but my eldest son turned out to be the black sheep of the family. In fact I expelled him from our household long before his disappearance. That is something you must know. The rest of the family is absolutely innocent. You must believe this," he informed the officers.

The officer observed him closely, and Naji later discerned him jotting down some thoughts on paper, "Father is innocent, ashamed of son's behavior... bring him in for questioning regularly, he will cooperate..."

Naji and Nuriya searched Monkith's room. They gathered up nearly all the letters, book summaries and journal entries they found, and buried them in their garden. Thus was their eldest son's existence metaphorically wiped out of Griyat.

Meanwhile after a few months of aimless wandering, Monkith met an Iraqi man named Jabber who had also escaped Iraq a few years earlier. Jabber offered to help him procure a residence permit for Syria. Monkith duly paid him one hundred and fifty liras for the entrance permit and another twenty-five liras to bribe the police to stamp it officially. With this newfound security, Monkith, worn out from constantly changing hotels, located a small, dilapidated room perched on an apartment building's roof, which the proprietor often used as a storage space and sometimes rented to poorer people for about one hundred and fifty liras per month. The wooden walls were supported by a mud consistency mixed with plants, which became hard upon drying. The room choked with damp humidity when the cold, relentless winter rain and snow brushed against the roof and water seeped through its walls.

As he flopped onto his bed and struggled to fall asleep, his dirty woolen blanket molded from humidity failed to warm him. He lay on his back and lifted his frozen legs against the walls. When this did not alleviate his pain, he brought his swollen, aching feet closer and hid his toes in his mouth to find warmth in his saliva as he sucked on them. After a time he gathered a few liras together and bought an old blow dryer, portable heater, metal teapot, and old broken radio from an Iraqi who was returning to Iraqi. He hooked the blow dryer to a pipe he found in a pile of rubbish and pointed it at his feet as he slept. Afraid that the pipe would break from the heat, he turned the blow dyer on for just a few minutes to unthaw his feet, and then he unplugged it. In the evenings to warm up his exhausted bones, he boiled water in the small metal teapot and let it simmer through the night. But one morning he awoke to find that the entire outer layer of the teapot had burnt and left behind a horrible, suffocating smell.

His friends who did not have places to sleep flocked to his room. He offered them his bed and moldy wool blanket and he himself slept on the cold floor. Monkith and his friends stayed up surrounded by the dim light given off by his small lamp, listening to the tunes, which surged from his broken radio. They cried and sang together as they listened to the cassettes of Iraqi singer Sadun Jabber:

My mother is faithful to me and takes care of me.
If you are dispossessed of your gold,
You can find more in the gold market.
If you are deprived of your lover,
Perhaps in one year you shall forget her.
But if you lose your homeland,
Where can you find another?
Oh, what the homeland does to me.
Oh, my God,
The fire of the homeland burns inside me.

In the meantime, Monkith found a job working in a plastic comb factory owned by the Haddad family. And a couple of months later, a stroke of luck occurred when he met an older Syrian man who put him in contact with the University of Damascus. When the Admissions Department saw his high school diploma, they told him he could choose among the most prestigious subjects: dentistry, electrical engineering, and the hard sciences. Monkith decided to obtain his bachelor of science in interior design, which in Arabic literally means "engineer of design." The degree meant little to him. He pursued it only to please his father who insisted he study engineering and the sciences. To fulfill his own dreams, he attended classes in sculpture in the Fine Arts Department and interned with the well-known Syrian sculptor Nashat Radoon.

But studying was no easy task considering the fact that he attended class from eight in the morning until four in the afternoon, and then worked in the comb factory from seven in the evening until seven the next morning. This left him with only an hour or so in the morning to rest. Despite his chronic cold, he continued to work his hardest, realizing that he was lucky to have this second shot in life. And so he rejoiced at the chance to live through the brittle chill of winter that seeped through his mud walls and to work long hours through the night at the comb factory.

Mr. Haddad's father had established the comb factory near the Hamidiyeh district prior to World War I, and since that time none of the handmade mechanical equipment or supplies of the family-run business had been updated. The workers used old, badly oiled metal machines to gash the combs. As Monkith slid the plastic under the extremely sharp cutter of the machine, he splattered water over it, so that when combined with the machine's heat, he could pierce the edges of the comb. As he splashed water, it spilled over his clothes and drenched his bloody hands already injured from the cutter. He was too exhausted and grateful for the job to lament the rheumatism, which would surely hunt down him in the future.

Monkith was the only Iraqi and the youngest worker in the factory. His income was the lowest. He worked ardently, aspiring to save money and travel to France or Germany. He never took a break so that he could finish making the required one thousand combs and leave as early as possible to catch up on his studies. Yet as many combs as he made, as bloody as his hands became, and as tired as he grew, his pile never seemed to stack high enough. The Egyptian manager, Ahmad, with a cold mocking smile, continued handing him more and more plastic to incise. Monkith's mound never seemed to have more than two hundred and fifty combs. He never fathomed what the secret was behind his inability to create a heap of combs as hard as he worked, until one evening, he caught Ahmad distributing Monkith's combs to the other workers. Monkith had secretly suspected Ahmad, for Ahmad had begged Monkith to sleep with him and when he adamantly refused, the infuriated Ahmad did all he could to hurt him. He questioned Mr. Haddad's trust of Monkith, and tried everything to raise doubts against the newcomer. But no matter what Ahmad said or did, Mr. Haddad's affection and confidence in Monkith never ruffled. He and his wife no longer had children at home, as both their daughters were abroad, and so they often invited Monkith to dine with them. They envisioned their own daughters alone in a foreign city in Europe and wished to help Monkith, so that God would assist their own daughters in finding the warmth of strangers.

But on that evening when Monkith first caught Ahmad furtively passing out his combs to other workers, who were exerting no effort, he had had enough. His hands were bloody, his clothes were soaked in water, and he was overcome by fatigue.

"God curse you! What the hell are you doing? You son of a bitch! You can't give my combs to the others," Monkith screamed.

"You ingrate! I have done no such thing, you dirty dog. You liar, now get back to work or you are fired," responded an infuriated Ahmad as he clenched his fists at Monkith.

With his bloody hands, Monkith threw down the plastic and stormed out of the factory into the pouring rain. His face and hands were bloodstained, his clothes drenched. The cold rain mingled with his tears and froze the blood on his face. The thought of returning to his damp mud room and searching for another job sickened his senses. It seemed like hours that he was wandering and then sitting in a bar, but he had lost all sense of time and he could not tell where he drifted anymore. He longed for warmth; he yearned for a sense of belonging. He sank into delirium and passersby looked at him with fright as he tumbled to the ground...

I fantasized that as I hobbled, I beheld a beautiful young woman in front of me on the street corner. Her eyes were outlined in heavy kohl and her lipstick was a blackish red. Her headscarf was wrapped loosely around her hair and a few pieces of hair hung loosely around her oval olive face. I gaped at her for just a moment, while she glanced at me from the corner of her eye. She then disappeared, but a moment later she ambled alongside me, beseeching me to pursue her. I followed her down the alley and the two of us were silent as we ascended the four flights of stairs that led to her small apartment.

She turned on the lights, and in silence, she removed her headscarf and let down her long black curly hair. She searched for cotton that she could soak in hot water to wipe off the blood that lined my face and hands. She sat me down next to the heater and offered me a robe to wear. Tenderly, she rubbed the cotton on my face. She kissed my forehead, my eyes, my hands. Her lips brushed against mine and they fused tightly together. I helped her shed her clothes and my robe slipped underneath us. I passed my arm around her waist. Our bodies were entwined, and it was not until later when she lit a cigarette and the two of us smoked, that we ended the magical moments' lull.

She confided in me: 'I have been married for four years now, but my husband is never around. He is a chauffer who works between Syria and Saudi Arabia. He comes every other week.'

I held her tight and listened to her stories. I returned every day when I had an hour or so between school and my odd jobs. I felt calm and at peace with her. She prepared Damascene delicacies for me and let me take warm showers and nap under soft, crisp sheets. Like her, I needed the kindness and affection I had lost ages ago. She too was frustrated – filled with sexual desire that her husband did not care for – he knew how to make money, but not love. For the first time in a long time, she felt the warmth of another human being. It was just a few months later when she announced that she was pregnant, and that shortly after the birth of the baby, she and her husband would move to Saudi Arabia.

On the day her child was born, her husband was traveling again. She called me, 'Darling, my sister has just left. You must come over soon, your son needs you...'

'My son needs me, my son needs me?' I wondered. I was still not sure what any of this meant.

For a few days before her husband arrived, I visited daily. I bought the infant a soft blue blanket and laid it underneath him. I peered down at the infant's small smiling face with large hazel eyes. The baby laughed when I tickled his feet. I wrapped the baby's tiny fingers around my hand, and the baby's feet and arms jumped up and down. I was scared to get too close, though, for the baby and his mother were leaving soon and she told me that I would never see them again. Several days later, her husband sent for them... 'Wait, my son, my son'... I ran after the car driven by a chauffeur, screaming 'my son, my son'...

He could not tell for how long he slept, but he woke up the next day with a pounding headache. The floors were lined with filth and he was sick with a fever. His hair and clothes were damp. He had no sense of time and what had happened the day before. With his battered nerves, he prepared to leave for class and then look for a new job. Everything seemed hopeless. He was lost. His mind was in shambles.

Meanwhile, back in Iraq Saddam ousted and assassinated the ailing Bakr, and assumed the presidency. He showered himself with one hundred and two names, to give the impression that he was more powerful than God, who only enjoyed one hundred names, of which man knows ninety-nine. Saddam's goal, of course, was to continue cultivating fear in the hearts of Iraqis. He passed a law that stated that all Iraqi students must return to their country immediately, or face a prison sentence of five years and be stripped of passport and nationality. And then he promulgated a second law that raised the prison sentence to fifteen years.

Syria and Iraq had enjoyed a brief period of political and economic union that was quickly severed when Saddam Hussein came to power in 1979. Shortly thereafter, all diplomatic ties between the two countries ended. A strong personal animosity existed between Saddam and Syrian President Hafez al-Assad. Syria, under the leadership of Hafez al-Assad, refused to send home Iraqis living within their borders. Unlike countries such as North Yemen, Jordan, Saudi Arabia and many nations of Eastern Europe, which cooperated with Saddam, Syria was a safe haven for Iraqis. Although Syria did not send Iraqi students back, about ninety percent of them decided to return home voluntarily. Upon their return, some were imprisoned or put to death by Saddam. Others would lose their lives fighting in the series of bloody and destructive wars that ensued in Iraq.

Monkith refused to turn back to Iraq. He did not place importance on nationality or citizenship. Freedom was all that mattered to him. As a result of his decision to stay in Syria, the Iraqi government revoked his passport and citizenship. But to stay in Syria he needed an official identity, so he began to buy a series of cheap fake Iraqi passports from those who sold passports for a living. Thus began many years of knowing that he was now not officially registered as existing anywhere in the world.

While the Syrians did not force Iraqis to return to their country, they required them to report once a week to the Syrian *mukhabarat* headquarters. It was always the same drill: awaiting them was a questionnaire filled with some one-hundred-and-fifty questions. Who were your father and mother? Your uncles, aunts, and distant cousins? Have you ever come into contact with any Iraqi *mukhabarat*?... Then came the verbal interrogations by the officers.

The stultifying weekly visit to the Syrian *mukhabarat* became part of Monkith's routine. One summer afternoon, he had the misfortune of being questioned by a grumpy, sleep-deprived officer with a bright red face. Dressed in a dark brown shirt, the officer sat at a wobbly metal table. The smell of *araq* seeped from the officer's breath as he began to read the questionnaire, hunting for some element of harassment. Then he looked Monkith directly in the eye and, in a strong village accent, grumbled: "You have written that you do not know any Iraqi *mukhabarat*. You seem sure of that, but does that mean that you have intentionally searched them out?"

Monkith, whose good nature always compelled him to joke, even when it was injudicious to do so, answered: "I am a student. If I start searching out Iraqi *mukhabarat*, what will you do for a living?"

That was it. The officer stared at Monkith for a moment and then jumped from his seat in a rage. He ripped the thick questionnaire into pieces and spit on it. Then he called his boss to punish the headstrong student who had the arrogance to crack a joke at the officer's expense.

A second policeman led Monkith down a hallway into another room. There was no one in the room at first, just a long brown table about four meters long, a familiar picture of Syrian President Hafez al-Assad hung on the wall, and a multitude of papers on the desk next to a cup of coffee. A moment later, an older man, tall and slim, wearing a clean white shirt, entered the room. Without glancing at Monkith, he took a seat at the desk and began to shuffle through his papers and sip from his coffee.

Then he lifted his head and asked:

"What is your name?"

"Monkith Saaid."

"What do you do?"

"I am an Interior Design student in the Fine Arts Department at Damascus University."

The officer noted that Monkith answered as if bored. To get his attention, the officer snapped: "I am going to bring in two men to make you forget the milk you drank from your mother's breasts! What do you think about that?"

Monkith responded dryly: "After living in exile far away from my family, depressed, starving, malnourished, and always afraid, with only the al-Hamra cigarette[30] to puff on, I believe I have already paid a high price for my life, and that nothing else can hurt me."

The policeman stared at Monkith – he was expecting some clenched fists and a less articulate answer. He was astonished to behold a cultured young man in front of him. He began to ask Monkith about his studies and his art. To his own surprise, Monkith found the older man to be quite cultured as well. By the end of their conversation, the powerful officer expressed a desire to help Monkith. He asked what he needed. Monkith answered that he did not lack anything, but he explained that the requirement to fill out the same questionnaire weekly was distracting him from his studies. The officer promised to take his name off of the interrogation list. That way, his weekly visits would be much less tiring, and he could focus on his studies instead.

Monkith was grateful, but he still faced daunting challenges. He was still one of the poorest students at Damascus University, and he lived on the very edge. Fortunately, though, during his second year of study, he had the opportunity to leave his humid clay room and move into the university housing located in Mesaken Berzah.

To put himself through university, he continued to work an odd assortment of evening jobs such as washing dishes in the Green Valley Restaurant[31] and hauling trash. His grueling schedule still allowed for little time to sleep before classes in the morning. His job at the restaurant did not last long, though. He began by washing dishes in the kitchen, but one day the owner spotted him, "My how you are handsome. You should not be washing dishes, we need to get you out on the floor, waiting tables."

That day Monkith quit. He did not wish to wait tables and appear before the customers. When washing dishes, in the shadows of the kitchen, he was anonymous. And this is what he desired. That is when he began hauling trash. An Egyptian friend named Hassan worked during the day with a laundry service and then from two to five in the morning he towed trash. He confided to Monkith that he earned a lot of money this way, about three thousand liras per month.

"I am engaged and want to marry soon. I dream of buying a house. And so I have to work any job I can get. What is more, I am the only son in my family, and so every month I have to send money to my mother and four sisters in Cairo. Do you want to start working with me?" Hassan asked. And Monkith readily agreed to join him.

Monkith and the others in the dark of the night wore masks as they collected trash, so no one could recognize them. During the break they all ate sandwiches. They spoke with each other through the veil of fake names. But years later he learned that they were all poor students like himself, choked with dreams, with only empty specters to lean on.

Every day after working his odd jobs, an exhausted Monkith met his friend, Osama, another poor student who like Monkith could not afford the bus. Together, from Mesaken Berzah they walked the several miles to the university at Baramkeh, munching tiredly on their plain loaves of bread. On their way, they passed a shwarma restaurant, whose plump chickens roasted in an open oven on the restaurant porch. The wonderful aroma of those roasting birds followed the two hungry students to the university, permeating their skin and their surroundings. Each time,

---

[30] These are among the cheapest cigarettes in Syria.
[31] Al-Wadi al-Akhdar in Arabic.

they commented on the torture of being forced to inhale the delicious smell of those chickens. They imagined the taste of meat, chicken, and cheese on their empty breads. One day Osama came up with a plan. He asked Monkith to hold onto his books. He ran up to the shwarma stand and dipped his bread close into the oily roast. Then the two young men ran off. Once they had put a little distance between the restaurant and themselves, they stopped and split the piece of bread now seeped in the tasty shwarma oil. They devoured it together, agreeing that it was the most delicious meal they had ever consumed.

At night when he returned to his dorm room he shared with a Kuwaiti philosophy student, he dealt with further abuse. His roommate's face and body were filled with large red pimples, and his personality was drowned in a vast sea of neuroses. Monkith owned a few shirts and pairs of pants at the time, and his roommate borrowed them without asking. And so Monkith would in the end just give them to him. Monkith ate stale bread and cheese in the evenings while the Kuwaiti, who received a large allowance from his family every month, dined lavishly. He drank whisky and devoured a roast of chicken in front of his starving roommate. He nonchalantly offered Monkith a bite, but Monkith's dignity would not allow him to accept. He watched as the juice of the chicken rolled down his roommate's red chin and pieces of chicken fell from his mouth onto his plate.

Luckily, a few months later Monkith moved into another room with a Turkish student in the same building. He began working for a photo studio and his situation began to improve significantly. He was able to eat better and even save some money. Through indirect means so he could not be traced, he sent money to his parents, brothers and sisters in Iraq, a country sinking further and further into a devastating war with neighboring Iran. Iraq, a country once mighty and proud, whose inhabitants were once counted among the richest in the Arab world, was now engulfed in poverty. His parents could no longer survive without help from their son living abroad. His responsibility to his family lay deep in his wounded heart, and sending food and money to them was a tradition he continued for many years to come.

One winter afternoon, as heavy raindrops fell from the sky, he sat at the university cafeteria waiting to meet the Jordanian gentleman who he had hired to deliver some blankets and food to his family in Iraq. It was on that day that he met a Jordanian woman named Morra who would change his destiny forever. She was sitting at the cafeteria with Amira, a Jordanian student he knew, and after he paid the older gentleman, Amira called for him to sit down next to them. She introduced him to Morra.

"So this is the Monkith you had spoken to me about – I was expecting something else!" Morra said laughing.

"You are extremely polite," replied Monkith sarcastically.

Nevertheless, they became friends and an attraction flourished almost instantly. This lovely girl with thick long brown curly hair and deep brown eyes seemed to be the woman of his dreams. He began to write about her in a small journal he kept in his vest pocket. One day they went to lunch. After the meal he left his vest on the chair and entered the men's room. While he was gone, Morra spied the notebook in his pocket, stealthily took it out, and began to read it. She was overwhelmed by his impassioned feelings for her. She was touched by the fear he expressed in loving her. When he returned, he grew red with embarrassment when he noticed the little notebook in her hands.

"Why are you scared of loving me?" she asked. But before she waited for an answer, she admitted, "I feel the same way you do. And I am also frightened." He took her hand, and for a moment they were locked in each other's gaze.

It was a cold night and there was a steady drizzle outside. Neither carried an umbrella, but that evening they walked for hours in the rain without feeling drenched, holding hands silently. The next day, minutes seemed to stand still when they were apart, and it felt like an eternity had passed when they finally saw each other after classes that day. In the spontaneous early days of their relationship, he only caught glimpses of the future troubles. There was something strange in the fact that Morra seemed to bask in the gloom of others and undergo a depression in the site of someone else's happiness. He convinced himself that he was imagining things, and when one day she recounted for him with elation that a man and woman had divorced in her building because she had accused the husband of flirting with her, he chose to ignore the alarm signals.

Morra was the eleventh child in a line of twelve children. Her father was seventy and his wife was over fifty when they conceived her. Her parents had passed away, and she now lived in Damascus with her younger sister Lina and older brother Ali. Several months after they were intimately involved, Morra introduced Monkith to them. Ali despised Monkith upon first setting eyes on him. He envied the poor young man's ability to work hard and succeed though he had no financial support from his family. Ali had an allowance from his older brothers, but had to repeat one year after the other at the university since he spent his days drinking whisky and gambling. He felt small and insignificant in front of his sister's successful friend and when the money from the family ran out, he forced his youngest sister Lina to cease her studies and return to Amman. He allowed Morra to pursue her studies, although she lived under the continual threat that her destiny was less important than her brother's and that at any moment she could be compelled to abandon her studies. For as her father had always told her before he died, and her brothers now reminded her, a girl was much less important than a boy.

Once at the beginning of their relationship, before pain engulfed them and honesty had subsided, Morra confided to Monkith: "I feel safe with you for the first time in my life. As a child, my parents and older brothers disregarded me. I didn't eat meals with them; instead, my sisters and I served them and then ate leftovers in the kitchen with the servants. As my father kicked me, he used to tell me I was his ugly brown girl. His ugly brown girl."

Tears fell from her eyes, and Monkith kissed her fervently. "My darling, you are so beautiful. Your father was wrong. By the way, you never told me what did he do for a living."

"My father worked with customs at the border between Jordan and Syria, and he accumulated his great wealth through bribes. When we ate our meals or when he bought us anything, he always chuckled and reminded us that he was raising us through bribes. Making money always seemed laden with dishonesty. I never knew that there were other ways," she whispered, blushing.

The feeling that she was not important as well as her traumatic childhood with a tyrannical father had scarred her, but by the time Monkith realized the extent of her psychological scars, he was in love.

One evening several months later, he and Morra had an argument. He had spoken to his friend Mona, and Morra accused him of sleeping with her. As much as he swore that he could never touch another woman, she did not stop screaming at him. He returned home devastated, cursing his luck for having been ensnared by her charms. At that moment, his former Kuwait roommate knocked on the door and asked if he could have a word with him.

"How are you, Monkith? Do you have a moment?" he said as tears welled in his eyes.

"Sure, how are you?" a haggard Monkith asked.

"Not very well. It has been four months since my family has sent me more money. Could you help me?" he asked with his head bowed down.

"Actually, my situation is a bit improved and I have saved a bit. Here, take whatever you need from this envelope," Monkith said looking his former roommate straight in his eyes.

The Kuwaiti began to cry. "You are killing me with your kindness. I know I once hurt you. When we lived together I received one thousand dollars monthly from my family. I savored my food in front of you although I realized you were poor and hungry. I knew you enjoyed drinking, but could not afford such luxuries. And so I drank my whisky in front of you."

"Please, don't worry about anything. It is all in the past, I have forgotten," Monkith insisted.

"No, please let me continue. You had so much pride that you refused to eat the chicken I offered you nonchalantly. I always thought you would come to me and ask for money, but in the end it is I who am asking you for help." The Kuwaiti uttered these thoughts as tears rolled down his black eyes.

"My friend, the past is now only a forgotten canvas. All that matters is that, thank God, I am able to help you. So please take what you need from the envelope and don't mention it again. I need to leave for work, but please feel free to rest here as long as you like," Monkith said quietly as he opened the door to leave.

The Kuwaiti removed three hundred liras from the envelope and one month later, he approached Monkith saying: "Please take this envelope. I can pay you back now. I took three hundred liras and now I am adding fifty more liras for interest. Thanks so much for helping me."

Monkith took the envelope and tore it up, tossing the pieces onto the ground, shouting, "You know, nothing you ever did bothered me. Even when you ate and drank in front of me when I was starving, I never held that against you. But the fact that you are handing me an envelope filled with interest, bothers me." He said this as he stomped on the torn shreds and without looking back at him, he walked to the photo shop.

Monkith's problems did not stop at chronic fatigue and a troubled relationship with Morra. To crack down on the local bombings and killings carried out by the Muslim brotherhood, the Syrian government imposed a curfew at night. But this curfew posed a problem for Monkith who was forced to work late at night.

Late one evening, after he had finished his work in the photo studio, Monkith met his friend, Feras Saaid. The two students stayed up in Feras' apartment until about five in the morning working on an interior design project. By the time they finished, they were exhausted.

Feras recommended that they sleep for a few hours and then go to the university campus around eight a.m. to finish their project. But Monkith disagreed, convinced that if they went to sleep now, they would sleep until noon. Not only would they fail to finish their project, but they would also miss their class. So Feras relented. To remove themselves from the temptation of the comfortable bed and couch, they set off for the university campus. Its gates were open, although the campus was empty. Instead of going to Monkith's room, they headed to the roof, where they could sit in the cafeteria and buy a cup of coffee when it opened.

Suddenly, there was a rush to the roof by the Syrian *mukhabarat*. Monkith and his friend were blindfolded. Their hands were tied behind their chairs. The police slapped them and yelled that they were dirty members of the Muslim Brotherhood.

Apparently, the evening before, the student members of the Muslim Brotherhood had passed out pamphlets at the university cursing President Hafez al-Assad and his regime. They called for an Islamic government. The next morning, the police arrived to search for those student members, and Monkith and Feras had the misfortune of being caught in the crossfire. The blindfolded students, who were deemed siblings by the police because of their common last name on their passports, were carried off in a car to an unknown destination. It was to no avail when they explained that Monkith was a Communist and Feras was a Christian – secular and religious beliefs that barred them from participating in the Muslim Brotherhood. Yet their reasoned pleas were in vain.

As they sat in captivity, both young men nodded in and out of sleep. The police became furious. They believed that the two offenders did not take their situation seriously. Thus, every other moment, the policemen slapped the students and yelled at them. They called them dirty dogs. They cursed them, along with their mother and father.

Finally, as noon approached, the police called the president of the university student union to collect information on the two young men in their custody. The president, who knew Monkith and Feras personally, laughed at the episode. Neither man belonged to the Muslim Brotherhood, he assured the callers. After several hours, the officers drove the two blindfolded students back to the university and dumped them outside the gate. Once Monkith and Feras removed their blindfolds and the police were out of earshot, Feras winked at his friend: "Hah, now don't you see that it would have been better if we had just gone to sleep?"

Restless

In 1983, Monkith was poised to receive his bachelor of science in interior design from the University of Damascus. But it was not as simple as that. He was required to procure some papers and a signature from Hazem al-Qubaysi at the Iraqi Baath head-quarters in Damascus in order for the university to grant him his degree. In the beginning, Hazem promised he would look into it. In the end, however, he refused, as he knew Monkith was a Communist and political dissident. Thus Monkith was denied proof of his graduation from the university. In any case, it was a degree that meant little to him – for he had found the professors full of insecurity in the face of promising students. But he longed to dispatch the diploma to his father one day, and tell him that he had obtained the degree just to please the old man. He dreamed of the day that he could inform his father that it was now time for him to pursue the arts. His mind was made up, and he could not postpone his destiny any longer. For a few months after graduation, he continued to work closely with his mentor Nashat Radoon, who recognized his protégé's innate talent, and taught him certain secrets of the trade.

At the Rawagh Gallery in Damascus, there was a group exhi-bition for Syrian artists. Monkith was still nervous and uncertain about his talent, but when the director of the gallery invited him to join the other artists, he agreed to participate. As he could not afford wood or bronze, he used stereo pore and gyps, the cheap-est material available to him, to sculpt three separate, incom-plete figures climbing a ladder at different stages. It was as if he was asking, who is stronger, the abbreviated man or the ladder? One panel consisted of the face of a man peering from inside, his hands holding tightly onto the ladder and the spectator could behold his two feet settled firmly on the ground. Another panel consisted of two hands and two feet, climbing a broken ladder. On the third panel, there was just one hand trying to grasp for breath, another hand clasping a broken step, and two feet perched underneath. Monkith himself did not attend the opening. He had invited his girlfriend Morra to accompany him, but she did not show up on time. When she came later in the evening to meet him at his room, she told him that he was nothing more than a failure and had no future as an artist. "Why don't you just commit suicide," she screamed as she stormed out of his room. That evening the darkness of his room drew him in and he swallowed countless pills before falling asleep. In the morning, he opened his startled eyes and saw Morra sitting next to him on his bed holding the empty container in hands. "Oh, you opened your eyes," she said sadly, "you'll have to try harder next time."

Although he never made it to the opening, he read in the newspapers that although the Culture Minister admired the strangeness of the work, no one knew how to describe it, nor could anyone determine whether it was a painting or a sculpture. Was it art? some asked themselves, and if so, where must it be placed? Some declared that it belonged to an Iraqi school of art; while Monkith wondered what in fact was an Iraqi school and why it was that his art should be placed there. Despite the criticism or complements, people noticed that there was a newly blooming young artist in their midst.

Monkith, however, grew restless. His relationship with Morra had deteriorated, and he was hunted down by the Iraqi *mukhabarat* in Damascus because of his Communist party affiliation. He fled to friendly South Yemen. North Yemen was not an option since its government was closely aligned to Saddam Hussein's political machine. The Iraqi *mukhabarat* network there was powerful. It sought out Iraqis and returned them to their native soil where they were harshly punished.

In South Yemen, Monkith was safe. In Aden, the capital of South Yemen, he took up teaching sculpture in the Fine Arts Institute. Yet, he soon grew restless in this country filled with humidity and deathly heat where the sun seemed to crown his head. He left South Yemen less than a year after his arrival. He passed a few days in Djibouti, Eritrea, and Somalia in transit to al-Habesha, renamed Ethiopia after a revolution by General Mangestu Hila Miryam toppled the Emperor Haile Silasi.

Monkith remained in Ethiopia for a few months, teaching English and art under the auspices of an independently run human rights organization. He lodged himself in one of the for-

259

mer Emperor Haile Silasi's castles turned hotels. In the early morning, he sat at his bedroom window with a bottle of *araq* and watched as the rising sun ushered in a new day. Each day, at the moment before the splendor of dawn, he was mesmerized by the mantle of royal blue reflected in a large pond beyond his window.

Giraffes, zebras, gazelles, and other wild animals gathered peacefully at the pond's waters. They played and roughhoused a bit, but the beasts that frolicked beneath his window never hurt each other. Little by little, the dark blue was transformed into a thick purple. The sun slowly began to rise, and little by little the animals abandoned the pond. By the time the animals had disappeared, the glorious dark red sun burst over the horizon and spread its rays across the sky and reflected onto the water. The cool shadows of the night gave way to an infernal heat and an oppressive humidity, which seemed to have no end.

To Monkith, a romantic leftist opposed to all forms of dictatorship and power, the harmony he perceived among the animals contrasted sharply with the world around him. Why couldn't humans live in a world where they could drink from one source and share with each other peacefully? Why couldn't the world be a place where no one hated the other, where each person had rights, and each took what they needed and left the rest to others? As he observed relative harmony among the animals, it struck him that, in many ways, the human species could learn a thing or two from the animals outside his window.

Alas, the sojourn in Ethiopia was not to last. When détente developed between Saddam Hussein's government and Ethiopia, members of the Iraqi *mukhabarat* attempted to arrest Monkith and send him back to Iraq. Once again, he was forced to flee to South Yemen, this time aided by his friends. At first, the Yemeni government refused him entry, for the country was struggling with its own fomenting civil war. Eventually, though, permission was granted. But the hospitality was a mixed blessing. The local water so troubled his kidneys that he was compelled to fly back to Syria.

Upon his arrival in Damascus, he learned that war had broken out in Yemen. In fact, it was a stroke of luck that he had taken the last plane back to Syria. When he turned on the television, he saw that the very house where he had lived in Toahi, the center of Aden, had been bombed the day he left. Many of his friends in South Yemen had been killed.

And so now in the middle of the 1980s, Monkith found himself back in Syria, the country of his university days, living in a bleak little room on Shah Bandar Square with a whimsical old landlady.

And the Window Was Always Open...

The window was always open. The discussions and bouts of drinking continued through the night.

The Iran-Iraq war loomed on. Monkith had heard no news from his family. He had only heard from Iraqi friends traveling in Syria that his grandmother Fatema had died one day as she was praying. The next day, they told him, his grandfather followed her to his grave. How he longed to be a child again and eat fish from his grandmother's slender hands. But how far away those lovely days of his childhood seemed to him now.

Monkith had slowly worked his way out of poverty thanks to the success of his polyester business. With the help of a friend in Jordan, he sent a huge lorry filled with food and clothes to his family in war-torn Iraq. For a moment his enterprise enjoyed a time of great prosperity. But then one day, an older Iraqi man named Abu Omar approached him. He held his daughter in his arms:

"My son, please take pity on me. Do you see this little girl in my arms? I don't even have milk for her. My family is starving. Please do something to help me. I will do anything if you hire me."

Monkith took pity on the man and the poorly dressed infant he held, "It is no problem sir. My polyester business is thriving. There is no reason we should not both be able to share in the profits. You shall be in charge of finances. Here is the key to the safe. What is mine is yours."

Monkith's trusting and detached nature proved damaging in this instance. Little by little, Abu Omar began to steal from Monkith. One day, when Monkith, who was not keeping tab of his money, went to collect the receipts, he saw that all of the factory money had been stolen. Within a matter of minutes, he went from comfortable to poor.

"Curse my fate. All the money is gone. Where is Abu Omar? He was in charge, he must have an explanation," Monkith cried out.

"Abu Omar is not at work today, and he will soon be leaving for Denmark," said one of the workers, who had foreseen this disaster.

"I swear, he will pay for this," screamed Monkith, "You tell Abu Omar when you see him, that he will pay for this. Do you see my dirty old shoe I am wearing? Tell him that it will leave its dark traces on his face, so that whenever he looks at himself in the mirror, he will remember me." A few weeks later when Monkith found him at a local café, he did indeed keep his word…

And so in the midst of the brutal Iran-Iraq war, he found himself suddenly destitute again. To make matters worse, his troubled relationship with Morra had gone from bad to worse forever. They broke up before he traveled to Yemen, but when he returned to Damascus over a year later, she contacted him. She told him how miserable she was without him. She had graduated from university and was now working as a teacher in Jordan. But she was expected to hand over all the money she earned to her older brothers who refused to work. They lived off the land their father had accumulated and preserved the tradition of living off of bribes. When Monkith agreed to try to start over again, Morra moved back to Damascus to escape the tyranny of her brothers. Monkith and Morra's relationship was rekindled briefly, though it never experienced again the magical moments of the first few months.

Monkith was still a young artist, building his reputation. Although his situation was improving once again as he slowly rebuilt the polyester business, he was uninspired by material possessions, and preferred to give away his money than burden himself with luxury. But Morra dreamed of "owning" an enormous villa and a husband who worked a regularly fixed schedule and honored her with comfort. In any case, Monkith certainly could not compete with an older, famous and wealthy Jordanian writer who had taken an interest in his girlfriend. The older man had wanted to marry a Christian woman, but when he met this pretty Muslim girl, he changed his mind. Morra enjoyed the game of cat and mouse she played with the writer behind Monkith's back.

One evening, Monkith struggled to drift into an agonized sleep. He was in Damascus and Morra was visiting her family in Amman. Nightmares filled his soul, and when he woke up shivering, he could feel in his heart that something was terribly wrong. Unable to fall asleep again, he transferred images from his nightmares onto an old piece of polyester. Through the night he carved a long, frightened arm, shooting upwards, with its sharp veins gushing forth. Every nerve and every muscle stood out on the arm. A head of an old man was cupped at the tip of the hands – a terrified head with its eyes and mouth wide open as if screaming wildly into the silence of the night. The screams pierced his ears and sweat gathered at his brows. Something was off. He felt Morra was not at home. She was somewhere else. But it was four in the morning, where could she be? He called her home, but no one answered. He tried again and again, until her younger sister woke up and picked up the receiver. The half-dazed girl whispered into the phone that her sister was not home; she was spending the night with her girlfriend, Sharifa. "I am sure Morra will call you tomorrow," she promised as she hung up the phone, not even waiting for his reply.

Three weeks later when Sharifa visited Damascus, Monkith asked her if Morra was with her that ill-fated night and if not where she was. She told Monkith that no, Morra was not with her, she was with the older writer who continued to woo her.

When Monkith finally learned of her betrayal, he broke up with her once and for all. But he was devastated. He became disgusted with his own shadow and could not longer look at himself in the mirror. Morra's words rang loud through his head, "You are a good for nothing artist, a looser, why don't you just end your grief and commit suicide?" Only the haze of *araq* could bring him a little relief from his ever-deepening depression.

He began to dig his own grave with both hands, always drunk and lost. He wandered the streets aimlessly. Repelled by his dreaded room, he left his key on the front door so that even when he was not there, his friends could continue to congregate and fill their evenings with drinking and discussions. For himself, he preferred to spend his evenings in the local bars.

Sometimes the tired Monkith stumbled into his room early the next morning and found strangers among the familiar faces. Sitting on his chair, sleeping in his bed, they turned to the "intruder" with curiosity. They asked him who he was, what he wanted? With no room to sit down or even sleep, he set out in a drunken trance to find some nearby alley or bench in Sepky Park where he might lie down.

Even the dreaded garden rat, which had stubbornly clung to the despised residence, met a dreary fate. It became addicted to the wretched *araq* that often spilled on the floor during an evening's soirée. After all the visitors left, the rat crept into the room and licked up the colorless "water." One night, it crawled out of the apartment in a drunken haze, and met its untimely death in the gutter of the nearby alley.

Monkith, who descended into the world of the living dead, was hardly in better shape than the rat. At the break of dawn, after finding himself still alive in some unknown place, he headed off in search of *araq*. His favorite haunt became a bar called Freydi's on al-Abed street, in the Salahiya section of Damascus.

Freydi's was part haven, part dungeon. The patrons formed a family of alcoholics trapped in a bar filled with the sickeningly sweet and sour odors of *araq* and beer. The atmosphere, with its cheap broken lights, flaking paint, tin plates nailed onto the table, and old-fashioned music, resembled a factory pumping out death. Freydi's was a way stop on the path to a certain and untimely end. The camaraderie masked the bar's role as an executioner hurrying its patrons towards their coffins.

The professional drinkers who regarded Freydi's as a second home bonded tightly together. One day one person paid, the next day another paid. They shared their food. They revealed the secrets of their miserable lives. They felt safe with one another, sensing the others' unlucky twists of fate that pushed them into despair. They cared for each other as if they were one family in the midst of a hostile and alienating world – a family, Monkith reflected, so different from his own.

Mostly men frequented Freydi's, although it had also been honored by a visit from the Syrian poet Daad Hadad. At the time she hovered at Freydi's, she was mending a broken heart. She loved an Iraqi who had left her and returned to Iraq. Eventually, life's hardships drove her mad and pushed her to an early death. It was not just poets, novelists, journalists, and artists who drowned their sorrows at Fredyi's. Ironically, it became a watering hole for once-powerful military men and government officials. These men, formerly part of the Syrian government's apparatus, had been laid off or forced into early retirement. They had lost their posts and with them, their confidence in life and in themselves. Their pasts were not held against them. All that was required of them to become loyal patrons of Freydi's was that they had lost all hope in life.

Joseph, the owner of Freydi's, was a chubby man with a perennially jovial expression. He always cracked jokes and tried to make his customers smile. After one too many friendly food fights, he had nailed the dinner plates onto the tables, and now he walked around throughout the evening, tossing water onto the tin plates to clean them. As he performed this task, he kept a close eye on his customers' needs. He understood what they wanted through their most subtle facial expressions. He intuitively sensed when someone needed a new drink, and he kept meticulous mental records of what everyone owed. If someone said they owed for five cups, he corrected them and said that it was four. Every time he saw Monkith, he complained with his usual sense of irony:

"My God, your cursed president Saddam Hussein owes me twenty-five liras that he did not pay the last time he was here."

Each time the exhausted, but good-natured Monkith answered:

"Okay, man, let me pay fifty liras to get rid of this irritating chatter of yours."

But Joseph chuckled and always refused to accept the fifty liras, saying that he wanted Saddam Hussein himself to pay him back.

Monkith was the youngest among the patrons. He became close friends with the other customers, sharing his secrets and listening attentively to theirs. Writer Abdullah Saqi spent mornings with him at Freydi's, since it served served araq from seven a.m. until one p.m. in the afternoon. At one p.m. the haggard friends left Freydi's together. They headed for other bars. Abdullah bade farewell to Monkith at two or three a.m. A few hours later, they met again at Freydi's.

Every morning, Abdullah tried to give Monkith an orange to eat for breakfast. But Monkith refused the acidic fruit and looked instead for a pomegranate. A bad stomachache following the drunken binge invariably plagued him, and he knew a pomegranate could help cure the pain. Once he felt better, he continued the bouts of drinking.

During this time in Damascus, there was a curfew that began at eight in the evening. The Syrian government was still trying to suppress the Muslim Brotherhood. And so Monkith, returning home drunk at off hours of the night, always violated the curfew. One very early morning, as Monkith was drifting to his dismal room in a drunken stupor, two members of the Syrian *mukhabarat* stopped him. Monkith clung desperately to his little plastic bag with bread, an empty bottle of *araq*, and Herman Hesse's *Steppenwolf*. The *mukhabarat* interrogated the practically unconscious young man: What was he doing out at that hour? What was he carefully guarding in his bag? For the bag stayed firmly locked in Monkith's hands as if it contained secret objects. The two men forced him to turn over the little sack and peered inside. Its strange collection of items made them gaze at the besotted young man in surprise. What could he possibly think was so important about an empty bottle of *araq*, a stale piece of bread, and a ripped paperback novel?

Monkith's answer only deepened the mystery. He told them that the contents of this bag were all he needed in life. Laughing, they let him go, though both parties knew this was not a final good-bye. They were sure to bump into each other again.

The famous Iraqi poet Muzaffar al-Nuwwab, who lived in Syria at the time, could no longer allow Monkith to slowly commit suicide in front of his eyes. Al-Nuwwab quickly set about organizing an invitation for Monkith to teach in Tripoli, in alcohol-dry Libya. When the offer came, Monkith accepted it with reluctance. He was already shattered.

After he severed ties with Morra, one evening by chance in the Salahiya district, he ran into Alia, a close friend from his university days. He asked if she would meet him the next day at the Hafez al-Assad monument.

"Hello Alia, I want to marry you! Will you marry me?"

"Well, Monkith, you're so romantic!" she said sarcastically.

"Aren't you going to bring me a present or whisper to me why you love me? No I will not marry you!"

"Okay, but can we stay friends?"

"Yes, we will always stay friends," she replied.

Before leaving Damascus, he stopped at one of his old haunts, the Rodha Café, and announced that he was distributing free books. People he knew and others he did not stopped by his room on Shah Bandar Square to see for themselves. Umm Fadi and her son Abu Baha were ready to be rid of Monkith, and made it clear that they wanted none of his belongings left behind. He tried to save the large sculpted panel wedged above the door that separated his room from Umm Fadi's – the figure of the man climbing a broken ladder, the old woman peering from thick bars, and the face of the women deformed by sorrow. He wished to give it to his bar hopping companion, Abdullah Saqi. But Abu Baha, anxious to be rid of the unkempt tenant, broke it into pieces and threw it out before he had a chance to pick it up. He obliterated him by throwing away his beloved memories even before he had departed.

On his final day in Damascus, surrounded by many of his friends in his nearly empty room, Monkith pulled his home-made faux window off the wall. He placed it on the ground. Everyone in the room laughed and cursed at him, saying:

"You scoundrel! How you fooled us all this time into thinking there was a real window in this room, and that the window was always open...

My dreams. Where are they? They have faded away like lucid writing erased on a chalkboard. Only piles of papers and note pads stacked before me. Scraps of crumpled sheets. Stories I have compiled over the past couple years. The day Monkith bought a donkey, his first kiss, his expulsion from high school, the story of Hamoudi and his four virgin wives... As soon as I think I have reached closure on my novel, in the late hours of the night he whispers a new story. My paper and pen make him nervous, though. Lately he is not very happy about me recording his stories. I have learned to listen closely to his tales and then register them in my mind as I slumber. I fall asleep repeating the details of his stories over and over again in my head. The next day I wake up and hastily jot down whatever I can remember on my paper. During the day, recollections from the previous night dart before me likes arrows. I catch them and write them down haphazardly on whatever sheets I can find, wherever I am. In the kitchen, in a bus, on the side of a street. Later I plan to piece everything together. I shall begin and end with the room in Damascus. I never decided it would be this way, this is just how the novel naturally flowed together. I ask Monkith if I can read him a chapter or two, to see if he agrees with the tone, but he refuses to listen to them. "I trust you," he says. "I don't need to hear what you are writing. I give you complete freedom to write as you wish. And in any case, I can't stand the constant sound of my name. That is my only advice – please avoid using my name. You are repeating it too often. Monkith, Monkith, Monkith is all I hear. I would even encourage you to change my name. Let me be anonymous." After reading my first draft, my sister also recommended that I change Monkith's name and create a fictitious character. But this suggestion I cannot take. I am proud to write his story. It is his story. The story of Monkith Saaid.

Sometimes I feel myself vanishing. I am not sure who I am anymore. Depression envelops my soul. I wonder if this body, which carries my soul, is really here. Monkith asks what is wrong, but I myself am not even sure. Whenever I walk by a mirror I turn out the lights so I cannot see myself. I wash my face, brush my teeth, comb my hair – all with the lights turned out. He comes and illuminates the bathroom, but I turn the lights off again and shut the door. I refuse to behold myself in the mirror. I am frightened of who I have become. Will I see myself as others see me? I don't know.

It has been weeks since I have been able to concentrate on my dissertation: "The Other as a Case of Cultural-Self Criticism in Eighteenth-Century France." The very name depresses me. I am drawn toward my novel "Two Grandmothers from Baghdad" – it is my forbidden love. How ironic... A forbidden love – like Monkith – a man I chose of my own will, despite my father's protest... A man I married in silence, without any announcement... While I struggle to work one hour on my dissertation, I lose myself in my novel – hours pile upon hours and I forget the time and place I began writing. Monkith comes and goes and I am still typing at the computer unwinding my stories like yarn twisted of fleece. My back burns from my stiff position, my arms begin to ache. Monkith kisses my cheeks, my neck and I am reminded that I am a woman. "So tell me, how is your dissertation going?" he asks softly as he places a tray of tea and cookies before me. He grows angry when I tell him that I have been working on my novel and that I cannot put it down, that it is more important to me than my doctorate degree in literature from Columbia University. When frustrated with writer's block, I throw a temper tantrum and fling my papers onto the ground. I announce that I don't care about my dreams anymore and threaten to quit everything – my novel, my dissertation – and tears wander in his big hazel eyes.

"Perhaps then your next story shall be about a woman once filled with dreams and ambitions. And this is what makes her attractive. She begins writing the story of an artist, her husband and partner. As she writes, she finds herself so thoroughly immersed that she begins disappearing under the canvases of his memories – the sheer tragedy of their weight. She forgets her own needs, desires. Perhaps she even goes mad." He looks into my eyes with a sadness I had never seen before. "So Rebecca, is that the story you wish you write?"

The Road Back to Baghdad

"You expelled me when I was young.
When I grew older you asked me for my blood.
Come, let us drink some wine.
Tomorrow we shall ponder serious matters."

Omr al-Qays

On September 25, 2003 I jotted down some thoughts in my journal: Last night after so many months of stiff silence, Monkith and I spoke to his mother and father. I told them how I longed to come to Baghdad and meet them, how I was almost finished writing my story, and hoped to see the village Monkith had described to me, the people he had conjured up for me, learn more about the childhood of the man I loved – this precious pearl I found in the deep sea of my restless journeys.

Relations with his family have been strained since two years earlier, when his brothers, Muhammad and Ahmad, ransacked our home and threatened our lives if we did not give them more money. Ahmad needed to pay for a visa for France, and if we did not do as we were told he said that we would have to face the bitter consequences. This was the same Ahmad who as a little boy could only fall asleep to his older brother's heartbeat. I shall never forget my fear, especially when Muhammad called and threatened Monkith that he would report all his political activities and statements against Saddam Hussein to the Iraqi *mukhabarat*. But Monkith was undaunted, and even when Muhammad told him he was recording the conversation, Monkith yelled into the phone, "You are nothing more than the son of Saddam Hussein. A coward making empty threats. Go and report me if you wish." But I was frightened. I screamed at Monkith not to utter such words into the phone, but he responded, "Don't worry. Saddam Hussein is spineless. He has created a generation of cravens in his image. Even if he disappears some day, it will take several generations to heal the scars of this beaten nation."

Despite his apparent composure, I knew something died inside Monkith's heart the day his brothers turned on him. He lost his sense of balance and confidence. I often heard him mumbling madly to himself in the darkness of the night. For he had spent his entire adult life first in Syria and then in Holland supporting them both financially and emotionally as if they were his own sons. He paid for their university education and he even gave them a large sum of money they could pay the government in return for military exemption. But Monkith said that he should have foreseen the alarm signals many years earlier when in Holland he had purchased a visa for Ahmad to come to live with him. Ahmad first went to Jordan and then called Monkith saying that he had lost his passport and would unfortunately have to return to Iraq. Could Monkith send him a large sum of money so that he could start a small business in Baghdad? Without a moment's hesitation, Monkith wired him the funds, which, Monkith later heard, both Ahmad and Muhammad used to pay for their wedding expenses and to purchase expensive cars. Ahmad never did open a business.

When our relationship with his two brothers ended, relations were also strained with his parents and sisters. His mother had traveled to Jordan to stay with Muhammad to try to find a way to make peace between the brothers, but after one month, she returned frustrated back to Iraq. One week later, war broke out in Iraq. Monkith and I watched the news of the bombings in Iraq, worried sick for his family, wishing that we had seen his mother before she left, regretting that so much tension had engulfed our relations with his parents and sisters. We knew A'dhamiyyah was heavily bombed and braced ourselves for the worst. But we had no news of them, as we were not able to get through for several months, until one day after the war, his father called and told us they were all safe. For the first time in a long time, Monkith and I we were able to truly breath again.

It was only yesterday that I told his family how much I yearned to meet them, and today, Abu Khalid, an Iraqi taxi driver who works between Iraq and Syria, and who escorted Monkith's parents to Damascus a couple of years earlier, called us and said that Monkith's father had informed him last night that we wished to come to Baghdad. And so Abu Khalid was planning to pick us up the next morning at five a.m. That way we would reach the Syria-

Iraq border at about nine in the morning, and that would be the safest time to travel into Baghdad. And in any case, the Americans did not allow cars to travel through Iraq in the night. I spent the afternoon running errands, buying sweets I was told did not exist in Iraq, packing our bags, and trying to convince Monkith that traveling to Iraq was the right thing to do.

Monkith, despite agreeing to go, still feels reluctant. He told me, "My father asked me when he visited me in Damascus why I don't ever want to travel to Iraq. I hold a Dutch passport now, so I could pass as a tourist. But then I asked my father about my childhood friends one by one, and one by one my father explained to me their sorrowful fate, either killed in wars or executed. And so I asked my father, why should I come to Iraq? I have nothing there. If I come, all I will do is weep. Perhaps this is why I hang on to my childhood memories – as a defense mechanism. These memories are, in the end, all I have left. Who knows, perhaps if I return to Iraq, I will destroy even these. I am only going for you – I know how curious you are to see where I grew up. And I realize how important this is for your novel. But after my experiences with my brothers, I feel as if I have lost Iraq forever."

"Monkith, forget the past." I told him. "You helped them leave Iraq. Muhammad is now teaching in Jordan and Ahmad has gone to France. Let us just wish them well. They will live with the regret that they lost your priceless friendship. But your conscience is clear – you did everything for them and your family all these years and now it is time for you to take care of yourself. Perhaps traveling to Iraq will help heal some scars."

But this evening I cannot sleep, and neither can Monkith. Neither of us can actually believe that we shall be traveling to Baghdad tomorrow. Neither of us knows what to expect. Is it wrong of me to risk opening up old wounds for Monkith for the purpose of the story I am writing? Is it wrong of me to wish to write this story for Monkith's daughter Maya so that she may have the chance to know her father, a chance that her mother has denied her for the past few years – ever since he met me? Will this trip to Baghdad be something I will eventually regret?

◆

As expected, Abu Khalid arrived at five in the morning – a thin dark man with clear green eyes, and an astonishing interest in other people's business. As I tried to sleep, I heard Abu Khalid asking Monkith one question after the other about what had happened to his relationship with his brothers, and I heard Monkith recounting the painful story over and over again – about how he brought his brothers to Damascus, but that they were so filled with jealousy and hate, how they began to show inexplicable hostility until in the end they robbed the apartment and made threats, and then our relationship was severed forever. All through the ride, Abu Khalid posed more and more questions, which Monkith duly answered, despite my insistence that he speak about other subjects.

A few hours later, we arrived at the Syria – Iraq checkpoint and with no difficulty at all the American soldiers let us through, waving at us and beaming. Perhaps it made them happy to see our smiling faces before them. For this was a time that the whole world was still in uproar over America's continual presence in Iraq, and President Bush's failure to catch Saddam Hussein. I was one of the Americans against the war. In one interview after another in Syria, I deplored the presence of war in the twenty-first century. After all, there had to be some diplomatic means to oust Saddam Hussein. And in any case, hadn't we Americans put him there in the first place? But as we rode past the soldiers, and we drove into Iraq, surprisingly, I felt no hostility toward my compatriots. Instead I looked at these young soldiers as the ones responsible for allowing a man exiled for twenty-six years to make an almost anticlimactic reentry – miraculous for its very simplicity. This man, who had escaped many years before, risking his life to cross the deathly cold winter desert, now entered without disguise. We traveled together into Iraq in the same banal way we drove into Lebanon or Jordan – with a bag filled with egg sandwiches, fruit, and a yogurt drink we had prepared the night before for ourselves as well as for our driver.

At about one in the afternoon, we reached Ramadiyah, a Saddam Hussein stronghold still filled with pocket resistance. The whole town was depressed and dirty. After we passed Ramadiyah, which still posed a danger, Abu Khalid stepped out of the car and called Monkith's parents reassuring them of our safety. We had passed Ramadiyah and were on our way to Baghdad. We would arrive in a little more than a couple hours.

On our way to Baghdad, we passed by some of Saddam Hussein's castles, and soon we were in A'dhamiyyah, northern Baghdad. All the while Monkith could not recognize his homeland.

"The only thing I can say is that it is obvious that the dictator who ruled all these years had as his one goal the destruction of this country," Monkith whispered as we headed into Griyat. He remembered nothing. The face of the village was scarred. All that remained of its former glory, of its magic, were the majestic palm trees gathered in thick clusters. But as with the rest of the country, the sky above them was gray, the ground below them dusty.

As the cab approached the Azawi household, Abu Khalid asked if Monkith realized where he was. He did not. But an instant later Abu Khalid announced that we were in front of his home. The glimmering grapevine trellis still overlooked the balcony of Monkith's former room, and the small palm tree his mother had planted in the garden when he was nine years old, reached up and shot up over the garden gate, which wore a dusty coat of brown. But the little birds nestled in the garden had flown away long ago when the young man who generously fed them had disappeared.

Abu Khalid beeped, the garden gate opened, his sisters, their husbands and children, poured into the street, crying and laughing. Each waited their turn to hug the long awaited visitor and the woman who now accompanied him. Manal's son Ali presented himself to us. He was now twenty-six years old, a newly graduated engineer. Tall and handsome, with bright green eyes and an innocent smile. Manal was pregnant with him on the day Monkith fled Iraq.

Monkith's eyes searched for his sisters who were hidden under their headscarves and long manteaus. Shrouded like many other Iraqi women since the early 1990s when Saddam Hussein, who gave himself the title 'Abd Allah al-Mu'min,[32]" had pro-

---

[32] The Faithful Slave of God.

moted a hypocritical religious revolution: banning alcohol, closing bars, and compelling women to veil. Those women who did not cover themselves properly were often raped by the *mukhabarat*, and so now even in Christian areas women chose to don the veil. One by one, Monkith recognized his sisters only from their distinctive eyes, smiles, and voices.

A woman, a little chubbier than the others, came forth and hugged Monkith and then me. It was Manal. I recognized her voice. We had spoken on the phone several times, but with her hazel eyes and clear skin, she was more stunning than I had imagined. But she was exhausted, mourning her six-year-old son Osama who had passed away of a mysterious illness several years before. I choked as I watched Monkith kiss his sisters Iqbal, Amal, and Ibtihal. Tears poured profusely from the eyes of his sisters, who had grown from the little girls he had left them as, into beautiful women with children of their own. Amal became an important fashion designer and beautician and the studious Iqbal was a lawyer. Ibtihal had smiling eyes and a natural knack for making others laugh. She had become the family storyteller and was now caring for her new infant son. She held her son tenderly in her arms and with her eyes sparkling in delight, she declared: "Well, I had three daughters, but my neighbor Umm Salem constantly spoke behind my back about what a pity it was I had no son. So at forty, I got pregnant once more just to show her I could also give birth to a son!" One little girl after another came forth to hug us and we struggled to learn their names. It seemed his sisters carried on Grandma Fatema's tradition of giving birth to daughters in abundance. When Iqbal put her hand on my stomach and asked if I would soon give birth to her nephew, I quickly pointed to the team of girls swarming around us, and said that if family genes had a say, I would most probably give birth to a girl. Manal chuckled and nudged me, "Rebecca's just like us. She also has an answer to everything!" And they all giggled as they hugged their brother and me ever so tightly. I barely knew them, but I felt so exuberant in the company of this wonderful and talented group of women, who I looked at as my own sisters, and as they held my hands and embraced me, the lumps in my throat gathered. I choked in order to keep myself from crying.

Monkith's brother-in-law, Hussein, came forth. Monkith embraced him tightly, thanking him profusely, telling me that this man was his true brother, who had the courage to stand by him when no one else would. Monkith asked about Hussein's friend Rashid who had also vouched for him so that he could leave Iraq. Alas, he was dead, murdered by the Baath. Hussein thanked Monkith for his support throughout the years, without which the family would never have survived. At a time when Saddam had said Iraqis should just eat shit, their family had meat, good white bread, and fruits and vegetables that others could not afford. The lorry filled with staples he had sent during the first Gulf War had fed the family for over a year. Monkith looked around and asked about his parents, and Manal said that they had gone to the doctor for their mother's weekly checkup. A moment later, they arrived. His mother limped towards her son and threw herself into his arms and then mine. His father came forward, hugged us, and welcomed us to his home.

His home… The home of Monkith's childhood. He could barely recognize it as he wandered around the house. As with the rest of the country, it looked raped and destitute. It bespoke of none of the gracious luxuries of a family supported by an eldest son who was abroad. He wondered what his brothers had done to all the money he had wired to his parents throughout the years. His parents appeared to be living like paupers. Apparently Muhammad had been in control of the money Monkith had wired all those years, distributing only a small portion to his parents and sisters, and saving the rest for himself. And after Ahmad's wedding, Monkith had sent money to buy him and his wife a bridal suite on the second floor. But with Ahmad moving to France, he abandoned his wife and son, and his wife returned to her parents. She sold all her furniture, and pillaged the remainder of the Azawi house for anything she could find.

Monkith felt like a ghost in this spoiled house. With the exception of a crack he had once made on a living room window with Manal's juggling set, Monkith's existence seemed blotted out. His own room was scorched. He was told that years earlier his brother Muhammad had set fire to Monkith's room, and all his childhood paintings were burnt. The cabinet he had locked all his treasures in was broken, and discarded in the empty hall-ways of the second floor, buried in a heap of cobwebs.

He learned that the day he left Iraq, his mother drowned in depression. Everything her eldest son left behind made her weep. Since the time he had gone to live with his grandparents, his room was locked and left untouched. Now Nuriya lay on his bed for hours mourning his absence. She enveloped herself in the chaos of his room, his torn socks piled on the floor, photo-graphs of Mervat Amin tacked on the walls, clay ashtrays hidden in his closet. As her health deteriorated, her husband took her to a doctor who recommended that in order for her to survive Monkith's emigration, she had no choice but to transfer all her love from him to her second son Muhammad. She had to con-vince herself that Monkith had died and that Muhammad had taken his place. When she and her husband buried Monkith's journals and letters to protect themselves from the *mukhabarat*, she believed that she had interred her eldest son. Little by little her love shifted to Muhammad, and Monkith's memory faded. Even his black and white photograph hanging on the mirror in the living room had the sinister look of a martyr's picture.

The very day we arrived, his parents sacrificed a lamb and distributed the meat to the poor, as was custom upon the arrival of a loved one from far away. Friends, neighbors, and rel-atives, near and far, poured forth to welcome him. He recog-nized very few of them. A seemingly middle-aged man came forward and hugged Monkith, who searched the stranger's face for familiar features. "Don't you remember me? I'm your cousin Sateh!" he whispered sadly. "Yes, yes, of course, I do," Monkith responded in disbelief. His cousin Sateh, who his father had always held up as an example of achievement, was currently unemployed. Only a few years older than Monkith, his face was now ravaged by time and hardship. The very same Sateh, who as a child was so religious that Naji looked at him in pride and gave him a leadership role when it came to recount-ing the history of Hussein's martyrdom, was now an atheist. He had spent three years in prison, since he was a member of the Da'wa Party, an anti-Baath Islamic party, and now he cursed anyone who mentioned the name of God. He cried on

Monkith's shoulders, but Monkith's tears were like stones stuck at the corners of his eyes.

Every home was mourning at least one martyr. Monkith sensed regret in his father's eyes as he stared at him. He imagined that perhaps his father was sad that he did not have a martyr that he could speak of – to be given the title *Abu Shahid*.[33]Perhaps, his father believed it was he, the eldest son, who should have been offered up in order to give his father this honor. This was what Monkith envisioned as his father complained about the fact that for years he had a weekly examination by the *mukhabarat* because of Monkith's escape. This is how Monkith felt as his father expressed disappointment that his eldest son had dropped Naji al-Azawi out of his name. "You did not respect me – you dropped my name from your name," his father said with sadness. "Rebecca," Monkith's father pleaded, "you must name your first son 'Naji' after me." I smiled and reminded him that there was a very good chance I would give birth to a girl like his own daughters. I glanced at Monkith who stared into space. His father then asked us eagerly if we wanted to visit his small shop around the corner, but Monkith said "perhaps later" as he rose and left the room. I was left alone with my father-in-law. This man who had been so hard on Monkith as a child and whom I had portrayed in all his severity, I now looked at with pity. He was suddenly an innocent, hapless child in my eyes. He huddled over the chair in his small frame and tattered white *galabia*. The skin around his clear blue eyes was devoured by time. I wondered if I had been fair in my depiction of him in my novel as he smiled and told me that he was very happy that I had entered his son's life.

Why couldn't his father understand that he had changed his name in order to ensure his family's safety? Monkith asked me that evening as we lay on the mattresses Manal and Hussein had brought for us from their home and placed on the second floor – in the room of his childhood, now raped and empty. The electricity had gone out for the third time that day. The room was

---

[33] Father of a Martyr

humid and dark, and Monkith lit his lighter and searched his bags for a bottle of *araq* and a box of cigarettes. Why did misunderstanding always have to exist between him and his father? Why did his father always have to think the worse of him? he wondered as we opened the window so that we could hide the smell of *araq* and cigarette smoke. We lay quietly together in the thick darkness of a room once familiar. In silence. I still could not believe that I was in Iraq, that I had met Monkith's family. That I had walked through the house he grew up in. I could not imagine the thoughts that must have been running through Monkith's head as he sat against the wall, sipping his *araq* and breathing heavily in his old room, which was filled with memories, both bitter and sweet.

Throughout the visit, Monkith told his family that I was writing a novel about his childhood, the local personalities, and legends in Griyat. He asked them if they remembered anything more. I described for them my stories about Umm Bassam, Hamoudi, Mehdiyeh, and Dr. Razak. "Dr. Razak," Ibtihal screamed out in laughter, "She even knows about him!" I asked questions, but I was impressed; no one knew more than Monkith. I felt that I was finally reaching closure on my story. When I asked Nuriya about Habooba and Fatema, she giggled and looked down. Her gentleness and shyness reminded me of my grandmother Zari Joon who I had spent time with several years ago in Iran. When I sat beside her, I forgot to ask about her stories but just nestled myself in her warmth. But Naji helped fill in the gaps with respect to his mother. He spoke of her with pride, telling me the story about how she was given the Persian name "Sheznah." I glanced at the good-natured Nuriya who just smiled and winked at me as her husband spoke about her mother-in-law who had tormented her in her youth. I took out a pen and piece of paper as Naji gave me the details I sorely needed.

"I would like to see these people, especially Dr. Razak. I feel I need to see him especially. Anyway, please tell me what happened to the inhabitants of this village", I pleaded.

As we sat in stunned silence, Monkith's brother-in-law Hussein told us that since the early 1980s, Saddam had planned to raze Griyat in order to build himself another castle. He

280

intended to relocate the inhabitants to a desert outside Baghdad called Nahrawan. But with one war after the other he became distracted from his plans. Although they were allowed to stay after all, the villagers still paid a heavy price for Baathi rule. By the time Saddam fell from power, at least four-hundred-and-seventy villagers had been executed, some for political activities, some for praying, and some turned in by innocent children who reported a family member who had cursed the President. This number did not include those villagers killed in the wars that ravaged the country, nor did it include the trauma and psychological scars that gnawed at most of them.

And so we heard that the feisty Umm Bassam, who used to chase her husband through the streets, had passed away after mourning the death of her sons who had either died in the wars or were killed for political reasons. Her husband was now handicapped and sat all day in a wheelchair staring through the window, lamenting the fact that with a pair of lifeless legs he was not able to make full use of his newfound freedom... The butcher Hajj Abbas was still as miserly as ever. Rumors spread that he no longer fed his own family meat. He had also opened a small vegetable and fruit store and it circulated that most of his produce was always at least two months old. He just did not feel comfortable throwing anything away.

Mehdiyeh, who had poisoned her unmarried pregnant niece Wahida, was now a widow grieving the mysterious deaths of her sons. According to the buzzing local gossip, because no one had taken criminal action against Mehdiyeh for her niece's death, it was left to Fate to exact divine retribution. Mehdiyeh was not required to turn over a sum or money or abandon her home. As the neighbors saw it, she would have to pay with life from her own family. Mehdiyeh's husband contracted a painful cancer and died a slow, agonizing death. One of her sons was killed in a car accident. Another died mysteriously. The Baath party executed two others. Because Aunt Mehdiyeh had poisoned Wahida, chimed the gossip in Griyat, God had avenged the girl's death, and misfortune piled upon misfortune in Mehdiyeh's life.

Uncle Annisse was still bitter and relations between him and his sisters were severed. Upon Fatema and Jawwad's death, he had taken revenge on his family for ending his relationship with his Kurdish fiancé Soad. He stole his siblings' inheritance and sold his parents' immense house for practically nothing to a stranger. Only Monkith's aunt Layla, who never married, lived with Annisse...

Sabiha, Monkith's first kiss at age eleven, was now three times divorced. Her two sons were killed in the Iran-Iraq war... All of Umm Hassan's daughters were married and had children of their own, but their brother Hassan was killed by the *mukhabarat*. The most beautiful woman in Griyat, Basima, and her husband had moved to Mosul. No one knew anything else about them... The elusive Dr. Razak, who had gone crazy because of his lost love, continued to roam the streets. He still appeared to be in several places at once...

Years earlier, Hatem, the movie-teller, had tried to escape with Monkith, but then had turned back. Monkith had already heard that the *mukhabarat* had killed him several years later. But now he also learned that the majority of his storytelling brothers were killed in the Iran-Iraq war. His older brother Latif had disappeared... Because he had worked closely with the Da'wa Party, the Baath executed Sheikh Khazal al-Sudani, the leader of the mosque who had caused Omar to commit suicide when Monkith was ten... Alas, a Baath party informer killed Moula Aboud, the old man who became rejuvenated like an adolescent when he turned one hundred and who used to wander the streets listening to the local gossip. It seemed he had overheard one too many stories...

The best news was about Hamoudi, who still owned his popular little vegetable store and continued to show extreme generosity towards his clients. He had given up on the idea of marriage. He repeated the popular saying that marriage is like a watermelon – you have no idea what to expect – either a sweet rosy red inside or a faded tasteless pink. So why bother taking the risk?

I was in tears by the time I had heard about the fate of people I had grown to love as I had written on them. That evening I could not fall asleep, and as we lay on the mattresses, Monkith said, "Well, now you know what it is like to ask about the fate of Iraqis. It is never that uplifting. Anyway, tomorrow I will take you to see Dr. Razak."

It was a while before Monkith's friend Fuad finally spotted Dr. Razak on a corner and picked us up to see. From the car, we saw that his white hair had grown long and he wore a dirty white *galabia*, yet his face looked more youthful than ever, even younger than Monkith's. As we approached, he began to scream and demand that we leave him alone. It seemed he could no longer recognize Monkith, the young man he had once called "Allah."

Later that day, we walked in the neighborhood with Amal. As we passed his school, Amal said that the school had tried to preserve Monkith's childhood paintings with pride throughout the years, but they were later destroyed during the Gulf War.

"How about visiting your uncle Annisse!" I asked. "Perhaps he can also tell me some stories about Fatema. What do you think?"

"Sure, he lives just around the corner!" Amal said. "We'll go there now!"

Words could not describe the goodness I saw in Amal. Despite the family tension, she was still willing to take me to see an uncle that she herself had not seen in years. An uncle who was not on speaking terms with her mother. I thought of the tension among my own relatives following the death of my grandfather. My uncle and his wife had forced my grandmother Zari Joon to move into the basement and they had usurped her comfortable first floor apartment. In the dark and cold basement, my grandmother was now robbed of her chief joy in life – glancing at the passersby on the streets from the kitchen window. I wondered if I could ever have the generosity to forget about these problems in order to help someone else. Somehow I doubted it. This made me cherish the generosity and warmth I witnessed in Amal even more.

When we arrived at the Annisse's gate, we heard the voice of an older woman on the other side.

"Who is it?" she cried out.

"It's me. I've come to see you!" Monkith said.

"Monkith! Is it you? This is a kind voice I have not heard in many years!" And she opened the gate and threw himself into his arms. And then mine and Amal's. "What a wonderful surprise!," Layla declared. "How do I look Monkith, have I aged?"

"No, you are just as beautiful as ever!" Monkith whispered as he hugged her.

And she was. With her deep blue eyes and clear white skin, she was radiant. When Monkith introduced her to me, she embraced me tightly, took my hand, and led me into the house.

Annisse came out to greet us. He was a tall, rather handsome middle-aged man. His hair was fully white, but not one wrinkle lined his face. After his heartbreak with Soad the Kurdish girl, he had refused to enter another relationship. It was only recently that he had married a distant cousin of Manal's husband, Hussein. As we sat at the table in the living room, a tall and gaunt lady walked by, took her purse, and without looking at us, left the house and shut the door behind her. Later Monkith told me that this was Annisse's wife, who still harbored resentment since Hussein and Manal had refused to attend the wedding.

But with Annisse, there was no tension. He smiled at Monkith with so much familiarity that it did not seem as if it had been over twenty years since they last saw each other.

"I had heard you were here, Monkith. Honestly, I should have come to visit you at your mother's. But you know the story. Anyway, I am glad that you have come to see me. I am grateful for that. But really it should have been me who came," he whispered shyly.

"I understand. But Annisse, it has been so many years. Why doesn't all of this tension just end. Is it worth it?" Monkith said to Annisse, who looked down. Layla brought us tea and hugged Monkith, me, and Amal again.

"You know I tried several times to leave to the Emirates to join Mohsen, but everytime the mukhabarat asked me 'So what is your relation to Monkith Naji al-Azawi, who is wanted?' And each time once I told them you were my nephew, they also banned me from traveling. This happened again and again. So I never was able to travel."

Monkith did not know what to say. He already realized that his politics had caused his family to suffer. Even when he changed his name he could not always protect them. I looked down, searching for a topic of conversation, but all thoughts fled. Layla abruptly ended the silence by talking about Annisse's son who was blind in one eye. The kids had begun making fun of him, so they had taken him out of school. He was very smart, but frustrated and he dreamed about leaving the country for help. I told them that in the future Monkith and I hoped to organize a trip for my father and other American doctors to come and treat patients in Iraq, and that when that happened perhaps we could help his son. Tears flowed from Annisse's eyes when he heard these words. This man who had acted cruelly to his sisters, was also a father who wished more than anything to save his son.

When we left, it seemed that all the ice was broken. Perhaps one day relations would be restored. As we turned to leave, Layla cried out "Please don't forget us!" A few meters from the house I jumped up and cried: "Can you believe it? I forgot to ask him about Grandma Fatema. Oh well, perhaps it is better this way. It is good he sees we visited him just to see them, not for anything else.

With Amal we strolled down to what remained of the Tigris. Saddam Hussein had taken water and transferred it to the Saddam River – nothing seemed to remain of that majestic river that had given life and taken so many lives in return. I remembered the legend of Salooeh and wondered if the children still believed that there was such a woman who lived in the depths. The river seemed so shallow and unpretentious – I could not imagine that it still struck awe. It was rather pity that I felt.

That afternoon when we arrived at the house, Monkith's father was distraught and cried out: "Monkith, where the hell have you been? One person after the other has come to visit you, and each time I have to say you are not here. Where is your respect for me? Even Hajj Abbas told me that this is not fair of you that you have come for only a few days and are not staying with me in the home but are just wandering the streets. Hajj Abbas said that perhaps you have come to Iraq for your own interest rather than to see your family! Monkith, think how this makes me look – so disrespected!"

"Good God. I see Hajj Abbas is up to his old tricks again! But you can tell him to go to hell. I am no longer affected by his gossip and vicious chatter!" Monkith yelled as he sat on the swing in the garden.

That afternoon Monkith's father led him to a site that the villagers wanted him to build a sculpture on, in honor of Griyat's four-hundred-and-seventy martyrs. We laughed with his mother over the irony of how as a child he was spanked for sculpting the red clay by the Tigris and that now he made his living off of that very play and was even asked by the villagers to erect a monument.

After three days, Monkith felt alienation and suffocation. He decided it was time to return home. It seemed, he told me, that after twenty-six years, he had adapted to exile. He had harmonized his soul with its loneliness. Exile had become his new homeland. And so after several days in Baghdad, he missed the country that had adopted him. As we waited for Abu Khalid to come and pick us up, his parents and sisters threw a cup of water behind us, as they had done twenty-six years before, "so that your enemy's heart becomes cold, so that your enemies do not continue hurting you. May you walk under the Quran for your safety."

But before mounting the cab, Monkith implored me to stroll along the Tigris one last time before we left. As we reached the river, he let go of my hand and began to search frantically for the rock he had carved and used to sit on as a young man. It was no longer there, though he was able to find the very spot he used to sit on and meditate. The sun was rising and as it dabbled beautiful, colorful hues onto the now humbled canvas of water, he held himself up by the tip of his toes and poised to fling himself high into the air and fly away. I held the hand of the flying man. I trusted him and sealed my fate with his.